FLEABAG
The Scriptures

Also by
Phoebe Waller-Bridge

Fleabag: The Original Play

FLEABAG
The Scriptures

Phoebe Waller-Bridge

SCEPTRE

First published in Great Britain in 2019 by Sceptre
An Imprint of Hodder & Stoughton
An Hachette UK company

3

Scripts copyright © Two Brothers Pictures Limited 2019

Post-script copyright © Phoebe Waller-Bridge 2019

The Confessional Kyrie © Isobel Waller-Bridge 2019

Guinea pig, fox and music score illustrations © Paula Castro 2019 @breedlondon

BBC and the BBC logo are trademarks of the British Broadcasting Corporation
and are used under licence. BBC logo © BBC 1996

The BBC series Fleabag was created by Phoebe Waller-Bridge and
produced by Two Brothers Pictures (an all3media company).

The right of Phoebe Waller-Bridge to be identified as the
Author of the Work has been asserted by her in accordance
with the Copyright, Designs and Patents Act 1988.

Fleabag: The Original Play is published by Nick Hern Books

A CIP catalogue record for this title is available from the British Library

Hardback ISBN 978 1 529 39480 1
Trade Paperback ISBN 978 1 529 32280 4
eBook ISBN 978 1 529 39481 8

Typeset in Avenir by Palimpsest Book Production Ltd, Falkirk, Stirlingshire

Printed and bound in Great Britain by Clays Ltd, Elcograf S.p.A.

Hodder & Stoughton policy is to use papers that are natural, renewable
and recyclable products and made from wood grown in sustainable forests.
The logging and manufacturing processes are expected to conform to
the environmental regulations of the country of origin.

Hodder & Stoughton Ltd
Carmelite House
50 Victoria Embankment
London EC4Y 0DZ

www.sceptrebooks.co.uk

For my family

Introduction

Fleabag is a television series based on the play
of the same name.

The first series appeared on our screens in 2016
and was an instant hit.

It tells the story of a woman living in London grappling
with family, work, sex, love and loss.

The second series aired in the summer of 2019 to
further critical acclaim.

It is a love story.

Enclosed in the pages of this book are the filming
scripts of the two series, alongside commentary from
creator Phoebe Waller-Bridge on the writing and filming
of the multi-award-winning show.

SERIES
ONE

EPISODE 1

INT. FLEABAG'S FLAT. CORRIDOR — NIGHT

Sounds of a woman breathing.

Shot of the inside of a front door. Fleabag's POV.

Shot of Fleabag a few steps away from the door, watching it as if she's ready to pounce. Smudged makeup, hair tousled.

Out of breath.

Shot of the inside of a front door. Fleabag's POV.

Shot of Fleabag. She turns to camera.

> **FLEABAG**
> (earnest, touch of pain. To camera)
> You know that feeling when a guy you like sends you a text at 2 o'clock on a Tuesday night and asks if he can 'come and find you' and you've accidentally made it out like you've just got in yourself, so you have to get out of bed, drink half a bottle of wine, get in the shower, shave everything, dig out some Agent Provocateur business, suspender belt, the whole bit, and wait by the door until the buzzer goes—
> (buzzer goes)
> And then you open the door to him like you'd almost forgotten he was coming over.

She opens the door to a HANDSOME MAN.

> **FLEABAG**
> (casual)
> Oh hi!

> **ARSEHOLE GUY**
> Hey.

> **FLEABAG**
> Hey.

Beat.

> **ARSEHOLE GUY**
> Hey.

> **FLEABAG**
> (to camera)
> And then you get to it immediately.

They start snogging violently.

INT. FLEABAG'S BEDROOM — NIGHT

They are going at it on the bed; we are looking at Fleabag's back while she is on top. In a throe of passion Arsehole Guy flips her over onto her side so she is facing us, with him behind her.

>   **FLEABAG**
>   (to camera)
> After some pretty standard bouncing you realise that he is edging towards your arsehole. But you're drunk, and he made the effort to come all the way here so, you let him. He's thrilled.

>   **ARSEHOLE GUY**
>   (whispered)
> I'm so thrilled.

INT. FLEABAG'S BEDROOM — MORNING

Fleabag lies in bed, peacefully.

She suddenly opens her eyes and talks to us.

>   **FLEABAG**
>   (to camera)
> And then the next morning, you wake to find him fully dressed, sat on the side of the bed, gazing at you...

REVEAL: Arsehole Guy is sat on the bed, gazing at Fleabag earnestly. Fleabag looks at him, and then back to camera.

>   **FLEABAG**
>   (to camera)
> He says that—

>   **ARSEHOLE GUY**
> Last night was incredible.

>   **FLEABAG**
>   (to camera)
> Which you think is an overstatement, but then he goes on to say that—

>   **ARSEHOLE GUY**
> It was particularly special because I've never managed to actually... up the bum with anyone before—

>   **FLEABAG**
>   (to camera)
> To be fair, he does have a large penis.

                    ARSEHOLE GUY
And although it's always been a fantasy of mine,
I've... never found anyone I could do it with.

                      FLEABAG
                    (to camera)
And then he touches your hair.

He touches her hair.

                      FLEABAG
And thanks you with a genuine earnest.

                    ARSEHOLE GUY
                     (earnest)
Thank you.

                      FLEABAG
                    (to camera)
It's sort of moving. Then he kisses you gently.

He kisses her gently.

                      FLEABAG
                    (to camera)
And then he leaves.

He leaves.

Beat.

Fleabag frowns.

                      FLEABAG
                    (to camera)
And you spend the rest of the day wondering—

CUT TO: INT. CAFÉ — MORNING

Fleabag sits with a cup of tea looking up into the distance
pensively. A moment of real consideration passes before...

                      FLEABAG
               (to camera, concerned)
Do I have a MASSIVE arsehole?

                   TITLES: FLEABAG

INT. BUS — DAY

Fleabag sits, reading a newspaper. On the page we see an
advert boasting: 'Thinking of getting a mortgage?' with an
inexplicably naked woman advertising it. Fleabag does not
react. Because none of us do.

She looks around and catches the eye of a MAN who is looking
at her over his paper. We can only see his eyes. He looks
away shyly. She looks at the camera and raises her eyebrows
slightly. Hello...

He pulls his paper down and smiles and reveals that he has
extraordinarily large front teeth.

She quickly looks away with a small grimace.

INT. BUS — DAY, LATER

Fleabag and BUS RODENT are getting off at the same stop.
They do a little awkward laugh at each other.

They stand next to each other.

> **BUS RODENT**
> (giggly)
> Wow... Um. This doesn't happen very often, does it?

> **FLEABAG**
> (really giggly)
> Nooo no... I er — I suppose it's... I suppose it's
> quite rare, yeah.
> (to camera)
> I hate myself.

> **BUS RODENT**
> Um, are you going to work?

> **FLEABAG**
> Oh, no actually I—

> **BUS RODENT**
> Ok, um. This is gonna sound crazy, um, but I think that
> I should take your number and I think I should call it
> and I think I should ask you if you wanna go out for a
> drink with me.

> **FLEABAG**
> Um... I—

> **BUS RODENT**
> Fuuuck me, you've got a boyfriend.

                              FLEABAG
Um, no . . . No, we broke up quite recently actually.

                             BUS RODENT
Oh my God, I'm so sorry slash really pleased.
Errrrm, how the hell did he manage to fuck that up?

INT. FLASHBACK, FLEABAG'S BEDROOM — NIGHT

Fleabag is lying in bed with her computer in her lap, eating
pizza. She is watching a video of OBAMA giving a speech.

He is very serious.

She is very serious.

She starts touching herself.

Suddenly a YOUNG MAN's head pokes up on the other side of
the bed.

                              HARRY
    What are you doing?

She flips the laptop down quickly.

                             FLEABAG
    Nothing!

Beat.

Harry gets out of bed.

                             FLEABAG
    Harry—

He grabs his bag and starts packing some things from a
clothes rail.

                              HARRY
    I know what you were doing.

                             FLEABAG
    I was watching the news!

                              HARRY
                            (genuine)
    Really?

                             FLEABAG
    Yeah!

                              HARRY
                           (genuine)
Really?

                              FLEABAG
Yeah!

                              HARRY
                           (vulnerable)
What was he talking about then?

Beat.

                              FLEABAG
What?

                              HARRY
                           (vulnerable)
Please. I — I just — need to hear this. What was he
talking about?

Long pause.

                              FLEABAG
Iraq.

Hurt and furious, Harry manically starts packing again.

                              HARRY
Don't say anything.

She doesn't.

                              HARRY
Please don't stop me leaving.

She doesn't move.

                              HARRY
                           (angrily)
Please don't.

                              FLEABAG
Ok.

                              HARRY
DON'T!

He pauses. Then picks up his stuff.

                              HARRY
I've really tried to be there for you through this. You
can't say I haven't tried.

She doesn't say anything.

                              HARRY
Don't say anything. And please don't contact me. Or turn
up at my house drunk, in your underwear. It won't work
this time.

                            FLEABAG
                          (to camera)
It will.

                              HARRY
                            (sadly)
I'm taking the posh shampoo.

He goes to leave, then stops at the door and looks at her.

                              HARRY
He was talking about democr—

HARD CUT TO:

They giggle and walk off in opposite directions. As she
walks, Fleabag checks her phone. She suddenly BOLTS it down
the street.

INT. AN OFFICE — DAY

Sounds of panting breath. Close-up of Fleabag, out of breath
and slightly sweaty. A man sits opposite her reading a docu-
ment.

Beat.

                         BANK MANAGER
Thanks for coming in today. We really appreciate you
considering us for your...
                         (reading it)
Small business start-up loan.

                            FLEABAG
No problem.

                         BANK MANAGER
I have read your application.

                            FLEABAG
Thank you.

                         BANK MANAGER
It was... funny!

                            FLEABAG
Oh — Ok — that wasn't my intention but...

BANK MANAGER

As you are probably aware, we haven't had the opportunity to support many — any — women-led businesses since the...

FLEABAG

Sexual harassment case.

BANK MANAGER

The sexual harassment case. Yes.
(beat)
Are you alright?

FLEABAG

Oh yeah, sorry, I just um — I ran from the station, so I'm just a bit... hot. But I'm really excited about, um...

BANK MANAGER

Water?

FLEABAG
(desperately wants water)
Uh, no, thanks I'm fine — actually, yeah, water would be great, if I could...

BANK MANAGER

Sure.

He doesn't do anything about the water.

BANK MANAGER

There are a couple of details that we need to iron out, and one or two bits and pieces I'm gonna need to see some more of. It says in here that you opened the business with your... that your partner in—

Fleabag pulls her top above her head. Realises she hasn't got a top on underneath and pulls it back down again.

BANK MANAGER

Ok. I'm sorry, that kind of thing won't get you very far here any more.

FLEABAG
(awkwardly laughing)
Oh no sorry. I thought I had a top on underneath.

BANK MANAGER

Yeah Ok, but—

FLEABAG

No seriously, in this case, genuine accident.

> **BANK MANAGER**
> I can see, given our history, why you might think that—

> **FLEABAG**
> No, seriously I wasn't trying to... I was hot!

> **BANK MANAGER**
> I take this kind of thing very seriously now.

> **FLEABAG**
> (laughing)
> I'm not trying to shag you, look at yourself!

Beat.

> **BANK MANAGER**
> Ok. Please leave.

> **FLEABAG**
> Oh — no, you don't understand, I need this — I need this
> loan.

> **BANK MANAGER**
> Please just leave.

Beat.

She gets up and starts to leave.

> **FLEABAG**
> Perv.

> **BANK MANAGER**
> Slut.

> **FLEABAG**
> WOW.

INT. LECTURE THEATRE — DAY

Fleabag runs down the stairs hurriedly and takes a seat next
to a serious, well-dressed woman — CLAIRE.

> **FLEABAG**
> (to camera)
> My sister. She's uptight and beautiful and probably
> anorexic, but clothes look awesome on her so...

Claire doesn't look at Fleabag.

> **CLAIRE**
> You're almost late.

> **FLEABAG**
> I had to do a flash poo in Pret.

> **CLAIRE**
> Ugh Christ, did you wash your hands?

> **FLEABAG**
> (wiping her hand on Claire's face)
> Course not.

> **CLAIRE**
> Oh my GOD. You are DISGUSTING. Fucking hell.

Claire takes antibacterial gel out of her bag.

> **FLEABAG**
> Course I washed my hands, it's not like I grew up
> without a mother.

Claire glares at her.

Beat.

> **CLAIRE**
> Heard from Dad?

> **FLEABAG**
> Nope.
> (to camera)
> Dad's way of coping with two motherless daughters was
> to buy us tickets to feminist lectures, start fucking
> our godmother and eventually stop calling.
> (beat)
> (to Claire)
> You look tired.

> **CLAIRE**
> Thanks. I've been sleeping really well recently.

Fleabag starts taking her coat off.

Claire eyes her top. Fleabag pulls the coat back on.

> **FLEABAG**
> (whispering, to camera)
> Shit.
> (she glances at Claire)
> I'm wearing the top that she 'lost' years ago. So. This
> is gonna be tense.

> **CLAIRE**
> (pointed)
> Do you want to take your coat off?

                    FLEABAG
No.

                    CLAIRE
Ok.

Beat.

Someone squeezes past them along the row. They're very
smiley and polite as they stand. They sit back down.

                    CLAIRE
So, any luck with—

                    FLEABAG
Oh GOD, can we just have two seconds—

                    CLAIRE
I WAS JUST GOING TO ASK HOW IT WAS GOING WITH THE CAFÉ?!

                    FLEABAG
                (simultaneously)
I KNOW, I JUST DON'T WANT TO TALK ABOUT IT YET.

                    CLAIRE
FINE. WE WON'T TALK THEN.

                    FLEABAG
FINE.

Beat.

                    FLEABAG
Hair looks nice.

                    CLAIRE
Fuck off.

Beat.

Fleabag stares at Claire.

                    FLEABAG
                (to camera)
The only thing harder than having to tell your super-
high-powered-perfect-anorexic-rich-super-sister that
you've run out of money is having to ask her to bail
you out.

Beat.

She looks at Claire.

                    FLEABAG
                (to camera)

I'm just gonna ask her.
                    (beat)
I'm just gonna ask her.
                    (beat)
I'm just gonna ask her. I'm just gonna come—

                    CLAIRE
Do you need to borrow money?

                    FLEABAG
                    (petulant)
NO.
                    (to camera)
Can't do it. Can't do it. Can't do it.

                    CLAIRE
So business is good then?

                    FLEABAG
                    (petulant)
Yeah! It's good, it's really good. It's really, really
good. Yeah, it's really good.

                    CLAIRE
Sounds like it's really good.

                    FLEABAG
It is.

INT. FLASHBACK, CAFÉ — DAY

Fleabag is at the counter. A YOUNG MAN has just sat down at
one of the tables.

                    FLEABAG
Hey.

                    YOUNG MAN
Hey.

He takes out his laptop.

                    FLEABAG
Can I get you anything?

                    YOUNG MAN
No thanks. I'm good.

Fleabag watches him. We stay on him while...

He plugs in his computer.

He then plugs in his phone.

He then takes out a Kindle.

He thinks, unplugs his phone.

Plugs in a multi-plug, plugs in his phone again and plugs in his Kindle.

> FLEABAG
>
> Are you sure I can't get you anything at all?

INT. LECTURE THEATRE — DAY — CONT.

Back with Fleabag and Claire.

> CLAIRE
>
> Is Harry helping?

> FLEABAG
>
> Uh, we broke up.

> CLAIRE
>
> What?! Again?

> FLEABAG
>
> Hm. If you see him, I'm a wreck Ok.

> CLAIRE
>
> God. Just don't get drunk and scream through his letter box again.

> FLEABAG
>
> Wow, thanks for the vote of confidence. Don't get drunk and shit in your sink again.

> CLAIRE
> (flipping out)
>
> When are you going to stop bringing that up?

> FLEABAG
> (laughing)
>
> When you do something better!

> CLAIRE
>
> I have two degrees, a husband and a Burberry coat.

> FLEABAG
>
> You shat in a sink.

Someone squeezes past. They're really polite again. They sit.

> FLEABAG
>
> Nothing is ever going to be better.
> (beat)
> I swear there are pants that give you thrush.

> **CLAIRE**
> What are yours made from?

Fleabag looks down at her pants.

INT. FLASHBACK, CHANGING ROOMS — DAY

BOO and Fleabag are concealed in adjacent changing rooms. We don't see them.

> **FLEABAG**
> (from her cubicle)
> I need to get sexy pants.

> **BOO**
> (from her cubicle)
> I hate my body I hate my body I hate my body. Fucking last-minute bastard trendy parties. Why do we do it to ourselves?!

They step out of their cubicles. Fleabag is holding her coat. Boo looks at Fleabag's outfit.

> **BOO**
> Oh God definitely not. That does nothing for you. I hate that.

Fleabag just looks at her.

> **BOO**
> What?

> **FLEABAG**
> These are my clothes, Boo. I've been wearing these all day.

> **BOO**
> Oh God. Were you wearing your coat?

> **FLEABAG**
> Yes, but... nothing here looked nice so I thought I'd just wear what I was wearing anyway.

> **BOO**
> Are you joking?

> **FLEABAG**
> Are you joking?

> **BOO**
> (unsure)
> Yes...?

Beat.

Fleabag chucks her clothes at Boo while shouting.

> **FLEABAG**
> OH MY GOD WHY DIDN'T YOU TELL ME. I'VE GOT TO GET A
> WHOLE NEW OUTFIT NOW. I'VE BEEN SO MANY PLACES TODAY.
> FUUUCK OOOFF.

> **BOO**
> (simultaneously)
> IT'S REALLY NOT THAT BAD IT'S REALLY NOT — OH MY GOD
> I'M SORRY. I LOVE YOU. I'LL BUY YOU PANTS I'LL BUY YOU
> SEXY PANTS!

Boo tries to hug Fleabag while she retreats back into her
cubicle.

> **BOO**
> I'M SORRY, IT'S A LOVELY DRESS.

INT. LECTURE THEATRE — DAY — CONT.

Fleabag still looking at her pants. Claire sees them.

> **CLAIRE**
> Ugh, you shouldn't wear such cheap materials, they don't
> let your fanny breathe.

> **FLEABAG**
> I know.

Everyone claps. A LECTURER settles on stage. She is a
middle-aged, confident, middle-class woman.

We INTERCUT with their reactions.

> **LECTURER**
> Gosh, look at you all! Thank you so much for coming to
> 'Women Speak — opening women's mouths since 1998'. Now,
> before we begin, I would like to ask you a question. I
> don't know about you, but I need some reassurance.

Lecturer laughs a little.

Fleabag grimaces at the laugh.

> **LECTURER (CONT'D)**
> So, I pose the question to the women in this room today:
> Please raise your hands, if you would trade five years
> of your life for the so-called 'perfect body'?

Fleabag and Claire raise their hands instinctively. Everyone stares at them.

They put their hands down guiltily.

> **FLEABAG**
> (whispering to Claire)
> We are bad feminists.

> **CLAIRE**
> I want my top back.

> **FLEABAG**
> Ok.

INT. LECTURE HALL — DAY — CONT.

Fleabag, with her coat tied tightly around her, walks towards Claire and hands back her top. Claire takes it.

> **CLAIRE**
> Won't you get cold?

> **FLEABAG**
> Nah, I've got really hairy nipples.

Pause. Claire looks sadly at her.

> **FLEABAG**
> What?

Weird beat. Claire suddenly tries to hug Fleabag. Fleabag flinches and ends up smacking her on the head.

> **CLAIRE**
> OW FUCK.

> **FLEABAG**
> What was that!

> **CLAIRE**
> What?! It was a fucking hug.

> **FLEABAG**
> Well why the fuck did you do that — that was terrifying! Never do that again.

> **CLAIRE**
> (hurt)
> I was just trying to—
> (this is not easy)
> Are you Ok?

FLEABAG
Yeah.

Beat.

CLAIRE
Do you want to go for a drink or...

FLEABAG
Uh, no I've got plans.

CLAIRE
(frosty again)
Ok. Fine. Sure. See you next time Women Speak, then.

She leaves. Fleabag feels a tinge of regret for turning her down. A woman from the lecture passes.

FLEABAG
Do you want to go for a drink?

The woman looks at her confused and hurries away.

Some time goes past. She gets a text. It reads: *Still smiling. :).* She grimaces.

INT. PUB — NIGHT

Bus Rodent now sits opposite Fleabag. He is talking animat-edly through his enormous teeth. They both have drinks.

BUS RODENT
(this speech was improvised by Jamie Demetriou)
Yeah my sister blows glass. She has done for a long time. The other thing — I've never like, been in a fight, well I've been in a fight, I've never been punched in the face — you know what I mean? I've been punched in the leg. And someone once threw some punch in my face. So, my colours this season are sort of brown, mainly, but like, you know, I wouldn't say no to a, to a maroon. I wouldn't like, jump down the throat of someone wearing something blue, it's just not for me.
(beat)
SO. I'm gonna go for a wazz.

He laughs and leaves as Fleabag smiles at him. As soon as he's gone she exhales with exasperation. She steals a twenty-pound note out of his wallet.

He reappears.

                         BUS RODENT
Same again while I'm up? Or a little cockytail? Or like
a, another shot?!

                         FLEABAG
Yeah, or we could just go back to mine?

                         BUS RODENT
Wow, erm thanks. Uh, I've actually got work, uh,
tomorrow, but, another drink here—

                         FLEABAG
Or we could just go back to yours?

                         BUS RODENT
                    (shaking his head)
Gotta be up really early so—

                         FLEABAG
Well I'll just get you a cab in the morning.

                         BUS RODENT
                    (laughing nervously)
Well, that's ridiculous, I can't—

                         FLEABAG
Ok, what the fuck is your problem?

                         BUS RODENT
Oh. Um, nothing. I um... I like you.

                         FLEABAG
                    (grabbing her bag)
Ok. You're a dick.

                         BUS RODENT
What's going on?

                         FLEABAG
You're pathetic.

She gets up and walks to the door.

                         BUS RODENT
Wait—

                         FLEABAG
Don't follow me.

                         BUS RODENT
Oh, I wasn't.
                    (picking something up from the floor)
You dropped this.

He hands her the twenty pounds she stole from him. She takes it and struts off towards the door, giving us a smug look.

                         BUS RODENT
    Um...

He looks after her, confused.

EXT. BUS STOP — NIGHT

Fleabag stands at the bus stop.

There is an incredibly DRUNK GIRL sitting on the kerb. Fleabag watches her.

Drunk Girl suddenly crashes to the floor. Her boob falls out of her top.

Fleabag helps her back up and puts her boob back in. They both settle.

The girl rests her head on Fleabag's shoulder.

After a while she looks up.

                         FLEABAG
    You Ok?

Drunk girl nods.

                         DRUNK GIRL
    Are you Ok?
                    (touches Fleabag's face)
    Sad face.

                         FLEABAG
    I'm fine.

The girl nestles into Fleabag's neck.

Beat.

                         DRUNK GIRL
    Aw.
                         (beat)
    You're such a lovely man.

Fleabag looks at the camera.

EXT. BUS STOP — NIGHT. MOMENTS LATER

Fleabag has hailed a cab for Drunk Girl. She picks her up.

>   **FLEABAG**
> Ok.
>   (Drunk Girl moves towards the cab)
> Stay there, you're Ok.

She opens the cab door.

>   **FLEABAG**
> Hey — do you, do you wanna come home with me?

>   **DRUNK GIRL**
> WHAT?! NO WAY! You naughty boy—

Drunk Girl gets into the cab and Fleabag watches it drive
away.

CUT TO: INT. FLASHBACK, CAFÉ — NIGHT

Boo closing the door. She joins Fleabag, who is pouring
wine, at a table.

>   **FLEABAG**
> Oooh, sing a song Boo Boo!!

INT. FLASHBACK, CAFÉ — NIGHT. MOMENTS LATER

Boo and Fleabag sit opposite each other with a glass of wine
each. They are happy in their little kingdom they built.

>   **FLEABAG**
>   (singing)
> Another lunch break another abortion!

>   **BOO**
>   (singing)
> Another piece of cake another two—

>   **FLEABAG**
>   (singing)
> Fuck it twenty—

>   **FLEABAG/BOO**
> —Cigarettes. And we're happy, so happy, to be modern
> women.

They laugh. Boo pulls Fleabag's face close to hers.

>   **BOO**
> Come here. Let's never ask anyone for anything. They
> don't get it.

                          FLEABAG
                     (nodding her head)
   Deal.

EXT. STREET — NIGHT — CONT.

Fleabag stands on the street. She looks at the camera.

                          FLEABAG
   Fuck it.

EXT. DAD'S HOUSE. FRONT DOOR — NIGHT

Fleabag is drunk. She is yelling through the letter box.

                          FLEABAG
   Helloliliiiooo!
                     (to camera)
   This is totally fine.

She hammers relentlessly on the door.

                          FLEABAG
   HELLLOOOO! OPEN UP!

Eventually the door opens. It's an exhausted man in his
fifties.

                          FLEABAG
   Alright Dad!

                            DAD
   What's going on?

                          FLEABAG
   Oh I'm, I'm absolutely fine!

                            DAD
   Ok.

                          FLEABAG
   I just, uh...

Fleabag starts tearing up.

                            DAD
   Yeah.

                          FLEABAG
   Uh — it's nothing. It doesn't — It's...

                         DAD
You know it's nearly two o'clock in the morning.

                       FLEABAG
Ok. Yeah, Ok. I'm— I don't wanna, I'm gonna. It was...
          (she turns but then turns back)
Oh fuck it. I have a horrible feeling that I am a
greedy, perverted, selfish, apathetic, cynical,
depraved, morally bankrupt woman who can't even call
herself a feminist.

She looks desperately at him. She needs him now.

                         DAD
Well... Um...
          (pathetic, trying to make a joke)
You get all that from your mother!

She laughs a sad laugh.

                       FLEABAG
Good one!

                         DAD
I — I'm going to call you a cab, darling. And um — don't
go upstairs.

He goes inside. Fleabag follows and climbs the stairs.

INT. SPARE BEDROOM/ STUDIO — NIGHT. CONT.

Fleabag walks into a room revealing GODMOTHER, with her back
to the door, painting thick black paint delicately onto a
canvas. Fleabag watches her.

                       FLEABAG
                    (to camera)
To be fair. She's not an evil stepmother.
                       (beat)
She's just a cunt.
                    (to Godmother)
Hi!

                     GODMOTHER
                  (really lovely)
Darling! I thought that must have been you. Everything
alright?

                       FLEABAG
                   (really nice)
Yeah! Just thought I'd... swing by.

GODMOTHER

Ah, how lovely. Lucky us.

FLEABAG

Oh, don't worry. Dad's already booking me a taxi.
(beat)
What you doing?

GODMOTHER

Oh, painting. I find the night-times very... peaceful.
(she laughs sweetly)
Usually!

Fleabag laughs too.

FLEABAG
(to camera)
Oop. Warming up.

Fleabag walks over to the bookshelves, looking at the objects on there.

GODMOTHER

Look. I know it's not really my place. But — are you Ok? Everyone's been worried...

Fleabag sees a small sculpture of a female legs and torso with large breasts but no arms.

FLEABAG

Poor fucker.

GODMOTHER

Yes. She's actually an expression of how women are subtle warriors... strong at heart. You know, we don't have to use muscular force to get what we want. We just need to use our—

FLEABAG

Tits.

GODMOTHER

Innate femininity.

FLEABAG

Tits don't get you anywhere these days. Trust me.

She picks up the statue.

GODMOTHER

It's very valuable actually.

FLEABAG

How much?

                              GODMOTHER
          Thousands.

                               FLEABAG
          Can I have it?

                              GODMOTHER
                               (laughs)
          No.

Godmother takes the statue off Fleabag and puts it back on
the shelf.

Beat.

                               FLEABAG
                 (gesturing to the thick, black canvas)
          What's that?

                              GODMOTHER
          Oh, um. My self-portrait.

They look at each other.

                               FLEABAG
          Oh!

Godmother smiles.

                              GODMOTHER
          Oo.
                         (wanting her to leave)
          I can hear your da—?

Godmother heads to the door. Dad's voice weakly from the
bottom of the stairs.

                             DAD (O.S.)
          CAB'S HERE!

                               FLEABAG
                         (a bit too loud)
          THANKS.

                              GODMOTHER
          Ah. Nice of him.

                               FLEABAG
          Bye.

                              GODMOTHER
          Bye.

They kiss on each cheek.

                         GODMOTHER
Um, please look after yourself.
                    (she holds Fleabag's arm)
You really do look ghastly darling.

INT. TAXI — NIGHT

Fleabag is in a taxi riding smoothly through London. The
DRIVER talks to her.

                         DRIVER
A café eh?

                         FLEABAG
Yeah.

                         DRIVER
On your own?

                         FLEABAG
Kind of.

                         DRIVER
Kind of? Go on!

                         FLEABAG
It's kind of a funny story actually.

                         DRIVER
Oh that's good! It'll keep me going! Shoot.

                         FLEABAG
I opened the café with my friend Boo.

                         DRIVER
Cute name.

                         FLEABAG
Yeah. She's dead now. She accidentally killed herself.
It wasn't her intention but it wasn't a total accident.
She didn't actually think she'd die, she just found out
that her boyfriend fucked someone else and wanted to
punish him by ending up in hospital and not letting him
visit her for a bit. She decided to walk into a busy
cycle lane, wanting to get tangled in a bike, break a
finger maybe. But as it turns out bikes go fast and flip
you into the road. Three people died.
                    (she laughs)
She was such a dick.

He doesn't know what to say. She laughs.

FLEABAG
So yeah... Kind of on my own.

He looks at her in the rear-view mirror. She drunkenly, and sadly, smiles. He drives on in silence.

She undoes her coat. She only has her bra on underneath.

She pulls out the little sculpture of the woman with no arms from her trousers. It sits on her lap.

Two women. One real. One not.

Both with their innate femininity out.

She looks at the camera and smiles.

END OF EPISODE 1

EPISODE 2

INT. TUBE — DAY

Fleabag sits on the tube.

'Sail' by AWOLNATION starts playing. We do not hear the
sound of the real world.

Each seat opposite is taken by random members of the public.
They all sit silently. A few people are standing.

It's your regular, bored, anonymous tube carriage of
commuters. No one engaging with each other.

Fleabag looks at each one individually.

At each break in the music each person breaks into a brief,
but eviscerating, sob before snapping back to their usual
expressionless face.

Just as we hit the climax of the music, it cuts out.

Fleabag looks sideways at the camera.

> **FLEABAG**
> (to camera)
> I think my period's coming.

TITLES: FLEABAG

EXT. CLAIRE'S HOUSE — DAY

The last echo of a DOORBELL fades. Fleabag is standing
outside. Claire opens the door. She is surprised to see
Fleabag, who never comes over. Plus no one ever just
'knocks' any more.

> **CLAIRE**
> Oh... kay...

> **FLEABAG**
> (smiling)
> Hi!

> **CLAIRE**
> Are you alright? What's happened? Are you hurt?

> **FLEABAG**
> No?

                              CLAIRE
        Oh good.

Beat.

                              FLEABAG
        Nice haircut.

                              CLAIRE
        It's better.

Another beat.

                              FLEABAG
        Can I come in?

                              CLAIRE
        Why didn't you text?

                              FLEABAG
        I just thought I'd pop by.

                              CLAIRE
        Tell the truth.

                              FLEABAG
        I need to speak to Martin.

                              CLAIRE
        Martin?

                              FLEABAG
                    (to camera, disgusted)
        Martin.
                       (to Claire, chirpy)
        Martin.

                              CLAIRE
        Why on earth would you want to speak to—

INT. MARTIN'S STUDY — DAY — CONT.

MARTIN (forties, American, twinkly, alcoholic) sits at an
old oak desk with piles and piles of paper everywhere.

He has both hands on his desk, watching something on his
laptop. There is something a little sweaty about him.

                              CLAIRE
        Martin?

The door opens and Claire and Fleabag enter. Martin looks up
and jumps up from his computer.

                         MARTIN
              (guilty and over the top)
    HELLO HELLO MY WIFE IN MY STUDY! Hello, give me...
                 (holds up two fingers)
    Two...

He looks closely at the laptop.

                        FLEABAG
                    (to camera)
    Gangbangs. Asian. I'd put a tenner on it.

                         MARTIN
        (looking at the screen, clicking something,
                  shuts the laptop)
    Finished.
                   (seeing Fleabag)
    Well hello you!

Fleabag holds up her hand in unenthusiastic greeting.

                         CLAIRE
    She wants to talk to you about something.

                         MARTIN
    Oh, well it must be my lucky day. You said she only
    talks to people she fancies!

Claire and Fleabag 'laugh'.

                        FLEABAG
                    (to camera)
    Ugh.
                    (to Claire)
    Can you leave us?

                         CLAIRE
    Why?

                        FLEABAG
    He's organising your surprise birthday party.

Pause. Claire is stony-faced. But secretly thrilled.

                         CLAIRE
    You know I... hate... Ok.

She leaves quickly, before she gives away how touched she
is, closing the door as she goes.

                         MARTIN
    I have a week to organise that now.

                         FLEABAG
Best of luck.

                          MARTIN
Nice top.

                         FLEABAG
                       (to camera)
Ugh.
                       (beat, to Martin)
Thanks. Do you deal in sculptures as well as paintings
and papier mâché?

                          MARTIN
Depends on the quality of the piece.

Fleabag pulls out the statue.

                          MARTIN
Fuck me.
                         (he takes it)
What a pair.

                         FLEABAG
I know, right.

He laughs.

                          MARTIN
Where d'you get this?

                         FLEABAG
Oh just I — stole it... From a market.

He laughs. Still examining.

                          MARTIN
Uh it's quite a piece. Who's the artist?

Fleabag shrugs.

                         FLEABAG
Just a... Market artist.

                          MARTIN
If I sell it I take 10 per cent. Deal?

                         FLEABAG
Deal.

                          MARTIN
Ok. Well. I'll get her photographed now.

                         FLEABAG
Don't tell Claire. Please.

                         MARTIN
                        (teasing)
Or what?

                         FLEABAG
Or I'll...

                         MARTIN
                        (grossly)
Ha! You got nothing on me, princess!

Fleabag laughs.

                         FLEABAG
Or I'll tell her you're watching gangbangs.

Beat.

He is totally taken aback.

                         MARTIN
                        (earnest)
Please don't do that again.

She smiles. She would.

                         MARTIN
                        (busted)
I wasn't. By the way.

He starts walking out, shaking his head. He leaves.

Beat.

Fleabag looks at the camera and then goes to Martin's
laptop.

Pulls up the screen. It flashes on. She looks at what he was
looking at, but we don't see it.

                         FLEABAG
                        (disgusted)
Ugh.

We see the screen. It's not an Asian gangbang. He's looking
at buying a necklace that says 'Claire' in big swirly
letters. Tacky. But sweet.

                         FLEABAG
                        (to camera)
Disappointing.

EXT. CLAIRE'S HOUSE — DAY

The doorway again. Claire is showing Fleabag out. Fleabag is holding a loo roll.

> **CLAIRE**
> Ummmm... Where did you get that?

> **FLEABAG**
> Oh I brought it with me.

> **CLAIRE**
> No you didn't. Give it back.

Fleabag gives it back.

> **FLEABAG**
> (to camera)
> Tight.

> **CLAIRE**
> Patch things up with Harry?

> **FLEABAG**
> Yeah we're... we're engaged.

> **CLAIRE**
> (horrified)
> God, what?

> **FLEABAG**
> (laughing)
> No we're not engaged. He's back at the flat packing up all his stuff again.

> **CLAIRE**
> (trying to come across caring — doesn't suit her)
> Well... I'm sorry. He really used to make you laugh.

> **FLEABAG**
> (to camera)
> He also used to say things like—

INT. FLASHBACK, FLEABAG'S KITCHEN — DAY

Fleabag's POV. Harry looks up lovingly.

> **HARRY**
> You're not like other girls... you can
> (taps his temple)
> keep up.

He sips a smoothie from a straw.

EXT. CLAIRE'S HOUSE. DOORSTEP — DAY

Back with Fleabag and Claire.

> **CLAIRE**
> (wistfully)
> I like Harry. I liked his songs.

INT. FLEABAG'S FLAT. BEDROOM — DAY

Fleabag stands, stunned, staring at the stripped bed and the emptiness of the whole room.

She looks momentarily lost.

Then she turns to us. She covers her loneliness. She doesn't want us to see.

> **FLEABAG**
> I admire how much Harry commits to our break-ups.

INT. FLEABAG'S FLAT. KITCHEN — DAY

The kitchen is totally bare. She opens the fridge. It's empty.

> **FLEABAG**
> I mean, this is a new detail, but he does usually go the extra mile. A few times he's even cleaned the whole flat.

INT. FLASHBACK, FLEABAG'S FLAT. KITCHEN — DAY

Harry is furiously scrubbing the floor on his hands and knees, sobbing.

INT. FLEABAG'S FLAT. KITCHEN — DAY

Fleabag looks at us.

> **FLEABAG**
> Like it's a crime scene. I've considered timing a break-up for when the flat needs a bit of a going-over...

INT. FLASHBACK, FLEABAG'S FLAT. BEDROOM — DAY

Fleabag and Harry are snuggled happily in bed watching a movie. She looks genuinely happy for a moment. Then she eyes around the room.

She grimaces at some dust on her side-table. She runs her finger through it.

She turns the movie off.

> **FLEABAG**
> I don't think this is working.

He looks totally ambushed.

> **HARRY**
> Wha—?

INT. KITCHEN — DAY

Fleabag in the kitchen. She is looking for something. She looks at some shelves.

> **FLEABAG**
> (to camera)
> But he always leaves...

She finds what she's looking for. There is a small toy dino-saur in there. She picks it up.

> **FLEABAG**
> (to camera)
> Him. To come back for.

INT. FLEABAG'S FLAT. BATHROOM — DAY

Fleabag sits on the loo holding the dinosaur.

> **FLEABAG**
> Gotta think about all the people I can have sex with now.
> (beat)
> I'm not obsessed with sex.
> (beat)
> I just can't stop thinking about it.
> (beat)
> The performance of it. The awkwardness of it, the drama of it. The moment you realise someone wants your body... Not so much the feeling of it.
> (beat)
> I've probably got about forty-eight hours before Harry comes back.

Slightly exhausted by having to fill her emptiness. She turns and pulls some loo paper. There's hardly any left — the cardboard roll falls to the floor.

FLEABAG
I should get on it.

EXT. STREET — DAY

Fleabag is rushing down the street. We are slightly behind her.

FLEABAG
(to camera, bit depressed)
I took half an hour trying to look nice... And I ended up looking...

The camera pans round to her face.

FLEABAG
(to camera, amazed)
AMAZING. Just one of those days. Gorgeous. Fresh-faced, new top, little bit sexy. On my way to open my café and— Oh God.

She sees a large, bruiser-looking man walking towards her. He is fixated on her. He is quite far away to begin with so it doesn't matter if we can't see his face clearly.

She starts strutting, pulls a face like 'ugh' to camera.

He approaches. He looks like he is building up to saying something.

FLEABAG
Yeah you check me out chub-chub cos it's neeeever gonna happen.

He gets a bit closer. He is starting to smirk.

FLEABAG
Oh God, he can't believe how attractive I am... Kinda worried I'm about to make a sex offender out of the poor guy.

She is clearly loving that he is checking her out. She holds her head up.

FLEABAG
(to camera)
Here we go. This better be good. Here we go.

He's about to pass. He shamelessly looks her up and down as he passes her.

MAN
(coughs)
Walk of shame.

Beat.

She is put out.

Because she was talking to us she forgets to look where she is going.

She is about to cross the road. A CYCLIST passes and dings the bell.

> **CYCLIST**
> OI!

It makes Fleabag jump.

EXT. FLASHBACK, ROAD — DAY

Boo stands on the side of the road. Bicycles and traffic fly past.

INT. CAFÉ — DAY, LATER

A MAN sits in the café. She watches him seductively.

She deliberately pushes a cucumber off the counter.

> **FLEABAG**
> (seductively)
> Oh. Dropped my cucumber.

He looks up and makes no comment. He goes back to his work. Not interested. She picks it up. Tries again —

> **FLEABAG**
> Just dropped my...

He's not listening. She gives up. The man walks up to the counter.

> **MAN**
> Um, could I get a cheese sandwich to go.

> **FLEABAG**
> Sure.

She reaches for some cheese sandwiches wrapped in clingfilm.

> **FLEABAG**
> That'll be... um... £12.55, please.

The man frowns.

                        FLEABAG
                      (explaining)
London.

He hands over a note.

                        FLEABAG
      Thanks.

He turns and picks up a picture of Boo and Fleabag. He
points to Boo in the picture

                    MAN
      Where do I recognise her from? Is she famous?

EXT. FLASHBACK, ROAD — DAY

Boo stands on the busy road and steps into the traffic.

INT. CAFÉ — DAY

Back with Fleabag and the man.

                        FLEABAG
                      (to camera)
      Boo's death hit the papers. Local café girl gets hit by
      bike, and a car, and another bike.
                      (to man)
      She used to work here.

He waits expectantly for his change.

                        FLEABAG
      I'm sorry, I don't have any change.

He shakes his head and goes. Fleabag sits down and looks
bored. She sighs.

                        FLEABAG
                      (to camera)
      The next man who walks in here is getting ridden to
      death.

The bell dings. Her dad walks in.

                        FLEABAG
      Dad?

                        DAD
      Hi.

                          FLEABAG
                          (to camera)
Not ideal.

                            DAD
Um... how're you... Uh... Darling.

Fleabag looks very confused. It's awkward.

                            DAD
You busy?

                          FLEABAG
A bit.

                            DAD
              (looking around at the empty café)
Well I won't... keep you... uh... I just want to talk
about... ah... when you... you dropped in the other
night.

                          FLEABAG
Ok?

                            DAD
I can't help thinking that I... I... We... I know that
we... don't have much of a chance to...
                        (beat, quietly)
Did you take the sculpture? Did you, um, take the sculp-
ture?
                        (more confident)
Did you take it?

                          FLEABAG
              (looks at camera, then back at Dad)
No? What sculpture?

                            DAD
                          (relieved)
Oh right... Good. You said no. That means I can go.
Alright. Great.

As he gets to the door he panics. He wants to ask her if she
is happy.

                            DAD
                          (turning)
Um... Are you... Happy... um
                          (beat)
Healthy?

She nods.

He smiles awkwardly and exits.

TWO YOGA GIRLS come in.

                    YOGA 1
     Hey, do you do like hot, organic-y food?

                    FLEABAG
     Of course. What would you like?

                    YOGA 2
     Um... like a risotto?

                    FLEABAG
     Sure. Grab a seat.

INT. SHOP — DAY

A cheap, microwave risotto in a fridge. Fleabag grabs it.

She turns and walks through the shop until she finds the tampons.

She stops and stares at the shelf. She goes for the small tampons sold in a yellow box, and then hesitates, eyes the camera, and then sheepishly puts them back and picks up the box of massive tampons sold in the green box.

Just then, Arsehole Guy appears.

                    ARSEHOLE GUY
     Hey.

She panics and quickly swaps the green box for the yellow.

They play it super cool.

                    FLEABAG
     Hi.

                    ARSEHOLE GUY
     Hey.

                    FLEABAG
     Hey.

                    ARSEHOLE GUY
     It's nice to see you.

                    FLEABAG
     You too.
                    (to camera, chuffed)
     Fucked me up the arse.

He gestures to the items she's holding.

ARSEHOLE GUY

What you getting?

FLEABAG
(flirty)

Oh just these. For my tiny, bleeding... vagina.

Beat.

He looks at her intensely.

ARSEHOLE GUY

Hot.

FLEABAG

You?

ARSEHOLE GUY

Stock cubes.

FLEABAG
(to camera)

Hot.

ARSEHOLE GUY
(beat, serious)

Hope it's a light flow.

FLEABAG
(flirty)

Oh, it never is.
(more intense)

It never is.

Beat.

He's not sure what they're doing any more. Neither is
Fleabag.

ARSEHOLE GUY

Listen, er... You around later?

FLEABAG

Uh...
(to camera)

YES FUCKING YES PLEASE YES.
(to him, calm)

Yes.

ARSEHOLE GUY

Cool.

FLEABAG

Cool. Bye.

He smiles and goes. She puts the yellow box back and picks
up the green ones.

                        FLEABAG
                     (to camera)
        YES.

INT. CAFÉ — DAY

Fleabag is staring at the risotto cooking in the microwave.
We can hear the yoga girls' conversation.

                        YOGA 1
        I'm just so — happy... with my body now. Like... I
        don't have to define myself by how I look because I've
        just got a fucking great body.

                        YOGA 2
        Yeah!

                        YOGA 1
        I can like do other stuff now.

                        YOGA 2
        That's so great!

                        YOGA 1
                     (suddenly serious)
        Mike wants to start trying for a baby.

                        YOGA 2
        Ok?!

                        YOGA 1
        No — I can't blow this body on a baby, Steph. I'm going
        to have to leave him.

They giggle, then notice something and scream.

In the middle of the room, there is a guinea pig, just
looking at them.

Fleabag rushes over.

                        FLEABAG
        Ah shit.

                        YOGA 2
        That is not hygienic!

                        FLEABAG
        Sorry.

YOGA 2

Ugh gross. We're leaving now.

They grab their yoga mats and rush out. Fleabag picks Hilary up and turns to camera.

FLEABAG
(to camera)
I suppose you should meet Hilary. Two years ago I—

INT. FLASHBACK, CAFÉ — DAY

Fleabag stands nervously in front of Boo, who is sat with a birthday cupcake and some tea.

FLEABAG
Ok. The most important thing is if you don't like it we can't take it back, Ok?

BOO
Ok.

FLEABAG
Happy birthday.

Hands her the box.

FLEABAG
Sorry. I panicked.

BOO
As long as I can wear it or eat it I'm happy.

FLEABAG
You can do both of those things.

Boo opens the box. She looks in, then at Fleabag in disbe-lief.

BOO
Oh my God — did you get me a — ?!! — what is this?! What the— what is it?

Lifting up the guinea pig.

FLEABAG
I dunno... something to love?

BOO
She's beautiful.
(affectionately smacking Fleabag)
You idiot.

She is thrilled with her present.

INT. CAFÉ — DAY

Fleabag puts the guinea pig back in her cage.

> **FLEABAG**
> (to the guinea pig)
> Escape artist.
> (to camera)
> I don't feel anything about guinea pigs, they're point-less, but Boo took Hilary very seriously as a gift and soon everything became guinea-pig related.

INT. FLASHBACK, CAFÉ — DAY

We see shots of Boo putting up a guinea-pig picture. She turns once she has hung it.

> **BOO**
> This is an excellent one.

INT. CAFÉ — DAY — CONT.

Fleabag looks at the same picture on the wall.

She misses Boo.

She snaps out of it.

> **FLEABAG**
> (to camera)
> Drink?

INT. ARSEHOLE GUY'S PAINFULLY COOL STUDIO FLAT — NIGHT

Fleabag is holding a drink. The studio is immaculate. Not a thing out of place.

Arsehole Guy glides in, also holding a drink and a piece of prosciutto.

> **ARSEHOLE GUY**
> Look, I'm sorry about the mess.

> **FLEABAG**
> No problem.

> **ARSEHOLE GUY**
> You want some prosciutto with that?

He approaches her and puts it in her mouth before kissing her. It's a bit awkward because she has prosciutto in her mouth.

He starts kissing her neck.

> **FLEABAG**
> (to camera)
> So reliable. Utterly inaccessible, relentlessly profound. All he wants is to get you in the bath and ask questions like—

INT. ARSEHOLE GUY'S BATHROOM — NIGHT

CUT TO: a close-up of Arsehole Guy's perfectly dampened hair and glistening face in the bath.

> **ARSEHOLE GUY**
> What are you afraid of?

Fleabag sits at the other end.

> **FLEABAG**
> (to camera)
> And you find yourself saying things like —
> (to Arsehole Guy, profoundly)
> I guess... losing the currency of youth.

He looks at her, intrigued, impressed. Fleabag looks to camera. Smashed it.

> **ARSEHOLE GUY**
> Ask me a question.

She thinks.

> **FLEABAG**
> (tongue in cheek)
> When did you realise you were so good-looking?

> **ARSEHOLE GUY**
> (serious)
> I knew I was different when I was about nine. But shit got real around eleven.

> **FLEABAG**
> Shit got real?

> **ARSEHOLE GUY**
> You know. Aunts got weird.

Fleabag frowns and nods.

                    ARSEHOLE GUY
I've got another question.

                      FLEABAG
Ok.

                    ARSEHOLE GUY
Do you ever feel lonely?

Beat.
                      FLEABAG
                     (earnest)
Yeah. Of course. Do you?

                    ARSEHOLE GUY
Never.

He sits up and leans forward.

                    ARSEHOLE GUY
Do you want some pineapple?

Fleabag looks to camera, then back at him.

                      FLEABAG
Yeah.

He stands up and gets out the bath. She looks to camera,
reacting to his body.

INT. ARSEHOLE GUY'S BEDROOM — NIGHT

They are in bed. They are passionate. He has his hands on
her tits.

                    ARSEHOLE GUY
God yeah... They're so small.

Fleabag frowns.

                    ARSEHOLE GUY
They're so small.

Fleabag frowns.

                      FLEABAG
What?

                    ARSEHOLE GUY
They're so small. God they're so fucking tiny.

                      FLEABAG
Yeah I guess—

                    ARSEHOLE GUY
                    (so aroused)
Oh my God they're hardly even there. Where the fuck even
are they?

                    FLEABAG

Bit much.

                    ARSEHOLE GUY

Excuse me.

He turns her around to FUCK HER UP THE ARSE.

                    FLEABAG
                    (to camera)
I'm having a Harry Panic. Madame Ovary is telling me to
run back to safe place. I can make baby in safe place.
But I've got to ride it out. Mustn't —
                    (beat)
Call. H—

INT. BAR — NIGHT

Harry sits opposite Fleabag. Who looks very morose and
proper.

                    FLEABAG

Thanks for coming.

                    HARRY

That's Ok. Are you Ok? Your message sounded urgent.

                    FLEABAG

Were you busy?

                    HARRY

No, I was in the interval of—

                    FLEABAG

Oh cool.

                    HARRY

Cats.

                    FLEABAG

Ok. Was it good?

                    HARRY

Really good actually. Really good.

                    FLEABAG

Sorry for interrupting.

HARRY

No it's Ok. I got the feeling it wasn't going to end well for the cats so — it's probably good to remember them like that — before they all — um. Sorry. Um. Are you Ok?

FLEABAG

Who were you with?

HARRY
(coy)

A work friend.
                    (beat)
A girl.

Beat.

She looks at the camera. Who...?

She pulls the little dinosaur toy out of her bag.

FLEABAG

I found this.

She places it on the table.

Beat.

HARRY

Thanks. I didn't realise I left it.
                    (beat)
Why's your hair wet?

She looks at him flirtatiously, running her hands through her hair.

HARRY

Don't look at me like that.

FLEABAG
(to camera, flirtatious)

Like what?
                    (to Harry)
Like what?

HARRY
(suddenly)

Look, I don't want to sound cold or cruel or... I don't want you to think I'm just off happy at the theatre all the time either. I'm not... But I'm not going to — I just — if this is about getting back together. I was serious. This time I'm just not going to come running back, I really just need some time away fr—

INT. FLEABAG'S FLAT — NIGHT

Harry is on top of Fleabag. They are 'making love'.

> **HARRY**
> (gently)
> I'm so glad you called.

> **FLEABAG**
> (gently to Harry)
> I'm so glad you picked up.

> **HARRY**
> I've missed you. I've missed you.

The 'lovemaking' is happening very slowly. Very... very... very... slow... ly. It's full of meaning for Harry.

> **HARRY**
> My gosh you feel good.

> **FLEABAG**
> Mmmm.
> (to camera)
> I wish he'd just fuck me. All he wants to do is make love.

> **HARRY**
> Are you Ok?

> **FLEABAG**
> (gently)
> Yeah I'm really good. I'm amazing.
> (to camera)
> He's wasting me.
> (beat)
> I was once fucking a guy who would breathe on every thrust—

CUT TO: INT. FLASHBACK, FLEABAG'S BEDROOM — NIGHT

Same shot, but OLDER MAN is fucking Fleabag. He says 'young' on each thrust.

> **OLDER MAN**
> You're so *young*. You're so *young*.

INT. FLEABAG'S BEDROOM — NIGHT

Fleabag with Harry making love. Fleabag frowns.

                    FLEABAG
I masturbate about that all the time. I masturbate a
lot these days. Especially when I'm bored, or angry, or
upset... or happy or...

She moves him off her gently. She starts masturbating. He
smiles.

                    HARRY
Shall I—

                    FLEABAG
No, could you just... stay there...

He frowns. He stops. She orgasms. He kisses her. She jerks
away, still enjoying her orgasm.

INT. FLEABAG'S KITCHEN — MORNING

Harry and Fleabag eat toast.

                    HARRY
Look, I think we should stop masturbating.

Massive pause.

                 HARRY (CONT'D)
Don't say anything yet. I just... I just think it would
help us focus on each other... Being more present.
Really successful couples do it.

                    FLEABAG
Um—

                    HARRY
I've hidden our vibrators.

                    FLEABAG
                  (to camera)
'Our.'

                    HARRY
I thought it would be fun.

                    FLEABAG
To find them?

                    HARRY
No. Just to try to not... touch ourselves. To try
and... Save our touches for each other.
                     (beat)
What do you think?

                    FLEABAG
I think you're being really sexy.

She mimes moving her hand towards her vagina.

                    HARRY
DON'T.

                    FLEABAG
I'm joking. I never masturbate! I don't know how!

                    HARRY
Also, I thought we should try and surprise each other
once every day. Just a sweet little something. To keep
it... You know.

                    FLEABAG
Are you getting this out of a book?

                    HARRY
                  (excited)
I've already planned your first surprise so...
              (really pleased with himself)
Don't eat too much before dinner...
See you later.

He smiles. Kisses her. Bends down to her vagina.

                    HARRY
And I will see *you* later too.

INT. CAFÉ — DAY

Fleabag looks through her mail. Claire enters the café.
Awkward.

                    FLEABAG
Oh. Hi.

                    CLAIRE
Just thought I'd... pop by for some lunch.

Beat.
                    FLEABAG
Bit weird.

                    CLAIRE
Yes well.
                  (beat)
How are you? Quiet day?

                    FLEABAG
Yeah I'm fine. You Ok? You look stressed.

                    CLAIRE
Well, I'm successful so... Do you have rye bread?

                    FLEABAG
No. But I have normal bread you could just puke up
after.

                    CLAIRE
Great.

                    FLEABAG
What do you want in it?

                    CLAIRE
Oh, just tomatoes is fine.

                    FLEABAG
Just tomatoes? Just a tomato sandwich.

                    CLAIRE
Yes. Is there a problem?

                    FLEABAG
Nope.

Fleabag tries not to smile. She makes the sandwich.

                    CLAIRE
Listen, I don't want to know anything about this party.
But if you could just um... Have it at mine this Friday
at 7:30 that'd be great. I can organise it and act
surprised but if you could just — you know what why
don't I just do it. I can organise it, do the food, and
act surprised and just to take it off your hands. I can
see that you're busy so...

                    FLEABAG
Ok, if you want—

                    CLAIRE
Well I don't want to but I think it would be easier for
everyone if I could just—

                    FLEABAG
Ok.

                    CLAIRE
I meant I've done it, it's done. It's this Friday at
7:30 at mine.

                    FLEABAG
Great.

Claire frowns. She picks up and looks at the FINAL DEMAND bills on the counter.

> **CLAIRE**
> How behind are you? If it's money that you need—

> **FLEABAG**
> I don't need money.
> (hands Claire sandwich)
> That'll be £25 please.

> **CLAIRE**
> London!

Claire gets out her wallet. Claire pays, then looks at Hilary.

> **CLAIRE**
> I can't believe that thing's still alive.

She starts to leave.

> **CLAIRE**
> Oh. Any news on Harry?

> **FLEABAG**
> Yeah we're back together.

> **CLAIRE**
> God I can't keep up.

Claire shakes her head and leaves.

INT. FLEABAG'S FLAT — NIGHT

Fleabag opens the front door.

> **FLEABAG**
> (calling out)
> Hello!
> (beat. Nothing.)
> Harry?

Nothing. She is about to go into the kitchen, when she stops. She spots the candles and a present wrapped up on the table.

> **FLEABAG**
> (to camera)
> Oh shit.

She hurry-creeps to the bedroom, past the bathroom, where we catch a glimpse of the oblivious Harry in the shower. She has an idea.

INT. FLEABAG'S BEDROOM — NIGHT

She finds a black t-shirt and ties it around her head so she looks like a ninja — whole face covered, with a slit for the eyes.

We follow her creeping out.

INT. FLEABAG'S KITCHEN — NIGHT

She grabs a huge knife from the kitchen. She is giggling to herself.

INT. FLEABAG'S CORRIDOR OUTSIDE BATHROOM — NIGHT

Fleabag swings open the door silently. Harry is in the shower facing away from her, rubbing his face.

We follow her into the bathroom.

She gets really close.

She gets closer. He stops rubbing his face. Sensing something. She is trying desperately not to giggle.

She gets really close. She holds up the knife over her ninja-mask-covered face

He turns around, he sees the ninja, AND TOTALLY FREAKS OUT.

> **FLEABAG**
> SUUURRPPPRRRRIIISEEEEEEEEE!!!

He SCREAMS, his hands flap about, he bursts into tears and drops to his knees shaking and crying.

Fleabag is both horrified she has scared him so much and in a fit of hysterical laughter. She tries to tear off the t-shirt-mask.

> **FLEABAG**
> It's me! It's me! It's me!

Harry continues to scream. He is in a proper panic. The shower is still running. She climbs in to hold him.

> **HARRY**
> Why would you DO THAT?! I THOUGHT I WAS GOING TO GET RAPED.

> **FLEABAG**
> (can't help her laughter)
> I'm so sorry! I'm sor— baby I'm sorry, I thought you
> wanted a surprise. It was a ninja surprise...

> **HARRY**
> Oh my God my heart is. I'm shaking so much. Oh my God.
> (beat. He takes a deep breath. Then starts to
> properly cry)
> Oh my God. Oh my God. Ok. It's Ok. Are you Ok? Oh my
> God. Did you — did you have a good day?

> **FLEABAG**
> (concerned laughing)
> Yes. Fine thanks. I'm so sorry. I didn't think you were
> going to react like that — sorry, it was a joke.

> **HARRY**
> It was a good joke. Jesus. I thought you'd be later.

> **FLEABAG**
> Yeah—

Harry jumps and screams.

> **HARRY**
> Oh GOD sorry. I just — I think I'm — I'm still in shock
> — I'm still — Ok.

They both sit, damp, in the bath under the shower. He
breathes deeply. Fleabag rubs his back and occasionally
giggles.

> **HARRY**
> (deep breathing)
> That was horrible.

> **FLEABAG**
> It was a surprise.

> **HARRY**
> I know. Thank you. It's fine.

She rubs his face and looks at the camera, trying to hide a
grin — whoops.

> **FLEABAG**
> Shall I go and get us some wine?

He nods.

EXT. STREET — NIGHT

Fleabag running back down a street being chased by someone.
She has just stolen a bottle of wine.

> **SHOP OWNER**
> I KNOW WHAT YOU LOOK LIKE! I KNOW WHAT YOU TOOK! THAT
> IS THE LAST TIME!!

INT. FLEABAG'S KITCHEN — NIGHT

Fleabag walks in.

> **FLEABAG**
> Splashed out on a special bottle for a special—

Harry is sitting dramatically with his towel around his hair
in the dark kitchen. His laptop is in front of him.

> **FLEABAG (CONT'D)**
> Harry?

Opening his laptop—

> **HARRY**
> I had to go into the history on my computer to find
> something I'd seen on the H&M website this morning and
> — I don't want to point fingers, but...

He takes a deep, brave breath and reads the history.

> **HARRY (CONT'D)**
> Anal, gangbang, mature, big cock, small tits, hentai,
> Asian, teen, MILF, big butts, lesbian, gay, facial,
> fetish, bukkake, young and old, swallow, rough,
> voyeur... and public.

Long pause.

> **FLEABAG**
> Why you being so sexy?

Beat.

She's taking the piss. He looks at her bravely.

> **HARRY**
> Don't make me hate you. Loving you is painful enough.

Beat.

Fleabag tries to hold it together but she can't help but—

FLEABAG

Ok, sorry... but I really think you should write that
down. I know it's not appropriate, but I really think
you should write that down. It's a really good for your
— a line for—

HARRY

I'm not going to write that down—

FLEABAG

No no, I'm serious. For your songs and stuff — it's
perfect. It's poetic yet real... Serious.

She mimes writing. He hates her.

Beat.

But he does it. He reaches for a pen and scribbles it down
in a notepad. He angrily dictates to himself.

HARRY

Don't make me—

FLEABAG

Hate you—

HARRY

YEAH I KNOW THANK YOU.
          (beat. He continues to write)
Loving you is painful...
          (throws the pen and notepad down)
WHAT AM I DOING?

He grabs his laptop and a bag and starts piling his things
into it. They speak at the same time. He is distraught while
packing away.

HARRY

Look, there is someone at work who loves me. She
told me she loves me and I said we couldn't be
together because I had to know and — do you want to be
alone?
          (beat)
You will never see me again.
          (he goes to leave)
I will always love you but I just can't take it any
more.
          (beat)
I-I don't hate you. I'm scared for you.

FLEABAG
          (to camera)
He's going to write that down.

Beat

He can't help but write it down.

He hates himself.

He leaves.

> **HARRY**
>
> I'm gonna go pack up my things up from the bedroom again, but I'm... I'm not going to clean. It's still in pretty good shape, so... If I don't see you after that — goodbye.

He exits.

Beat.

Fleabag stands there. Harry comes back through the door.

> **HARRY**
> (sincere)
>
> Forever.

He leaves the room again. Fleabag looks at his dinosaur. She looks at the camera.

> **FLEABAG**
> (to camera)
>
> He'll be back.

Harry opens the door again.

Beat.

He walks slowly past her. He takes the dinosaur. He tries not to look at her as he walks out.

Fleabag is left standing alone. She is shocked. This time really is forever.

END OF EPISODE 2

EPISODE 3

EXT. CEMETERY — DAY

Fleabag is jogging through the cemetery. She stops to stretch.

>   **FLEABAG**
>   (to camera)
> Jogging.

>   *TITLES: FLEABAG*

EXT. CEMETERY — DAY

Fleabag and Claire sit next to each other on a bench. Opposite them is a grave with fresh flowers on it.

Fleabag is still in jogging gear and trainers. Claire is in her work clothes.

>   **FLEABAG**
> I did a fart the other day that was exactly like Mum's.

>   **CLAIRE**
>   (deadpan)
> A door opening or suspicious duck?

>   **FLEABAG**
> Door opening.

>   **CLAIRE**
> Means you're getting Mum's bum.

>   **FLEABAG**
> God, I'd be lucky. My bottom dropped ages ago. My farts used to be like (loud and strong) PAH. Now they're just sort of... fighting their way out.

>   **CLAIRE**
> I haven't farted in about three years.

Fleabag reaches into her pocket and takes out a tiny box with a tiny cake in it.

>   **FLEABAG**
> Happy Birthday.
>   (to camera)
> She won't eat it.

> CLAIRE
>
> Thanks.

She starts eating it. Fleabag looks surprised.

> CLAIRE
>
> So it's a 7 p.m. arrival tonight for a 7:30 surprise,
> Ok?

> FLEABAG
>
> Yeah, I got your email.

> CLAIRE
>
> It's really a business birthday thing. It won't be much
> fun so just — don't expect a party-party.

> FLEABAG
>
> I won't.

> CLAIRE
>
> And maybe just wear trousers and don't drink too much.
> There's this huge promotion in Finland. So this party —
> is quite a serious — I mean it's basically a business
> meeting.

> FLEABAG
>
> Sounds like a blast. Can I bring a date?

> CLAIRE
>
> Harry?

> FLEABAG
>
> No.

> CLAIRE
>
> Who?

> FLEABAG
> (grins)
> Don't know yet.

Claire smiles in a weary way for Fleabag.

> CLAIRE
>
> It's really inappropriate to jog around a graveyard.

> FLEABAG
>
> Why?

> CLAIRE
>
> Flaunting your... life.

They both look at the grave. Claire takes a deep breath.

                              CLAIRE
God, I can't wait to be old.

                             FLEABAG
If it's any consolation you look older than you are.

Beat.

Claire gives her a sideways look. She is not going to rise
to her.

Claire's phone rings.

                              CLAIRE
                         (to the grave)
        Sorry.
                          (to Fleabag)
        Sorry.

She picks it up and walks away out of shot.

                              CLAIRE
                          (on phone)
Hello, Claire speaking...

                             FLEABAG
                          (to camera)
Mum died three years ago. She had a double mastectomy
but never really recovered. It was particularly hard
because she had amazing boobs. She used to tell me I
was lucky cos mine would never get in the way.

Claire sits back down, her call over.

                             FLEABAG
                          (to camera)
        My sister's got whoppers.

She looks at her sister's breasts.

                             FLEABAG
But she got all of Mum's good bits.

Claire comes off the phone.

                             FLEABAG
What's Martin given you?

                              CLAIRE
A cursory stroke would be nice.

                             FLEABAG
What? No bang-bang?

                              CLAIRE
He's still got that thing on his...

                              FLEABAG
What...

                              CLAIRE
On his...

                              FLEABAG
Come on, you can do it.

                              CLAIRE
I don't have to say—

                              FLEABAG
Come on.

                              CLAIRE
No. Not here.

                              FLEABAG
Say it. Come on.

                              CLAIRE
No.

                              FLEABAG
Please—

                              CLAIRE
Penis.

                              FLEABAG
Thank you.

Beat.

                              CLAIRE
He says he has a thing on his penis.
                    (to the grave)
Sorry.

Fleabag gives the camera a look.

EXT. CEMETERY — DAY — CONT.

Fleabag and Claire are now walking together.

                              CLAIRE
Christ. Look at that man. Tragic.

A MAN cries heavily by a grave.

> **FLEABAG**
> Nah he's a con.

> **CLAIRE**
> You can't call someone who is grieving a con.

> **FLEABAG**
> That is shit grieving! No one grieves like that unless they're in a film or from Italy!

> **CLAIRE**
> (simultaneously)
> Look at him, he's properly grieving. Who are you to pass judgement on his grief?!

> **FLEABAG**
> Trust me, he's at a different grave every day. Can't get enough of it.

Beat.

Claire stares at her.

> **FLEABAG**
> What?

> **CLAIRE**
> You come here every day?

Fleabag shrugs slightly.

> **CLAIRE**
> Don't do a jumpy outy surprise thing. And don't sing 'Happy Birthday'. I couldn't bear it.

Beat.

She smiles shortly.

> **CLAIRE (CONT'D)**
> I'm um... I'm actually looking forward to it.

Fleabag smiles at her. Ugh.

EXT. STREET — LATER — DAY

Fleabag is walking down the street, dialling a number on her phone.

> **FLEABAG**
> (on the phone, emotional)
> Hi, Harry, it's me. Ummm... Listen I know we're broken
> up but it's, it's Claire's birthday tonight and I
> thought that um...

Fleabag approaches a couple sitting on a bench with a dog
beside them. The dog is looking directly at Fleabag.

> **FLEABAG**
> (distracted by the dog)
> Er I thought that maybe you'd like to come to her...
> birthday party. Anyway give me a call and um, hope
> you're Ok. Bye.

As she walks past, the dog continues to look at her. She
looks back.

The dog is looking back at her over his shoulder too.

She is surprised at how flattered she feels. She goes a bit
coy.

She looks back again. He looks back at her too.

She turns to camera, getting serious.

> **FLEABAG**
> (to camera)
> Can't go out with a dog.

EXT. CAFÉ — DAY

Establisher of Fleabag's café.

INT. CAFÉ — DAY

Fleabag sits at the counter. She has her back to us. She has
her leggings pulled down and is taking pictures of her
vagina.

> **FLEABAG**
> (to camera)
> My boyfriend before Harry used to make me send him
> pictures of my vagina wherever I was. Ten or eleven
> times a day. One day when I was temping, he asked me to—

INT. FLASHBACK, OFFICE — DAY

Fleabag walking quickly down a corporate corridor towards a
disabled toilet. Her phone goes. We see the message.

Send me one of your favourite bits of your body

She stops and looks exhausted. She starts to turn when her phone beeps again. She reads.

Your pussy or tits please

INT. FLASHBACK, DISABLED LOO — DAY

Fleabag is in the disabled toilet taking pictures of her vagina.

She chooses one and sends it.

She's about to go when she gets another text.

Oh my God, I'm wanking! Send me another...

Unbuttons her top. Bored. Takes a photo of her tits. Sends it. Another text.

ANOTHER ONE. ANOTHER ONE!!!!

Fleabag unbuttons her top again, looking at us.

INT. CAFÉ — DAY

Fleabag takes a photo of her vagina. She scrolls through the photos she's taken.

> **FLEABAG**
> (to camera)
> Time to throw the net out...

She sends multiple photos. Suddenly Martin enters in a panic. He is dishevelled and drunk.

> **MARTIN**
> I AM IN SO MUCH TROUBLE.

Fleabag stands and hurriedly pulls up her leggings.

> **FLEABAG**
> Jesus Christ!

> **MARTIN**
> WHAT AM I GOING TO GET CLAIRE?! I AM MEANT TO GET HER THE PERFECT PRESENT. I AM NOT DRUNK.

> **FLEABAG**
> (to camera)
> Always drunk.

> MARTIN

I AM NOT DRUNK.

He knocks something over accidentally.

> FLEABAG
> (to camera)

Which is odd cos Claire's so straight.

> MARTIN

Smack me in the face. Really hard.

> FLEABAG

Really?

> MARTIN

Yes.

A customer walks in just as Fleabag SLAPS Martin in the face hard.

The customer makes a muffled 'oh God' and leaves.

> MARTIN

Fuck. Think you've given me a semi.

He laughs. Fleabag's grossed out.

> MARTIN

Can I get a water or a sandwich or something.

> FLEABAG
> (to camera)

I mean, the man's got a problem.

Martin stands by the sandwich fridge dancing at the sandwiches and takes one.

> MARTIN

Speak to me. Speak to me...!

> FLEABAG
> (to camera)

But no one wants to admit there's a problem because then they don't get to have crazy nights with fun drunk Martin.

> MARTIN
> (to sandwich)

Chicken... Are you chicken?

> FLEABAG
> (to camera)

He's one of those men who is explosively sexually inappropriate with everyone but makes you feel bad if you

take offence because he was just 'being fun'. Honestly,
you could tell him you were going to pop to the loo.
And he'll say—

INT. FLASHBACK, PARTY — NIGHT

Martin is sitting with Claire, Fleabag and two other women.

> **MARTIN**
> (jovially)
> Yesss you pop to the loo, pull down your knickers and I
> will come in and FUCK YOU!

He laughs uproariously. Everyone sort of half-laughs,
including Claire.

INT. CAFÉ — DAY

Martin looks at Fleabag's café.

> **MARTIN**
> I mean this place is ridiculous. Does anyone ever come
> in here? I mean it is creepy as fuck!

> **FLEABAG**
> Why don't you get her a guinea pig? It was a surprise
> hit here.

> **MARTIN**
> What? You think she'd like a pig? Can I take this one?

He steps towards Hilary.

> **FLEABAG**
> *No*. Not that one.

> **MARTIN**
> CHRIST WOMAN! Something wrong with that one. Got death
> in its eyes.

> **FLEABAG**
> Yeah. Vet says she's depressed.

> **MARTIN**
> (to Hilary)
> Aren't we all, girl.
> (to Fleabag)
> You know guinea pigs can die of loneliness.

> **FLEABAG**
> Can they?

This hits Fleabag. She looks at the camera.

INT. FLASHBACK, CAFÉ — DAY — CONT.

Boo is holding Hilary in front of Fleabag.

>   **BOO**
>   Hold her.

>   **FLEABAG**
>   No!

>   **BOO**
>   She needs it!

>   **FLEABAG**
>   No!

INT. CAFÉ — DAY — CONT.

Martin has had an idea. He's right up close to Fleabag.

>   **MARTIN**
>   Sssssshhh, I have an idea.

>   **FLEABAG**
>   (to camera)
>   Urghhh — he's sexually inappropriate and he eats raw
>   sausages, but no one's made her laugh like he does, so
>   I guess I have to give him that.

CUT TO: INT. FLASHBACK, END OF SAME PARTY — NIGHT

Martin is drunkenly putting Claire's coat on her. He is
teasing her by always handing her the wrong hole to put her
arm into. She can't help but release a little laugh.

>   **MARTIN**
>   I'll just put your... Where're you going?! What are you
>   doing? Stop it!
>   (puts coat on Claire's head)
>   There — there we go!

INT. CAFÉ — DAY — CONT.

Martin is now very upset, eating sandwiches right up in
Fleabag's face.

>   **MARTIN**
>   (almost crying)
>   I'm an innocent man. I bought her a necklace with her
>   name on it, which she found and told me not to buy. I
>   bought her a book that she already has and she says not

to buy her any clothes because she probably won't wear them. SHE SCARES ME.
                          (almost crying)
This sandwich is so good.

                    FLEABAG
Look this is London. Just fuck off and buy something weird and expensive.

                    MARTIN
No no, it's gotta be good, alright, HELP ME!

                    FLEABAG
Pay me and I'll help you.

                    MARTIN
Fuck off.
                    (beat)
How much?

                    FLEABAG
Sixty pounds.

                    MARTIN
Seventy.

                    FLEABAG
Done.

                    MARTIN
YEAH!

INT. SHOP — LATER — DAY

Martin is staring blankly at a wall of shoes.

Fleabag looks at him expectantly. He turns. Hollowed out.

                    MARTIN
I don't know who she is.

Beat.

                    MARTIN
Is she...?

Picks up a red loafer.

                    FLEABAG
No.

                    MARTIN
What about...

A wedge.

>   **FLEABAG**
> No.

>   **MARTIN**
> Just get whoever you are. Who are you?

>   **FLEABAG**
> I dunno...
>   (beat)
> I want to be that person.

She points to really cool shoes.

>   **FLEABAG**
> I have been that person.

She points to some awful shoes.

>   **MARTIN**
> Huh.

>   **FLEABAG**
> But most of the time I am that person.

She points to some boring boots.

>   **FLEABAG**
> Like everybody else.

>   **MARTIN**
> They're good right? Chic?

>   **FLEABAG**
> Chic means boring.
>   (to camera)
> Don't tell the French.

>   **MARTIN**
> What about these?

He holds up another awful pair.

>   **FLEABAG**
> No! God.

Fleabag looks at her phone.

>   **MARTIN**
> Nooo, stop checking. Alright? Nobody loves you. Help me
> here.

>   **FLEABAG**
> Who is this person?

She holds up a gold trainer, admiring it.

                    MARTIN
    FUCK NO!

                    FLEABAG
    THIS IS PERFECT. Get her something she'd never get
    herself. Surprise her.

                    MARTIN
    She'll think I've gone nuts.

                    FLEABAG
    No, she'll think you see her as this person. And
    everyone wants to be this person.

He fiddles around with the shoe.

                    MARTIN
    I dunno... Aren't these for children?

                    FLEABAG
    No!

                    MARTIN
    Let's keep going. I saw some more stuff she'll hate over
    there.

Fleabag puts the shoe back. Then freezes. Beyond Martin, a
young man is helping his girlfriend try on shoes.

It is JACK. Fleabag's face drops.

Fleabag can't stop staring at Jack, who is kneeling by a
girl and helping her choose a shoe. They are clearly a
couple.

Jack looks up and catches Fleabag's eyes. His face drains of
colour. His girlfriend turns to look at Fleabag.

INT. FLASHBACK, BOO'S FLAT — MORNING

The girls are still up and really high. They are giggly.

                    BOO
    My neighbour is really fit.

                    FLEABAG
    Which one?

                    BOO
    The fit one.

                         FLEABAG
The one with the sexy big belly?

                           BOO
No no, he's the other neighbour. He's like... he's
like... Ok. I'm gonna hold his face in my head so you
can see him.

                         FLEABAG
Ok.

Fleabag frowns but totally goes with it.

Boo really thinks hard.

                         FLEABAG
I'm not getting anything.
                          (beat)
Make your face his face.

                           BOO
Yeah Ok.

She tries really hard to morph her face into his. Her face
doesn't change that much.

                         FLEABAG
Is he mixed race? I'm getting mixed race.

Boo gasps with joy — he is!

                           BOO
Yes he is!

They laugh. There is the sound of his door opening. They
jump up.

                           BOO
That's him!

                         FLEABAG
Come on.

                           BOO
Noooo. Ok.

EXT. FLASHBACK, CORRIDOR — DAY — CONT.

Fleabag and Boo are in the doorway. Their faces are squidged
in the door.

Jack walks past checking his mail. He suddenly notices them.

                        JACK
Jesus!

                        BOO
                (intensely whispered)
I'm really sorry. We're really high.

                      FLEABAG
We just really wanted to know what you looked like.

He points to his face.

                      FLEABAG
She thinks you're lovely.

Boo winces. He focuses on Boo, then smiles at her and then
goes. They close the door laughing.

INT. SHOP — DAY — CONT.

Jack is still looking at Fleabag. Fleabag is in shock. Jack
waves.

Meanwhile Martin has come back and has put on a pair of
heels.

                      MARTIN
                (admiring them)
Oh my God. Look at my ELEGANT feet!

Fleabag can't deal with the proximity to Jack. She grabs her
bag and legs it.

EXT. STREET — DAY — CONT.

Martin chases Fleabag down the street. He's still wearing
the heels.

                      MARTIN
                (calming her)
Hey hey hey hey hello hey HEY!

He makes her stop.

                      MARTIN
What's your problem? Who was that?

                      FLEABAG
Er ... No one, it was — What? No, no one. I just need to
go and get a drink — or something.

                              MARTIN
        Ok. Well. Excellent. Can I go get my shoes?

                              FLEABAG
        Yeah?

Fleabag waits for him as he runs back.

INT. BAR — DAY

Fleabag and Martin are sat in a bar. Fleabag downs a drink.

                              MARTIN
                            (recovering)
        Woah. Easy tiger.

                              FLEABAG
        Coming from you.

Beat.

                              MARTIN
        So come on. Who was that heartbreaker?

                              FLEABAG
        He used to go out with Boo. And then he slept with
        someone else and... she...

EXT. FLASHBACK, ROAD — DAY

Boo stands by the busy road and walks into it.

INT. BAR — DAY

Back with Fleabag and Martin.

                              MARTIN
                            (sensitively)
        Yeah. Yeah, I know. Ok. Fuck.

Beat.

                              MARTIN
        I've never really said how sorry I was-

                              FLEABAG
        You should get the trainers.

He realises she doesn't want to talk about it.

                          MARTIN
She'll say I don't know her.

                          FLEABAG
You don't.

                          MARTIN
You're just as bad. It's never clear what she wants — I
should just get her some perfume.

                          FLEABAG
                     (losing patience)
Jesus, just fuck her. Please. For the love of a good
woman. Just wrap your willy up in a bow and screw her.
She's going insane.

He sits back. He looks at her, defensive suddenly.

                          FLEABAG
What is it?
                          (beat)
You having an affair?

He smiles in a slightly smug, defensive way.

Beat.

                          MARTIN
Think you're a clever little puss don't you.

                          FLEABAG
A little marital poke isn't going to kill you.

                          MARTIN
Would it kill her to take me out to dinner? You girls,
Jesus. Anyone said that to her they'd be hung.

                          FLEABAG
If they were hung she probably wouldn't be complaining.

Beat.

He didn't like that. He laughs — holding back his rage.

                          MARTIN
A little advice from a married man... You should prob-
ably get yourself out there, sweetie.
                          (beat)
You're juuust tipping your prime.

There is a weird beat between them. Martin holds up his
glass. He's trying to cover the weird beat, but ends up
making it worse with this suggestion.

>   MARTIN
> Another drink?

Her phone beeps. At last! She grabs it.

>   FLEABAG
>   (to camera)
> Bingo.
>   (to Martin)
> Excuse me. I have a date. Get the trainers. The shop
> closes in an hour.

She leaves.

EXT. STREET — DAY

Bus Rodent and Fleabag are walking down the street. Bus
Rodent is very out of breath.

>   BUS RODENT
> Whooooaaaa, I was not expecting to see you again.

>   FLEABAG
>   (to camera, embarrassed)
> Shut up.

>   BUS RODENT
> Don't get me wrong. I'm chuffed to my boots. But
> um... And thank you for the text. Saucy. And sorry I'm
> late.

>   FLEABAG
> Oh no, it's fine. It was last-minute! It's really nice
> to see you—

>   BUS RODENT
> No no I'm such a toolbox. I'd like to say I was
> trying to save a puppy or something, but I just
> got my coat caught on someone else's coat outside
> the tube — we had to separate ourselves. It was
> fucking intense. I had to give him my coat. What are
> we doing?

>   FLEABAG
> Well it's my sister's surprise birthday party—

>   BUS RODENT
> Cool, yeah, love surprises. Go on.

>   FLEABAG
> I just thought I need to get her a present first.

> **BUS RODENT**
> Woahh, what are you going to get her? I know this
> beeeeautiful soap shop. I mean this stuff just gets you
> straight. In. The. Bath.

> **FLEABAG**
> Oh, I was thinking more like—

INT. SEX SHOP — DAY

Bus Rodent, surrounded by sex toys, looks terrified. He
can't cope with being in a sex shop.

> **BUS RODENT**
> (slightly under his breath, totally freaking out)
> Um. Yah... Yah... These places. All the time... Yah.

> **FLEABAG**
> You Ok?

> **BUS RODENT**
> N—yes.

> **FLEABAG**
> Sorry, I won't be long.

He waves his hand like he's super chilled and it like
totally doesn't matter.

The WOMAN who works there approaches. They all greet each
other.

> **WOMAN**
> Hi. What you craving?

> **FLEABAG**
> Oh just a really, really, cheap thrill.

> **WOMAN**
> (slightly flirtatiously at Fleabag)
> For you?

> **FLEABAG**
> (to camera)
> Hello.

Bus Rodent notices them flirting.

> **BUS RODENT**
> (defensive)
> No. It's for her sister.

The Woman looks amused by his jealousy.

                          FLEABAG
                         (to Woman)
It's for my very sexually frustrated sister. Just a
basic bunny would be great.

                          WOMAN
Ok, I'll see what I can dig out. You go browse.

Beat.

Fleabag smiles and turns to look at the goods for sale on
the wall. Dildos, whips etc.

As she looks at the vibrators, behind her, Bus Rodent is
freaking out. He switches a vibrator on, and then can't
switch it off and panics.

                          FLEABAG
Oh I think you just — at the bottom.

He finds the off switch. They laugh awkwardly.

                        BUS RODENT
It's always a twist.

Fleabag turns. He's found a new sex toy.

                        BUS RODENT
Whoa.

                          FLEABAG
I know.

                        BUS RODENT
You should totally get one of those.

Beat.

                          FLEABAG
A vagina?

                        BUS RODENT
Yah!

She looks again at the penetrable vagina he is suggesting
she might need. She decides to try some intelligent banter.

                          FLEABAG
Ah I've already got one.

                        BUS RODENT
                       (not getting it)
Really... you — you've got one?

                    FLEABAG
I take it with me everywhere.

                    BUS RODENT
No you lie! You do not have one on you now...?

                    FLEABAG
Yup.
                    (to camera)
Never gonna get it.

                    BUS RODENT
Where?

                    FLEABAG
Where is my vagina?

                    BUS RODENT
Yeah!

                    FLEABAG
Where is my vagina?

                    BUS RODENT
Yeah!

Beat.

                    FLEABAG
Ah you got me! I don't carry a vagina around with me!
                    (beat)
That would be way too provocative.

They laugh.

                    FLEABAG
                    (to camera)
Didn't get it.

Woman walks up with a vibrator. Bus Rodent starts panicking
again.

                    WOMAN
Ok, this one is really great. It's half price because
it's quite relentless. It called the Burrower.
                    (beat)
Basically, it doesn't stop until you come.

Bus Rodent panics, feels a bit sick.

                    BUS RODENT
Excuse me.

He exits.

>   **FLEABAG**
> Oh don't worry about him. He'll be fine in a
> minute.

EXT. CLAIRE'S HOUSE — EVENING

Bus Rodent is more than fine. He is REALLY fine and totally
enthusiastic.

They are walking towards Claire's house.

>   **BUS RODENT**
> Oh my God I LOOOVE surprise parties! I love them I love
> them! I love them. Will your parents be there?

>   **FLEABAG**
> My dad might be—

>   **BUS RODENT**
> Ugh intense! Parents adore me. I want you to be totally
> in love with me by the end of the night. Ok?

There is a beep of a car.

Fleabag and Bus Rodent see Claire waiting in the car. She
waves them up to the house and taps her watch.

>   **BUS RODENT**
> Who's that?

>   **FLEABAG**
> That's my sister.

He starts ducking behind the cars.

>   **BUS RODENT**
> Oh noooo, are we are going to ruin the surprise?! Oh
> nooooo! Get down!

>   **FLEABAG**
> It will be fine—

CUT TO: INT. CLAIRE'S HOUSE — LIVING ROOM — EVENING

Claire walks in to—

>   **EVERYONE**
> SURPRISE!

>   **CLAIRE**
> My God thank you so much! I'm SO surprised.

> FLEABAG
> (to camera, impressed)

She's very good.

Godmother and Dad stand close to each other, her arm around his back.

> GODMOTHER

How divine. What a lovely husband you have.

> DAD

Where is he then?

They all turn to see the back of Martin swaying with a drink.

> GODMOTHER

Ah. Busy.

> CLAIRE

I'm blown away. I had absolutely no idea.

Everyone smiles. Claire turns to talk to a guest. Godmother turns to Fleabag.

> GODMOTHER
> (sweetly)

Hello.

> FLEABAG

Hello.

Fleabag smiles. Dad smiles. Bus Rodent smiles at everyone. They all stare at his teeth.

> BUS RODENT

Dad. Hi.

They shake hands.

INT. CLAIRE'S HOUSE. KITCHEN — EVENING

The party is in full swing. Godmother, Bus Rodent, Dad, Martin and Fleabag all stand around. Claire is in the background, on her computer with some business-looking people.

> BUS RODENT
> (mid-conversation)

Thank you for asking. I'm essentially a doc maker. Docs.

Martin roars with laughter.

DAD
Oh really. What is your latest project?

BUS RODENT
Well sir, I'm interested in life. And how it affects
lots of people in all sorts of different ways.

Dad smiles encouragingly.

BUS RODENT (CONT'D)
Yeah, it's awesome.

MARTIN
How did you two meet?

BUS RODENT
Oh I met her on a bus. So easy to pick up girls these
days. I was like 'hi' and she was like 'TAKE MY NUMBER'.
I was like yeah.

Everyone laughs.

GODMOTHER
I'm just going to see if there are any wines to try.
It's lovely, I'm just going to see if there are any
others.

Fleabag watches Godmother move across the room.

FLEABAG
'Scuse me. Can't resist.

Fleabag follows her.

Godmother is looking for more wine.

FLEABAG
Found anything nicer?

GODMOTHER
Oh I was so sorry to hear about Harry. Lovely Harry.
Love Harry.
(beat)
Exciting news about his new job.

Fleabag looks to camera. She doesn't know what Godmother is
talking about.

FLEABAG
Oh yes very exciting.

GODMOTHER
I was so pleased that you found someone else so fast. I
just can't stop conjuring an image of you sitting around

in that café. Just all alone. Feeling so terribly
lonely. Just can't stop picturing it.

FLEABAG
I don't think you have to be alone to be lonely. Dad
always taught me that.

GODMOTHER
Did your father tell you that one of my pieces has gone
missing?

FLEABAG
He did. It's awful. I'm so sorry.

GODMOTHER
So sweet of you.
                    (beat)
Very sweet.

Bus Rodent comes over, munching on a canapé.

BUS RODENT
May I cut in?

GODMOTHER
Yes of course.
                (admiring them)
Do you know you are the most perfect-looking pair.

Godmother moves off.

BUS RODENT
Such a great gang.

FLEABAG
Do you want some normal food...?

BUS RODENT
No... No. What I really want to do is this—

He tries to gallantly twizzle her around and kiss her, but
they crash into a load of glasses. There's a crash.

FLEABAG
                (shouting)
NO SORRY NOTHING HAPPENED.

BUS RODENT
I was trying to be sexy!

FLEABAG
No it was, it was really sexy!

                    BUS RODENT
    Was it?

Claire comes over.

                    CLAIRE
    What broke? What broke? Show me.

                    FLEABAG
    Nothing, I just slipped. Claire, this is my frie—

                    CLAIRE
    Yes we've already met.

Martin appears. He is drunker than before.

                    MARTIN
    MY WIFE MY WIFE. My wife. All your desires are wrapped
    up in... Here.

He hands her a shoe box.

                    CLAIRE
    Ok.

                    FLEABAG
    Open it!

He hands it to Claire. She opens it.

                    CLAIRE
    Well gold has always—

She pulls out the statue. Fleabag glares at Martin. He
grins. Claire is touched.

                    CLAIRE
    Wow. That's really rather wonderful. Thank you. What is
    it a paperweight or...?

                    MARTIN
    It is a shrine to your BODY. Because I love your body.

                    CLAIRE
                  (she smiles)
    Thank you.

Fleabag takes it.

                    FLEABAG
    WOW! Wow. This is really. Can I — can I see this? Wow I
    think it's really — probably a bit inappropriate for
    your guests to see your body. I'll just... Shall I put
    it somewhere safe? Ok?

She shoves it a drawer.

Claire and Martin have an awkward kiss on the cheek.

EXT. CLAIRE'S GARDEN — NIGHT

Fleabag is smoking.

Martin comes out grinning.

>   FLEABAG
> Smooth.

>   MARTIN
> I told ya I'd find you a buyer!
>   (beat)
> Your boy is hilarious. Smart. Funny—

>   FLEABAG
> Fuck off.

>   MARTIN
> You'd fuck anything wouldn't you.

Beat.

>   FLEABAG
> Just don't tell her you got the statue from me.

>   MARTIN
> How much you want for it? Finger up the ass? Nipple
> tickle?

He laughs. Fleabag just smokes.

>   MARTIN
> Come on! Lighten up.

>   FLEABAG
> She's going to leave you one day.

He is stopped in his tracks. He almost lets his guard down
but he can't. He guffaws.

>   MARTIN
> You looking forward to that?

Fleabag just stares at him.

He pantomimes staring back at her.

He is right up at her face. He is drunk. There is tension
between them. He is playing with fire in the proximity of
his face to hers. She is not moving.

He stops pulling faces, but remains close to her lips.

He leans right in. He's not even sure if he's going to do it... But then he does.

He kisses her.

She doesn't move. She doesn't kiss back or recoil. She just bears it.

He pulls away. He looks pathetic. He's just realised what he's done.

>   MARTIN
> You're an asshole.

He turns away and stumbles back inside.

EXT. CLAIRE'S HOUSE — NIGHT — CONT.

Fleabag is walking away. Claire comes out.

>   CLAIRE
> HEY!

Fleabag is worried she knows what happened. Claire catches up with her holding a coat.

>   CLAIRE
> I think you took my coat!

Fleabag looks down at it.

>   FLEABAG
> Oh.

>   CLAIRE
> Sorry. I just — my coat.

>   FLEABAG
> Oh. Sorry.

Fleabag takes it off and gives it back to Claire. Who takes it and hands her hers.

>   CLAIRE
> Why are you leaving so early?

>   FLEABAG
> I have to give Hilary some Earl Grey... She's not feeling well, so... Oh I got you this.

She pulls out a present wrapped in a bag for Claire.

                              CLAIRE
    I wasn't expecting anything...

She unwraps it. It's the Burrower.

                              FLEABAG
    It's called a Burrower. It basically won't stop until
    you come.

                              CLAIRE
    Sounds horrendous. Thank you.

                              FLEABAG
    Good birthday business?

                              CLAIRE
    Oh huge. Yeah I don't want to jinx it but... Huge.
    Could be life-changing.

There is a moment between them. They both smile.

                              FLEABAG
    Great. Ok. Happy Birthday.

                              CLAIRE
    Thanks... Are you Ok?

                              FLEABAG
    Yeah?

                              CLAIRE
    Tell the truth.

Bus Rodent appears.

                            BUS RODENT
    Are we leaving?

                              FLEABAG
    Yes.

                            BUS RODENT
    Birthday girl! Awesome party, thank you so much, we had
    such a great night.

They hug. Claire's still holding the Burrower. It gets
trapped between them as they hug.

                            BUS RODENT
    What's that?
                            (realising)
    Oh.

Beat.

                              FLEABAG
Goodnight.

                              CLAIRE
Goodnight

                              BUS RODENT
Night.

Claire returns to the house. Bus Rodent touches Fleabag's
hair.

                              BUS RODENT
Shall we?

INT. CAFÉ — NIGHT

Bus Rodent is pounding away at Fleabag from behind. They are
both clothed. She is leaning over the counter. It's a rushed
job.

                              FLEABAG
                          (to camera)
Surprisingly bony.

                              BUS RODENT
I'm nearly finished... I'm nearly finished...

                              FLEABAG
                          (to camera)
It's like having sex with a protractor.

                              BUS RODENT
I'm finishing... I'm finishing... I'm — I'M DONE. I'M
DONE.

He catches his breath.

                              BUS RODENT
I'm done. Are you done?

                              FLEABAG
Oh yeah.

                              BUS RODENT
Amazing. That was amazing. That was amazing.
                          (beat)
That was amazing.

He looks at her, realising.

                              BUS RODENT
Oh for fuck's sake.

                                    FLEABAG
What?

                                   BUS RODENT
You don't go through life with teeth like these and
not... know when someone's pretending.

He walks away.

                                   BUS RODENT
WHAT THE FUCK IS THAT? I'LL KICK IT. I'LL KICK IT.

Fleabag looks to the floor and sees Hilary in the half
light. Bus Rodent tries to kick her suddenly.

                                    FLEABAG
No! NO!

She pushes him aside and picks up Hilary.

                                   BUS RODENT
Uh... Do we catch that or is that yours? That is a rat!

                                    FLEABAG
It's a guinea pig.

                                   BUS RODENT
That is a rat!

Fleabag holds Hilary, shaken.

INT. FLASHBACK, CAFÉ — NIGHT

Boo is happily stroking Hilary as Jack strokes her hair.

INT. CAFÉ — NIGHT

Later. Fleabag sits alone with Hilary on her chest. Music
begins to play.

INT. FLASHBACK, CAFÉ — DAY

Montage of Boo and Fleabag with Hilary, having a great time.

INT. CAFÉ — NIGHT

Back with Fleabag. She starts to smile and strokes Hilary.

EXT. CEMETERY — MORNING

It's a new day. Fleabag jogs and notices the crying man again.

She waves. He waves back.

END OF EPISODE 3

EPISODE 4

INT. CLAIRE'S CAR — DAY

Fleabag and Claire are in the car.

Claire is driving. They are mid-argument.

> **CLAIRE**
> You cannot know this. No one can hold a map in their head.

> **FLEABAG**
> I CAN. It's three turnings away.

> **CLAIRE**
> You're so going to get this wrong. Stop it.

> **FLEABAG**
> What?

> **CLAIRE**
> I can feel you judging my driving.

> **FLEABAG**
> I'm not judging your driving.

> **CLAIRE**
> Let go of the handle then.

> **FLEABAG**
> Oh we were supposed to go down that turning.

> **CLAIRE**
> WHAT? YOU SAID THREE TURNINGS.

> **FLEABAG**
> Yeah well I missed one.

> **CLAIRE**
> JUST USE YOUR PHONE. YOU HAVE A SAT NAV ON YOUR PHONE.

> **FLEABAG**
> Oh my God THERE. Mindful oh God Farm. There it is. We're going the right way. I was right.
> > (to camera)
> I was right.

Claire sees it and shuts up. They sit in silence.

> **FLEABAG (CONT'D)**
> Do you know what the lesbian app for Grindr is called?

Claire doesn't respond.

FLEABAG (CONT'D)

Twat-nav.

CLAIRE
(bursting into tears)
DON'T MAKE THIS FUN.

INT. CLAIRE'S CAR, PARKED ON HARD SHOULDER — DAY

The car is now parked up on the side and Claire is crying in the way that people cry when they wish they weren't.

She is desperately trying to hold it down, which only makes her hyperventilate.

CLAIRE
It's Ok. I'm fucking Ok. I'm excellent.

Fleabag looks suspiciously at the camera.

CLAIRE
I know I seem mental, but I'm fine.

FLEABAG
Ok...

CLAIRE
I just — I just sometimes need — need you not to—

FLEABAG
To take the piss-

CLAIRE
DON'T FINISH MY SENTENCES — take the piss—

FLEABAG
Out of you when you're—

CLAIRE
YOU DON'T ALWAYS KNOW WHAT I'M GOING TO SAY Ok?

FLEABAG
Sorry.
(to camera)
Out of her when she's driving.

CLAIRE
Out of — me while I'm driving.

Pause. She wipes her eyes and looks in the mirror. She breathes out. Relaxes.

                    FLEABAG
I'm sorry. Is it home or work or Martin or —

                    CLAIRE
It's fine. It's fine. Martin's being lovely.

                    FLEABAG
Really?

                    CLAIRE
It's fine.
              (beat, calming down)
I'm Ok.

Fleabag nods.

Beat.

                    FLEABAG
              (to camera, terrified)
Fucking psycho.

                TITLES: FLEABAG

EXT. RETREAT HOUSE/CAR PARK — DAY

The sisters are walking up a path carrying their
bags.

                    FLEABAG
Wow. Dad really splashed out this time.

                    CLAIRE
He must be about to do something awful.

                    FLEABAG
No, it's just Mother's Day.

This jolts Claire slightly. She hadn't realised.

                    CLAIRE
Oh.

                    FLEABAG
Happy Mother's Day.

A few moments go by. They don't speak.

                    FLEABAG (CONT'D)
We're not supposed to bond on this, are we?
                    (beat)
Because I really don't think that's going to end
well.

                    CLAIRE
We're not supposed to talk at all. It's a silent
retreat. God help us.

They walk for a bit.

                    CLAIRE
How's everything at the café, are you—?

                    FLEABAG
You really don't have to—

                    CLAIRE
Thank you.

Some very peaceful people walk calmly by.

                FLEABAG/CLAIRE
                  (very politely)
Hi. Hi. Morning.

The calm people smile and nod and continue off.

Claire rings the bell.

No one comes to the door.

Claire rings again.

                    CLAIRE
   Come on.

Claire looks at her phone.

                    FLEABAG
They're probably going to think we're a couple.

                    CLAIRE
The fact that your mind even goes there is beyond
disturbing.

                    FLEABAG
Hey! We'd make a really cute couple.

Claire sighs and shakes her head.

In the distance they hear a man shout.

                              MAN (O.S.)
SLUUUUUUUUUUUUTS.

They both frown and turn around. There is no one there.
They both frown.

                              FLEABAG
                          (shouting back)
       YEEESS?

She turns to Claire.

                              CLAIRE
We're gonna die here. We're going to be raped and die.

                              FLEABAG
                            (shrugs)
       Every cloud.

                              CLAIRE
            (through her teeth, to the door)
       Just open the fucking door it's been fucking
       forev—

The door is opened by a MONK.

Both girls smile super politely.

                              MONK
       Welcome.

As they walk in —

                          CLAIRE/FLEABAG
       Thank you so much. Really wonderful. Really beautiful
       grounds. Extraordinary energy.

INT. RECEPTION — DAY

There is a sign saying 'Talking Zone' and an hourglass
counting down to silence.

The RECEPTIONIST is writing in a big leather book.

                          RECEPTIONIST
                      (very softly spoken)
       I see you've been gifted this retreat. How lucky you
       both are.

The girls smile.

                          RECEPTIONIST
       I hope after this weekend you'll feel rested, inspired—

                          CLAIRE
Do you have wifi?

                        RECEPTIONIST
No. Would you... like two single beds or a double...?

                          CLAIRE
Two singles.

                          FLEABAG
A double please.

                          CLAIRE
Actually, do you have a separate room?

                        RECEPTIONIST
I'm afraid not. Everyone has to share here. It's part
of the communal fee—

                          CLAIRE
Singles then. Do you get newspapers in the morning?

                        RECEPTIONIST
                          (laughs)
No. We try and keep the outside world on the outside
during your stay here. You'll appreciate it in the end,
I promise. So, here's your key. I hope you have a
restful weekend.

                          FLEABAG
You too.

They move off.

                          FLEABAG
Wow. No papers.

                          CLAIRE
You don't read the news.

                          FLEABAG
Yes I do.

                          CLAIRE
What happened yesterday?

                          FLEABAG
Sting wore white jeans and a puppy got stuck in a fan.

Claire looks at her blankly as they walk up the stairs.

                          FLEABAG
                        (to camera)
Big day.

INT. DORM — DAY

Claire is laying out all her moisturisers.

Fleabag has one moisturiser.

It takes ages. Claire has so many lotions.

> **FLEABAG**
> What's that for?

> **CLAIRE**
> My neck and chest.

> **FLEABAG**
> What's that for?

> **CLAIRE**
> My legs and knees.

> **FLEABAG**
> What's that for?

> **CLAIRE**
> The ends of my hair.

> **FLEABAG**
> What's that?

> **CLAIRE**
> For my under-eyes. What's that?

> **FLEABAG**
> That is for my face and body. What would you do if
> someone stole all those?

> **CLAIRE**
> I'd kill myself. Why are there no plugs in here?
> > (beat)
> Don't touch my stuff.

Fleabag is fiddling with some of Claire's things. She's
holding a pouch and finds some batteries.

> **FLEABAG**
> What are these for?

> **CLAIRE**
> Nothing.

> **FLEABAG**
> Hm.

                          CLAIRE
What?

                          FLEABAG
Well it's... Why would you bring such
tiny batteries?

                          CLAIRE
I'm just prepared.

                          FLEABAG
Just I've only ever see them used for remote
controls...

                          CLAIRE
Yes well—

                          FLEABAG
Or alarm clocks or—

                          CLAIRE
Yes alright.

                          FLEABAG
And vibrators—

Claire goes bright red.

                          CLAIRE
YES ALRIGHT.

Beat.

                          FLEABAG
You didn't have to ask for a separate room.

                          CLAIRE
What?

                          FLEABAG
If you want to have a wank I can give you some space.

                          CLAIRE
                       (mortified)
Oh my God.

                          FLEABAG
If you want to take ten minutes, I'll just go into the
bathroom and moisturise my wrists for a bit.

                          CLAIRE
You are so immature.

Claire opens the door to the bathroom.

> **FLEABAG**
> Oh give it a minute.

The smell hits Claire.

> **CLAIRE**
> OH GOD. Seriously WHAT IS WRONG WITH YOUR INSIDES?

> **FLEABAG**
> Why did you bring the tiny BATTERIES?

Claire storms out. Fleabag looks at the camera — chuffed. She sits on the bed. She looks at the batteries.

INT. FLASHBACK, FLEABAG'S LIVING ROOM — DAY

Boo is standing on the sofa taking the tiny batteries out of the clock.

> **BOO**
> Ah ha!

She throws them to Fleabag, who is packing a vibrator.

> **FLEABAG**
> You're a genius.

> **BOO**
> Always know where the reserves are.

She grins.

INT. MEDITATION ROOM — DAY

Close-up of the RETREAT LEADER (forty, serious, gentle).

> **LEADER**
> Let go of your past.

Beat.

> **FLEABAG**
> (to camera)
> Bit on the nose.

There are about twenty women and one man all sitting on the floor. Some of them in proper yoga poses.

> **LEADER**
> Now is the time to let it go. Open up your senses. Close your mouth and live... now.
> (beat)

Welcome to the female-only 'Breath of Silence' retreat...
Women: Don't Speak.

Pause. The ONLY MAN gets up, embarrassed.

>   **ONLY MAN**
> Sorry, I think I'm meant to be at—

>   **MALE VOICE (O.S)**
> FUCKING SLUT!!!!

>   **ONLY MAN**
> That one...

He runs out.

>   **FLEABAG**
>   (to camera)
> Shame.

>   **LEADER**
> The first major consideration is 'why are you here'.
> Can anyone here answer that question?

Fleabag puts up her hand. Claire looks at her,
suspicious.

>   **FLEABAG**
> I want to shut the noise out and reconnect to my inner
> thoughts on the road to feeling more at one with myself.

Claire gives her a look. Fleabag nods profoundly at her.

>   **LEADER**
> Excellent attitude. Well you're in the right place.
>   (beat)
> This weekend is about being mindful. It's about leaving
> your voice in your head. And trapping your thoughts in
> your skull. Think of it as a thought prison in your
> mind.

Fleabag and Claire look at each other. Christ.

>   **LEADER**
> Firstly we are going to teach you how to breathe.
>   (beat)
> Then we will have a short meditation. Then we will find
> our sanctuary in the partaking of menial tasks. All in
> perfect silence.

Claire is unmoved.

>   **LEADER**
> Principal rules are: No talking. If you need to commu-

nicate with any of the other superiors you can write on
that board.
                    (points to a tiny board)
Under no other circumstances must you communicate. Even
with each other.

                         FLEABAG
What if there is an emergency—?

                         LEADER
Thank you all for coming here today. No matter what
happens, a word must not be heard.

EXT. GROUNDS — DAY

Everyone is outside doing menial, and apparently mindful,
gardening work. They occasionally look up and nod at each
other. Fleabag is working on some grass.

A wasp attacks a woman in the background. She is trying not
to scream. She is shushed by the Leader.

                    MALE VOICE (O.S.)
    ARGHHH.

The women look up. They are not impressed.

Fleabag, intrigued, leans over the hedge.

She wanders away from the women and down a path to find a
room of men, shouting at blow-up dolls who are sat in
chairs.

Nobody notices her.

INT. WORKSHOP — DAY

Fleabag creeps along the corridor and peers through some
glass doors.

We watch it all from her slightly-too-far-away POV.

There is a workshop of about forty men in motion. All the
men are shouting 'SLUT' or other sexist insults to the
blow-up dolls in the chairs.

                    WORKSHOP LEADER
Back here, back here! Back to me.

They all stop and listen to the very enthusiastic,
highly energised WORKSHOP LEADER.

WORKSHOP LEADER
(they quieten down)
Ok. Now wherever it's come from; your upbringing. Your
experiences with women. *Now* is the time to turn that
around. To reprogramme your mind, your body and your
mouth, to be the better man. Alright?
(beat, he holds up a blow-up doll.)
So — this is Patricia, yeah? She's a friend. Now
Patricia has just earned a promotion at work, beating
six other candidates. She's the youngest person ever to
achieve this role. What should we not say when we meet
her?

The men speak up at random.

JAMES
Clever little munchkin?

WORKSHOP LEADER
Excellent.

MARK
Who did you have to blow to get that job?

WORKSHOP LEADER
Ok.

FRANK
SLUT you FUCKING STUPID SLUT.

Beat.

WORKSHOP LEADER
Ok. Ok. What should we say to her?

Long pause. The men seem slightly confused.

Longer pause.

Then Bank Manager from Episode 1 steps forward.

BANK MANAGER
Well done, Patricia.

All the other men nod and murmur, 'Well done, Patricia'.

Fleabag squints at Bank Manager. She recognises him. She
smiles.

WORKSHOP LEADER
Very good. Well done, Patricia.

He turns and sees her.

INT. FLASHBACK, BANK MANAGER'S OFFICE — DAY

Flashback to Episode 1.

> **BANK MANAGER**
>
> Please leave.

> **FLEABAG**
>
> Perv.

> **BANK MANAGER**
>
> Slut.

> **FLEABAG**
>
> WOW.

INT. WORKSHOP — DAY

Back at the workshop. Fleabag and Bank Manager smile a little in recognition.

Suddenly a man notices her.

> **FRANK**
> (to Fleabag)
>
> SLUT.

All of the other men notice her and begin to act shifty and nervous.

> **WORKSHOP LEADER**
>
> Guys. It's Ok.

A very NERVOUS MAN nervously interrupts him.

> **NERVOUS MAN**
>
> Oh my God. Um excuse me miss, you can't be here. You really can't be here. It's for your own good.

> **FRANK**
> (whispering)
>
> Ok!

Fleabag nods, waves to Bank Manager and backs off.

INT. MEDITATION ROOM — DAY

Touching workshop. Everyone is sat opposite a partner. Fleabag and Claire are together.

On the tiny board is written: 'I've been stung by a wasp'.

>   **LEADER**
> And now, hands up! Mirror your palms. Look each other
> in the eye. And... touch.

Fleabag winks at Claire.

>   **FLEABAG**
>   (to camera)
> Literally her worst nightmare.

Fleabag touches Claire's palms, who shudders.

INT. DORM — NIGHT

Fleabag and Claire are whispering. Fleabag is in bed. Claire
is getting ready for bed.

>   **FLEABAG**
> Are you alright? Talk to me!

>   **CLAIRE**
> It's nothing.

>   **FLEABAG**
> God. I can't feel my feet.

>   **CLAIRE**
> Do you remember when we used to go top to toe?

>   **FLEABAG**
> Yeah. Kids are so weird.

>   **CLAIRE**
> We used to do that all the time.

>   **FLEABAG**
> Yeah, when we were TEN and CUTE. Now we're thirty and
> angry.

>   **CLAIRE**
> God, I'm not suggesting that we—

>   **FLEABAG**
> Just no. Ok.

Claire gets under the covers.

Beat.

Fleabag looks suspicious — we hear a buzzing sound start,
coming from under Fleabag's covers.

Claire looks over. Fleabag waggles the vibrator at her.

                    CLAIRE
Stop stealing my things!

                    FLEABAG
I'm just checking it's working!

                    CLAIRE
Oh it's working, it's definitely working.

There's a loud knock on their door.

                 VOICE (O.S.)
Shhhh.

Fleabag puts the vibrator on again, laughing. She hands it back to Claire.

                    FLEABAG
Have fun!

Claire puts it on the bedside table.

                    CLAIRE
It's actually a really thoughtful present. Thank you. And Martin getting me that sculpture. He must have bent over backwards to get something like that. I feel very lucky.

Beat.

                    FLEABAG
I have to tell you something.

                    CLAIRE
What?

                    FLEABAG
I stole that sculpture... From a certain somebody's studio. And then I tried to sell it through Martin. But Martin took it and gave it to you. Just don't put it pride of place when Dad... well when they come over, Ok, because—

                    CLAIRE
Right.

Claire switches off the lamp and turns over to go to sleep.

                    FLEABAG
Claire?... Claire?

                    CLAIRE
Shhh. Go to sleep.

> **FLEABAG**
> (to herself)
Shit.

INT. DORM — MORNING — 6 a.m.

A loud gong goes off. Fleabag jolts awake. The clock says 6 a.m.

Claire is already dressed.

> **CLAIRE**
> (whispering)
> The sooner we get o—

Fleabag mimes at her to be silent.

> **CLAIRE**
> (whispering)
> The sooner we get on with it, the sooner we are out of here.

> **FLEABAG**
> That's a really nice outfit.

> **CLAIRE**
Thanks.

She exits.

INT. MEDITATION ROOM — DAY

Everyone sits in the hall with their eyes closed except Fleabag.

> **LEADER**
> (sing/speak)
> Delve into your past.

Everybody does.

> **LEADER**
> Think of something you can't let go of in the past.

She frowns. The Leader mimes for Fleabag to close her eyes.

> **LEADER**
> A moment of noise. A moment of tension.

INT. FLASHBACK, FLEABAG'S BEDROOM — NIGHT

We see a woman's hands unbuckling a guy's trousers.

INT. MEDITATION ROOM — DAY

Fleabag opens her eyes. She is a bit shocked.

She shakes the flashback off.

> **FLEABAG**
> (to camera)
> Not for now.

Fleabag closes her eyes again.

> **LEADER**
> Now a moment when you were peaceful.

INT. FLASHBACK, FLEABAG'S BEDROOM — NIGHT

Boo and Fleabag are lying in bed facing each other. They are whispering.

> **FLEABAG**
> If you could change anything in the world what would it be?

> **BOO**
> My thighs.

Fleabag pisses herself.

> **FLEABAG**
> (laughing)
> In the whole world?

> **BOO**
> Don't tell anyone I said that. You?

> **FLEABAG**
> I've always been insecure about my face. You know that.

> **BOO**
> I know, you shouldn't!

> **FLEABAG**
> Thank you but—

> **BOO**
> No seriously! There's nothing wrong with your nose!

Beat.

Realising—

BOO

I mean there's nothing—

FLEABAG

Sorry?

Boo realises what she has said.

BOO

I mean...

FLEABAG

What?

BOO

I don't know.

FLEABAG
(starting to laugh)

OH MY GOD.

BOO

NO I ALWAYS SAY THE WRONG THING.

INT. KITCHEN — DAY

Claire and Fleabag and the other women eat soup silently.

It's too hot for Fleabag. She yells. The other women stop and stare at her.

INT. CORRIDOR — DAY

Everyone is cleaning the floors. The Leader walks around them nodding.

CLAIRE
(whispering)

What is this? I don't even do this in my own home.

FLEABAG

Oh it's very simple. We've paid them to let us clean their house in silence.

Claire laughs loudly. Everyone looks round at her. Her laughter suddenly morphs into crying.

                              FLEABAG
                           (to camera)
JESUS.

INT. SMALL OFFICE — DAY

Claire and Fleabag sit opposite the Leader like two naughty
children. The tired, but understanding Leader takes a deep
breath.

                              LEADER
     I don't want to come down on you like a school teacher,
     but I'm afraid your flagrant lack of respect for the
     one rule we have here is now affecting the other
     students — clients—

                             FLEABAG
Inmates.

                              CLAIRE
Cleaners.

                              LEADER
                        (finds the word)
     Participants. Do you have a problem with the programme?

Beat.

Both the girls look down.

                              LEADER
     I suggest you try sitting here in silence for the next
     hour. It will benefit you. I swear by my soul. It will.

She stands up and leaves. When they think she's out of
earshot, Fleabag turns to Claire.

                             FLEABAG
     I went through your bag.

                              CLAIRE
What?

                             FLEABAG
     I couldn't find anything so you're just going to have
     to tell me what's going on with you.

Pause.

                             FLEABAG
     Talk or I'll scream.

                              CLAIRE
I got the Finland promotion.

                             FLEABAG
What Finland promotion?

                              CLAIRE
HOW CAN YOU ASK THAT I'VE TOLD YOU ABOUT IT—

                             FLEABAG
                         (simultaneously)
OH MY GOD I'M JOKING — I KNOW THE FINLAND PROMOTION.
THAT'S AMAZING!

                              CLAIRE
Thank you.

                             FLEABAG
Does that mean you are a millionaire now?
                          (to camera)
Handy.

                              CLAIRE
Don't be ridiculous. Yes, it would.

                             FLEABAG
Money makes you cry?

                              CLAIRE
I'm turning it down.

                             FLEABAG
What?! Why?
                          (to camera)
Martin...

                              CLAIRE
Martin says it would be unfair on Jake.

                             FLEABAG
                          (to camera)
Jake's her stepson. He's really weird. Probably clini-
cally but no one really talks about that. He freaks out
if she's gone for longer than a day and has this thing
about trying to get in the bath with her.

CUT TO: INT. FLASHBACK, CLAIRE'S BATHROOM — DAY

Claire is in the bath. The door creaks open. She looks
nervous and grips the side.

A young teenage boy walks through the door and tries to get
in.

                              CLAIRE
NO. NO. NO JAKE. NO—

INT. SMALL OFFICE — DAY — CONT.

Fleabag looks at Claire. Appalled.

                              FLEABAG
                         (to camera)
          He's fifteen.
                         (to Claire)
          He's not your son!

                              CLAIRE
          That's not the point.

                              FLEABAG
          GO.

                              CLAIRE
          I KNEW you'd say that!

                              FLEABAG
          This is what you've always wanted! No more power-suits.
          Fuck load of snow. The perfect place for your cold, cold
          heart.

                              CLAIRE
                         (simultaneously)
          I know. I know.

                          CLAIRE (CONT'D)
          I know! I CAN'T. I have responsibilities.

                              FLEABAG
                 (can't believe she is turning this down)
          Oh come ON. Don't let other people get in the way of
          what you really want. Finland is what you really want!

                              CLAIRE
          My 'husband' isn't... 'other people' Ok.
                         (beat)
          My 'husband'... is my life.

                              FLEABAG
          Your *'husband'* tried to kiss me on your birthday.

Claire looks like a train has hit her.

Long pause.

                              CLAIRE
                         (weakly)
          Did he?

Fleabag nods.

CLAIRE
(harder)

Did he?

Fleabag nods.

Beat.

Claire gets up and walks out.

INT. DORM — EVENING

Fleabag enters the dorm. Claire is not there.

Fleabag sits on the bed.

MALE VOICE (V.O.)

SLUT.

(beat)

SLUT.

(beat)

SLUT.

She looks out and sees a group of men gathered on the grounds.

MALE VOICE

SLUT.

She smiles.

EXT. RETREAT GROUNDS, SLIGHT MOUND — EVENING

Fleabag walks through the grounds. She sees Bank Manager among the group of men. He's standing up and holding his Patricia doll.

BANK MANAGER

SLUUUUT.

FRANK stands up.

FRANK

SLUUUUT.

Fleabag lights a cigarette as she watches from a distance.

WORKSHOP LEADER

Up on your feet. We're going to say, 'Sorry, Patricia'.

EVERYONE
Sorry, Patricia.

WORKSHOP LEADER
Lovely. Give yourselves a round of applause.

They all clap themselves.

WORKSHOP LEADER
Alright guys, well done. We are going to head back to
that house better men. Yeah.

They walk towards the building. Bank Manager stands slightly
separate to them, in his own thoughts, holding his Patricia
doll.

He looks up to see Fleabag watching him. Frightened, he
pauses.

The male Workshop Leader approaches and gently encourages
him...

WORKSHOP LEADER
Go on. You can do it. You're ready.

EXT. RETREAT GROUNDS, SLIGHT MOUND — EVENING

Bank Manager is now sitting next to Fleabag on the mound,
both smoking.

BANK MANAGER
Yes, I thought I recognised you.

Fleabag zips her mouth shut. Can't speak.

BANK MANAGER
Fair enough. Probably for the best. So is your
business... Surviving?

She shakes her head.

BANK MANAGER
I'm sorry.

He lights a cigarette. Takes a drag. Throws it.

BANK MANAGER
So you're doing the whole silent escape thing?

Fleabag indicates she cannot talk again.

BANK MANAGER
Indeed. Going well?

She raises her eyebrows.

She points to him. You?

> **BANK MANAGER**
> I uh... I touched a colleague's breast... more than
> once... at a party... I — they asked me to go on a
> workshop — I'm just a very... disappointing man.

Fleabag smiles. She pushes out her breasts to him.

> **BANK MANAGER**
> No... Thank you. I'm trying to quit. Those, on the
> other hand...

Pause. He takes another cigarette.

> **BANK MANAGER**
> They keep asking me. What do you want from this? What
> do you want?
> > (beat)
> I'm not telling them what I want...

Fleabag looks at him.

Beat.

A beautiful track starts playing quietly under his next
dialogue.

> **BANK MANAGER**
> I want to move back home, I want to hug my wife, I want
> to protect my children, protect my daughter, I want to
> move on, I want to apologise to... everyone, I want to
> go to the theatre, I want to take clean cups out of the
> dishwasher... and put them in the cupboard... At home.
> And the next morning I want to watch my wife drink from
> them. And I want to make her feel good. I want to make
> her orgasm again. And again. Truly.

He smiles. She smiles.

Pause.

> **FLEABAG**
> I just want to cry... all the time.

He looks at her. His smile falls slightly. He looks away. He
understands her. He nods slightly. She looks vulnerable. He
looks at her again. She looks at him. She zips her mouth
shut. He zips his mouth shut. They both look out.

INT. DORM — NIGHT

Fleabag is sneaking back into the room. She sees Claire asleep in her bed. She watches her for a second.

She climbs into her own bed. Then changes her mind.

She gets out and goes to Claire's bed and climbs behind her like they did when they were little.

She puts her arm around Claire.

Beat.

Claire opens her eyes and folds Fleabag's arm under her arm.

They lie like this for a few poignant moments.

INT. DORM — NEXT MORNING

Fleabag wakes up in Claire's bed. Claire is not there.

>   **FLEABAG**
> Claire?

All her things have gone except two small batteries left on the side table.

Fleabag sits up. Confused. She gets up.

INT. RETREAT CORRIDOR — DAY

Fleabag enters a room where all the women are scrubbing the floors.

>   **FLEABAG**
> Have you seen my sister?

They all turn in shock. One of them shakes her head, the other one points to the door.

Fleabag turns and runs.

INT. MEDITATION ROOM — DAY

Fleabag looks around and sees the board. There is a small essay in tiny writing there.

She approaches. Squinting.

Claire has written: *Gone home. Left some money at reception. Just needed a bit of quiet. C.*

Fleabag looks at the camera. Worried.

Fleabag sits down. Puts her hands into her pants. She pulls her phone out. Dials a number.

> **BOO (V.O.)**
> (voicemail)
> *Hi, this is Boo. I can't come to the phone right now, but please leave me a messiagio and I'll get back to you.*

Beat.

> **FLEABAG**
> (to camera)
> Someone should probably disconnect that.

END OF EPISODE 4

EPISODE 5

INT. DOCTOR'S OFFICE — DAY

A male DOCTOR is checking Fleabag's breasts. She is taking it very seriously.

> FLEABAG
> (to camera, grinning)
> I mean, we're all being very grown up about this but um—

> DOCTOR
> Let me know if you feel any discomfort.

> FLEABAG
> No, it's lovely, thank you.

She laughs. He looks uncomfortable.

> DOCTOR
> Your father informed me of your family history.

> FLEABAG
> Yep. Evil boobs everywhere.

He doesn't react.

> DOCTOR
> Arm up please.

She lifts it. She looks down at her breasts.

The Doctor starts the check on her breast. He is touching it mechanically, but all the way around.

> FLEABAG
> (giggling)
> Heyyy! Stop it!

He stops.

> FLEABAG
> Sorry I'm just ticklish.

He literally could not look more bored.

> DOCTOR
> I examined your sister this morning.

> FLEABAG
> Did you? Did she... Is she alright, did she seem alright?

> DOCTOR
> Yes. Why?

> ### FLEABAG
> Oh just — can't get hold of her.

> ### DOCTOR
> She seemed very busy.

> ### FLEABAG
> Sure.
> (beat, to camera)
> Dad books us boob appointments once a year to make sure
> our tits don't turn on us like Mum's did. It's a bit of
> a hassle, but at the end of the day it's nice to be
> touched.

Beat.

> ### FLEABAG (CONT'D)
> (joking with him again)
> Bet you look forward to seeing Claire. A LOT more to
> touch, if you know what I mean.

He tries to smile.

> ### FLEABAG
> I'm sorry. It's — just — there are worse jobs.

> ### DOCTOR
> Look... I check for cancerous lumps in mammary glands.
> Any pleasure I derive from that is entirely dependent
> upon whether or not I am about to save your life.

Beat. Fleabag is humbled.

> ### FLEABAG
> Of course, Doctor.

> ### DOCTOR
> You can put your clothes back on.

> ### *TITLES: FLEABAG*

EXT. DAD'S HOUSE — DAY

Fleabag runs up the street towards Claire.

> ### CLAIRE
> I've been waiting out here for nearly ten minutes.

                        FLEABAG
You left me on a fucking silent hill.

                         CLAIRE
Yes well I had to — Did you get back Ok? God this is so
stressful.

                        FLEABAG
                      (to camera)
Mum's memorial lunch.

                         CLAIRE
I should have worn my other coat.

                        FLEABAG
                      (to camera)
Visiting Dad is hell for Claire. I see it more as a
sport.

                         CLAIRE
It's so inappropriate that she should be here.

                        FLEABAG
Have you spoken to Martin?

                         CLAIRE
Oh it's fine, everything's fine, everything's totally
fine.

                        FLEABAG
Sounds like it's fine.

                         CLAIRE
Can you please just give me some space, you're standing
SO close to me.

                        FLEABAG
Ready?

                         CLAIRE
No.

Fleabag rings the bell.

                         CLAIRE
Don't tell Dad about Finland. And don't provoke her.
Let's just get out of this alive, Ok.

Fleabag grins.

It opens. Godmother is there. She puts her hand over her
heart, overcome with emotion on this difficult day.

                              GODMOTHER
        Girls.

                              FLEABAG
                          (to camera)
        Got to hand it to her.
                          (to Godmother)
        Hi!

                              GODMOTHER
                          (re the flowers)
        Oh you shouldn't have.

                              CLAIRE
        Oh! They were actually for Dad—

                              GODMOTHER
        Oh are those freesias?

                              FLEABAG
        Yeah they were always a sort of favourite of Mum's—

                              GODMOTHER
        Oh gosh how special, how lovely. Aren't they stunning.
        Let's just leave them...

She just puts them on the step. She looks at them.

                              GODMOTHER
        There.
                          (looks at them)
        Lovely!
                          (beat)
        Come in.

The girls enter the house looking at each other.

INT. HALLWAY — DAY — CONT.

Godmother is taking Fleabag's coat. There is the sound of
sawing in the background.

                              FLEABAG
        Who's Dad sawing in half?!

                              GODMOTHER
        Oh, just the tree.

                              FLEABAG
        Sorry?

Beat.

                    GODMOTHER
The tree in the back garden.

                      CLAIRE
Why are you taking the tree down?

                    GODMOTHER
                     (smiley)
Felicity tried to use it to get out.

They all look at the cat cowering in the corner of the
hallway. Fleabag sees that the cat flap has been taped up.

                    GODMOTHER
She's very expensive.

Godmother takes Fleabag's coat.

                GODMOTHER (CONT'D)
This is nice.

Fleabag gives a suspicious look to camera.

                     FLEABAG
                   (suspicious)
Oh thank you.

                    GODMOTHER
                 (taking Claire's coat)
Oh this is beautiful.

She smiles. Fleabag looks at Godmother's hairpiece. Everyone
is sweet as pie in this exchange.

                    GODMOTHER
I hope you don't mind my being here but my Pilates fell
through so—

                 FLEABAG/CLAIRE
Oh of course. No it's lovely.

She strokes both of their arms.

                    GODMOTHER
It's a sad day. A sad, sad day.
                  (beat, cheerily)
I'll get the champagne.

CUT TO: INT. LIVING ROOM — DAY — CONT.

Fleabag and Godmother and Claire sit in silence.

An unopened bottle of champagne sits on the coffee table with three glasses.

                    FLEABAG
                   (to camera)
This is my favourite bit. Wonder who's going to—

                    CLAIRE
That's a lovely cushion.

                    GODMOTHER
Thanks. It's an original.

                    CLAIRE
                   (bemused)
Gosh.

Pause.

Fleabag relishes the awkwardness. She grins at the camera.

                    FLEABAG
I love your hat.

                    GODMOTHER
It's a hair-scarf.

                    FLEABAG
Looks like a hat.

                    GODMOTHER
                 (still smiling)
Well, it's a hair-scarf.

                    FLEABAG
Ok.

Pause.

                    GODMOTHER
Is Martin coming?

                    CLAIRE
Oh. No. He's away.

The girls look at each other. Fleabag is concerned.

                    GODMOTHER
I'm very excited to meet your new chap. Is he the...

She gestures gently to her front teeth.

                    FLEABAG
Oh no. He's a different one.

                    GODMOTHER
Oo! You do turn over fast.

                     FLEABAG
                  (to camera)
Dad'll come in with some weird canapés in a second.

Beat.

Dad enters with a tray of weird canapés.

                       DAD
    Girls!

He puts the tray down.

                  DAD (CONT'D)
    Hello hello!

They all stand up, but then don't know where to go.

                     CLAIRE
    Hi!

                     FLEABAG
                  (simultaneously)
    Hi!

He smiles at them awkwardly. Godmother smiles endearingly
and stands next to him.

                       DAD
    Sorry about all that noise. Have you got a drink?

Godmother jumps up.

                    GODMOTHER
    Oh sorry!
                    (to Fleabag)
    I forgot your glass.

She exits. Dad turns, slightly nervous.

                       DAD
    You're both looking... very healthy... very good and
    healthy and um...

They smile.

                  DAD (CONT'D)
    Did you... talk to Dr Samuels about your...

He gestures to their breasts.

                    FLEABAG
Yes.

                    CLAIRE
              (simultaneously)
Yes.

                     DAD
They're happy.
                 (still gesturing)
Getting along alright...

              FLEABAG/CLAIRE
Yeah, yep.

                     DAD
Good. Excellent.

He smiles and awkwardly continues.

                 DAD (CONT'D)
You are... my... daughters.

They both nod.

              FLEABAG/CLAIRE
Yep / Yes we are.

Dad looks emotional for a second.

                     DAD
Sit down. I think I should... say a few words about
your mother—

Godmother enters with another glass and starts opening the
champagne.

                   GODMOTHER
                    (sweetly)
Ignore me... Ignore me... Ignore me...

                     DAD
This day is not an easy one—

She pops it loudly with a little 'woo!'.
Godmother holds up her glass.

                   GODMOTHER
Cheers.

                    CLAIRE
              (holding up her glass)
To Mum.

FLEABAG

To Mum.

The girls look at Dad. He looks nervously at Godmother, who
smiles sensitively.

DAD
(quickly)

To Margaret.

Beat. Godmother is visibly jealous. She can't bear it when
he says her name.

GODMOTHER

Dearest Margaret. Just the most... generous woman.

She puts her hand on Dad. He smiles.

DAD

Yes she certainly was a—

GODMOTHER
(quickly)

Yeah she was great.

Fleabag and Claire look at each other. Fleabag and Claire
drink.

INT. LIVING ROOM — DAY

Later. Dad has relaxed a bit. He is at the end of a conversation with Claire about Mum.

DAD
(laughing)

It was the voice she used for the pigeons. She always
made them sound so rude. But very, very funny. She used
to take the girls round the park and point at the um...

FLEABAG

Oh the squirrel voices were the best—

CLAIRE
(doing squirrel voice)

RUN RUN RUN RUN.

Dad and Fleabag join in. Godmother smiles awkwardly.

GODMOTHER

Yes my ex did a similar thing. Voices and fun. Really,
really funny man. Really funny.

Fleabag frowns.

                          GODMOTHER
Can I help you with the food?

                            DAD
Oh yes, yes I should — yes.

                          GODMOTHER
And take that off.

Godmother leaves the room. Dad quickly follows, taking off
his jacket as he goes.

Claire and Fleabag are alone. Claire gets out her phone.

                          FLEABAG
So are you going to Finland? You're going to have to
talk to me eventually.

Claire ignores her.

Fleabag notices Claire has a plait in her hair.

                          FLEABAG
                        (to camera)
Plaits. Either she's got her period or some serious
shit's gone down.
                        (to camera)
She always does something slightly different around her
period. She gets really bad PMT. Mum used to call it
her Monthly Confidence Crisis but it's PMT. The only
way she can get through it is to reinvent herself in
some small way.

INT. FLASHBACK, DAD'S HOUSE. KITCHEN — DAY

Dad and Fleabag talk in the kitchen.

Claire in full Lycra, breathing deeply, looking defiant,
enters. Dad and Fleabag look very awkward.

INT. LIVING ROOM — DAY — CONT.

Fleabag grins.

                          CLAIRE
What?

                          FLEABAG
I'm doing a wee on this cushion.

                          CLAIRE
WHAT??

Fleabag laughs.

> CLAIRE
>
> Sort of wish you were.

Claire takes the statue out of her bag and puts it in front of Fleabag, who panics.

> FLEABAG
> (whispering)
> What are you doing?!?!

> CLAIRE
>
> Just put it back where you got it from, Ok?

> FLEABAG
>
> NO.

> CLAIRE
>
> Just do it. I don't want it in my house. I'm doing you a massive favour. She could really go to town on you for this.

> FLEABAG
>
> Come on. What's she gonna do? DRAW me?

Claire smiles slightly at the joke and gestures to the door.

> CLAIRE
>
> GO.

> FLEABAG
>
> No.

Claire goes to put it back herself and Fleabag jumps up.

> FLEABAG
>
> Ok Ok Ok Ok.

She takes the statue and puts it under her top and exits. Claire follows.

INT. STAIRS — DAY - CONT.

The girls are sneaking up the stairs. Fleabag's sneaking is very pronounced.

> CLAIRE
>
> Why are we sneaking?

> FLEABAG
> (whispering)
> We're not allowed upstairs.

                              CLAIRE
        Of course we are.

INT. GODMOTHER'S STUDIO — DAY

Fleabag and Claire walk in. There are paintings and sculptures and books everywhere.

Claire looks around the room. Claire focuses on one
painting.

                              CLAIRE
        God I keep forgetting that she's actually talented.

                             FLEABAG
        I know. It's infuriating.

                              CLAIRE
                (gesturing to put the statue down)
        Go on then.

Fleabag wipes her fingerprints off the statue, and places it
on the floor, as though it's fallen off the shelf.

                        CLAIRE (CONT'D)
        Where's her head?

                             FLEABAG
        She's got your boobs. She doesn't need one.

Claire smiles. They go to leave.

                             FLEABAG
        Hey — is everything Ok — with Martin?

                              CLAIRE
        You've invited someone today?

                             FLEABAG
        Yeah. But he's horrifically hot. You're gonna puke when
        you see him.
                          (beat)
        Are you on your period?

                              CLAIRE
        Why would you ask that?

                             FLEABAG
                     (to camera)
        The plaits.
                     (to Claire)
        No reason.

                              CLAIRE
Say it.

                              FLEABAG
The plaits.

Beat. Claire touches her plaits and turns away.

                              FLEABAG
                        (laughing a little)
Hey. Do you think she's ever painted Dad naked?

                              CLAIRE
                           (short)
I think you should take your nose out of other people's
marriages.

Fleabag is hurt.

Godmother walks in.

                              GODMOTHER
Oo! Sneaking a preview are we?

                              CLAIRE
Sorry! I spilt my champagne and I got distracted on the
way to the bathroom.

Beat.

She looks at Fleabag.

                              FLEABAG
Me too.

Beat.
                              CLAIRE
It's really beautiful work.

                              GODMOTHER
Thank you. Let me show you to the loo.

                              CLAIRE
Oh that's alright. We grew up in this house.

                              GODMOTHER
It's all changed now though!

Claire leaves.

                              GODMOTHER
Your father is in the kitchen.

> **FLEABAG**
>
> Ah great. I'll go and torment him.

Godmother laughs.

INT. KITCHEN — DAY — CONT.

Fleabag enters while her Dad is looking at the canapés.

> **FLEABAG**
> (to camera)
> He hates being in a room alone with me. Watch this.
> (to Dad)
> Hi.

He turns around and immediately panics, bending his legs a little and moving quite a lot.

> **DAD**
>
> Oh! Oh!

He panics, looking subtly for an exit.

> **DAD (CONT'D)**
>
> I just need some—

He tries to leave.

> **FLEABAG**
>
> What do you need?

> **DAD**
>
> Just some... um...

He is standing next to the salt.

> **DAD**
>
> Sa-lt.

> **FLEABAG**
>
> There it is.

> **DAD**
>
> Oh! Here it is! So um... how are you, darling? Have you got... enough... clothes?

> **FLEABAG**
> (she smiles)
> You can never have enough clothes.

> **DAD**
>
> And how's the café?

                         FLEABAG
Um... Well the lease is up in a couple of days and...
I don't really think I can afford to... I think I'm
going to have to accept that it's—

                           DAD
I'm sorry about that darling, but of course we're just
a little bit tight on the purse-strings too...

                         FLEABAG
Oh no no, I wasn't asking you for any—

                           DAD
... We've just been keeping it quiet. We haven't been
able to buy anything, or do anything.

He smiles. She notices a picture of a beautiful farmhouse on
the dresser.

                         FLEABAG
Oo what's that?

                           DAD
Oh that's um... A tiny little house that we're buying
in... in France.

Beat.

Fleabag smiles.

                         FLEABAG
Lovely.

Beat.

                           DAD
I just wanted to talk to you about this... exhibition—

                         FLEABAG
What exhibition?

He accidentally knocks over a tray of canapés.

                           DAD
Oh no!

Dad goes into a panic.

                         FLEABAG
                        (laughing)
Jesus Dad.

                           DAD
Pick it up pick it up! Help me.

FLEABAG

It's Ok!

DAD

Please please please pl—

FLEABAG

Ok!

DAD

She mustn't — see it — she mustn't find out.

They get on their knees and start scooping up the canapés. Fleabag eats one.

FLEABAG

Mmm five-second rule!

DAD

NO! I've never bought into that rule! It's disgusting!

He looks up at her. He eats one. They both laugh.

Godmother enters.

GODMOTHER

What are you doing?

FLEABAG

Oh just a little family tradition.

GODMOTHER

Oh! What odd fun. What are the rules?

The DOORBELL rings.

GODMOTHER

Oh thank God. That'll be your man.

Fleabag and Dad look at each other.

INT. DINING ROOM — LATER — DAY

Everyone is sat round the table. We don't see who the guest is yet.

FLEABAG
(to camera)

I mean, I didn't want to show off but um...

Arsehole Guy is revealed in all his handsome glory.

                    GODMOTHER
               (really fancies him)
Gooooosh! You really are... So how did you two meet?

                     FLEABAG
                  (to camera)
Fucked me up the arse.

                  ARSEHOLE GUY
I used to manage a bar, and I just found her, crying in
the toilet one night.

Pause.

              ARSEHOLE GUY (CONT'D)
            (to Dad and Godmother)
How about you two? How did you two meet?

                     FLEABAG
Through our mother actually.

Beat.
                       DAD
How's work, Claire?

                     CLAIRE
Oh, fine. Nothing new.
                 (to Arsehole Guy)
She used to be our godmother.

                    GODMOTHER
                    (sweetly)
Still am!
                     (beat)
But then their parents split up.

                     FLEABAG
Mum died.

                    GODMOTHER
And we just became even closer friends.

Another awkward beat around the table.

               GODMOTHER (CONT'D)
You know — and I can say this because I'm an artist —
but you really are very good-looking.

                  ARSEHOLE GUY
Thank you...

                    GODMOTHER
Very.

Beat.

                          ARSEHOLE GUY
Thank you.

                            GODMOTHER
   Very.

                             FLEABAG
Thank you.

Godmother smiles and looks between Fleabag and Arsehole Guy.

                            GODMOTHER
                             (smiling)
   I mean, almost... *too* good-looking!

He's chuffed. Fleabag gets the jibe.

Godmother puts her hand on Dad's hand and smiles.

                          ARSEHOLE GUY
   Excuse me. I've got to do that old human thing.

He gets up and walks out charmingly.

                             CLAIRE
   How's the exhibition going?

                               DAD
   Ah yes... I er... wanted to talk to you about that.

Arsehole Guy reappears.

                          ARSEHOLE GUY
                             (joking)
   Talking about me?

They all laugh and react. 'All good things,' 'Hey!' 'As you
were.' He goes.

They go silent.

He then appears again.

                          ARSEHOLE GUY
   And again!

They all react and laugh again and he goes.

                             CLAIRE
   Have you found a venue?

                             FLEABAG
What exhibition?

                         GODMOTHER
Thank you so much for asking. We have actually found a—

                            DAD
There are some elements of the work that I wanted to
talk to you about...

Dad looks nervous.

                         GODMOTHER
It's a sexhibition. But don't panic! It's nothing scary.
It's simply a journey through my physical and sexual
life climaxing in a few pieces inspired by and moulded
on your father.

Dad takes a mouthful and nods optimistically at the horrified girls.

                         GODMOTHER
And there are photos — I've taken a photo of my naked
body every year for the past thirty years.

                         FLEABAG
Why?

                         GODMOTHER
Well, I think it's important for women of all ages to
see how my body has changed over the years. I think they
have to have a healthy perspective — on my body.
                         (to Dad)
Don't they?

                            DAD
Oh absolutely.

                         GODMOTHER
I don't have to tell you that your father is a deeply
sexual man.

She takes his hand.

                          CLAIRE
No, you don't.

                         FLEABAG
Just did.
                       (to camera)
Knew it.

                         GODMOTHER
I'm very lucky. I will be touched until the day I die.
And so will you, Claire. It's really all that humans
want. Is to be loved. And to be touched.

This hits Fleabag.

INT. FLASHBACK, FLEABAG'S BEDROOM — NIGHT

The same flashback as in the previous episode. A woman's hands unbuckling a guy's trousers.

INT. DAD'S HOUSE. DINING ROOM — DAY

Back with Fleabag. Shaken.

The cat meows, trying to escape out of the window.

> **FLEABAG**
> Tell Dad about your promotion Claire.

> **CLAIRE**
> There's nothing to tell.

> **GODMOTHER**
> What promotion?

> **FLEABAG**
> Finland.

> **GODMOTHER**
> Oh. Odd place.

> **DAD**
> Any news?

> **CLAIRE**
> No.

> **FLEABAG**
> She got it.

> **GODMOTHER**
> (clapping)
> Ooooooooooo!

> **CLAIRE**
> Fuck's sake.

> **DAD**
> Congratulations Claire!

> **CLAIRE**
> Thank you!

> **GODMOTHER**
> Clever girl.

CLAIRE

Can we not.

DAD

It's so exciting!

FLEABAG

She's turning it down.

Pause.

DAD

Why?

GODMOTHER

Why?

DAD

Why, why not, why Claire?

GODMOTHER

Claire, are you pregnant?

FLEABAG

Why aren't you getting on a plane to your cold, rich future?

Godmother and Dad protest more.

CLAIRE

Because YOU CAN'T JUST FUCK OFF ON AEROPLANES AND LEAVE YOUR WEIRD STEPSON AND BROKEN SISTER TO FEND FOR THEMSELVES Ok.

Beat. Claire is emotional. She holds it down.

Fleabag drinks some wine.

FLEABAG

Excuse me.

She gets up and walks to the door.

INT. TOILET — DAY

Fleabag is in the toilet. She closes the door. She sits with her head in her hands.

INT. FLASHBACK, FLEABAG'S BEDROOM — DAY

Fleabag walks into her bedroom. Boo follows.

> **BOO**
> She's your sister. It's your job to annoy her.

> **FLEABAG**
> No I'm just so annoyed with myself. I just wish I could meet myself and just have a go at myself.

Boo takes Fleabag's coat, scarf and hat. She leaves the room.

Beat.

She comes back in wearing all of it. Fleabag smiles.

> **BOO**
> Do your worst.

Boo suddenly goes badass.

> **BOO (CONT'D)**
> COME ON BITCH!

> **FLEABAG**
> (going for it)
> You don't take yourself seriously.

> **BOO**
> Oooo pussy.

> **FLEABAG**
> You need to reach out to your family. You need to stop provoking your sister, just grow up. YOU DO NOT TAKE YOURSELF SERIOUSLY AS A BUSINESSWOMAN. YOU NEED TO PAY YOUR FUCKING BILLS. YOU NEED TO BE NICER TO HILARY. YOU NEED TO GET A NEW HAT.

> **BOO**
> Is that better?

> **FLEABAG**
> Yeah that's better.

INT. TOILET — DAY

Fleabag still sitting there. She hears a scratch on the door. She opens it.

The cat is there.

She lets it in and picks it up.

She stands, opens the window, puts the cat out of the toilet window and closes it.

                    FLEABAG
Ok. Off you go.

INT. DINING ROOM — LATER — DAY

Pudding is on the table.

Godmother is pouring Arsehole Guy some wine.

                    ARSEHOLE GUY
The artwork in this house is stunning. Who is it?

                    GODMOTHER
If I tell you, will you promise to come to my
sexhibition?

                    ARSEHOLE GUY
                (charming as hell)
It's not your work!

                    GODMOTHER
Will you come?

                    ARSEHOLE GUY
It would be an honour.

Beat.

                    GODMOTHER
                (to Fleabag)
How's your little restaurant?

                    FLEABAG
It's a café.

                    GODMOTHER
Oh don't do it a disservice.

                    FLEABAG
I'm not. It's a café.

                    GODMOTHER
Oh. Sorry.

                    FLEABAG
It's fine. It's fine.

                    GODMOTHER
Your father tells me you're struggling.

                    DAD
I - I think we all are!

> **GODMOTHER**
> Oh well yes. But I — now there is only one of you — God,
> I can't imagine what you have been through.

> **ARSEHOLE GUY**
> Sorry have I missed something?

> **GODMOTHER**
> Well — her dear little friend died and left her to run
> the café on her own.

> **CLAIRE**
> Jesus.

> **ARSEHOLE GUY**
> God that is truly awful. How did she die?

> **GODMOTHER**
> Oh she killed herself—

> **FLEABAG**
> It was an accident.

Beat.

> **GODMOTHER**
> Well. Maybe it's time to let the little restaurant go.
> Give it up. Sell it. Have a little holiday.

INT. FLASHBACK, CAFÉ — NIGHT

Fleabag and Boo are drinking and smoking in the café.

> **FLEABAG**
> We did this.

> **BOO**
> Mhm. And whatever happens, we never let it go. Ok?

INT. DINING ROOM — DAY

Back in the dining room.

> **CLAIRE**
> Excuse me.

She exits.

INT. TOILET — DAY

Fleabag is back smoking in the toilet. She blows the cigarette smoke into the room.

INT. HALLWAY — LATER EVENING

Fleabag is getting her coat. Godmother is coming down the stairs.

> **GODMOTHER**
> Have you seen Felicity?

> **FLEABAG**
> Oh no, sorry.

> **GODMOTHER**
> Gosh, all sorts of things go missing in this house, don't they!

> **FLEABAG**
> (smiles)
> Big house.

> **GODMOTHER**
> Yes. Lovely house.
> (beat)
> Oh the sculpture turned up.

> **FLEABAG**
> Did it?!

> **GODMOTHER**
> Yes... Must have just toppled off the side.

> **FLEABAG**
> Well if you rid a woman of a head and limbs you can't expect her to do anything other than... roll around.

Beat. Godmother laughs and looks at Fleabag and smiles.

> **FLEABAG**
> What?

> **GODMOTHER**
> (with a gentle curiosity)
> Oh... Your father and I often say, when you've had a few drinks you're so like your mother.

Beat.

Fleabag pushes Godmother hard. Godmother is knocked backwards into the coats but regains her balance and slaps Fleabag right across the cheek.

They are both shocked.

Fleabag takes a deep breath.

They realise Dad is watching, terrified.

> **GODMOTHER**
> (sweetly)
> Oh whoops. Look at these.

She starts picking up the coats that have dropped on the floor.

Claire comes down the stairs.

> **DAD**
> So, the party's moved to the hallway, always a good sign.

> **CLAIRE**
> Does anyone mind if I leave? I've got a dicky tummy.

> **DAD**
> So swift.

She takes her coat off Godmother.

> **CLAIRE**
> Thanks.
> (to Dad)
> I'm not going to kiss you because I'm probably very ill.
> (to Fleabag)
> You too. Come on.

> **DAD**
> Goodbye then... my... my daughters.

> **FLEABAG**
> Goodbye.

EXT. DAD'S HOUSE. DINING ROOM — EVENING

Fleabag and Claire exit the house. Godmother and Dad follow out after them and stand on the steps.

> **GODMOTHER**
> What a lovely occasion!

> **FLEABAG**
> Yeah. See you at the sexhibition.

> **DAD**
> Ugh — there's absolutely no need to—

> **GODMOTHER**
> (simultaneously)

Y-yes lovely...

> **FLEABAG**

No no. I'll definitely be there. I will *definitely* be there.

Godmother and Dad stand as a couple in the door.

Arsehole Guy squeezes out from behind them holding two helmets.

> **ARSEHOLE GUY**

Hold up! Were you trying to keep me overnight?!

Godmother laughs.

> **GODMOTHER**

Very good-looking! I might never see you again but you're very good-looking!

> **DAD**

Yes, yes, very good-looking!

Everyone is waving now, even though they aren't moving and are right by the door.

EXT. STREET — EVENING

They close the door. Claire, Arsehole Guy and Fleabag walk down the path and onto the street.

> **FLEABAG**

Thanks, I owe you.

> **ARSEHOLE GUY**

No I owe you. It's been really nice to spend a day with a normal family. I actually feel quite emotional. Will you stay with me tonight?

> **FLEABAG**

Sure.

> **ARSEHOLE GUY**

I'm going to go warm up the bike. Lovely to meet you Claire.

> **CLAIRE**

You too...

He walks out of earshot.

                              CLAIRE
Um — what's his—

                              FLEABAG
Fucked me up the arse.

                              CLAIRE
Oh that —

                              FLEABAG
Yeah.

                              CLAIRE
I totally see that now.

Beat.

                              FLEABAG
I'm sorry I was uh—

                              CLAIRE
Listen to me. I'm going to leave Martin. I'm going to
give you the money for the café. And I'm going to go to
fucking Finland.

Fleabag smiles.

                              FLEABAG
Ok.

                              CLAIRE
Oh and —

She pulls out the statue from her bag and hands it to
Fleabag, who is stunned.

                              FLEABAG
That is the coolest thing you've ever done.

                              CLAIRE
I know.

                              FLEABAG
Thanks Claire.

                              CLAIRE
Shall we...?

                              FLEABAG
We can try.

They tentatively hug. It's awkward at first but then they
relax.

                    CLAIRE
I'll see you at the sexhibition.

                    FLEABAG
Yeah.

Claire walks away. Fleabag gets onto the back of Arsehole
Guy's motorbike, who's waiting for her.

As they drive off Fleabag spots Felicity the cat climb
through a fence and walk on the street, free. A new queen of
London.

Fleabag looks at the camera and the bike drives off.

                    END OF EPISODE 5

EPISODE 6

INT. ARSEHOLE GUY'S BEDROOM — NIGHT

Fleabag, hands against a wall, is having sex with Arsehole Guy. He is being really 'sexy'.

He is trying to navigate the sex by taking her from behind but it's clearly not sexy and she looks distressed.

> **ARSEHOLE GUY**
> Ah yeah.

> **FLEABAG**
> Yeah...

> **ARSEHOLE GUY**
> Look at me, I wanna see those tiny things again.

He turns her around and throws her onto the bed.

> **FLEABAG**
> (to camera)
> Stay sexy. Always stay sexy.

He joins her on the bed.

> **ARSEHOLE GUY**
> Those tits!

He gets on top of her and starts having sex again. Her head is banging against the headboard.

> **ARSEHOLE GUY**
> They're so fucking tiny. May I uh —

He turns her over and takes her from behind again, more slowly.

> **ARSEHOLE GUY**
> Erm...

She suddenly looks confused.

He looks confused, but keeps going.

She turns to camera.

> **FLEABAG**
> (to camera)
> Oh God. There is always the stage, when someone's falling in love with you, that they lose their erection. They get confused.
> (beat)
> They panic.
> (beat)

The stakes get too high. The blood rushes from their dick to their heart...

>   **ARSEHOLE GUY**
>   (looking down)
> Oh Jesus.

>   **FLEABAG**
>   (to camera)
> And everything is fucked.

TITLES: FLEABAG

INT. ARSEHOLE GUY'S BEDROOM — MORNING

Fleabag lying in bed looking at a pencil on the bedside table.

INT. FLASHBACK, CAFÉ — DAY

Boo and Fleabag are in the café.

Boo has been cutting some vegetables up. She is holding Hilary and feeding her the veg.

Fleabag is reading the paper.

Fleabag gasps.

>   **BOO**
> What?

>   **FLEABAG**
> Oh no, I don't think Hilary's gonna wanna hear this.

>   **BOO**
> No, go on.

INT. ARSEHOLE GUY'S BEDROOM — MORNING

Fleabag in bed. She smiles at the memory.

INT. FLASHBACK, CAFÉ — DAY

Fleabag and Boo sit as before.

                    FLEABAG
No...

                      BOO
Go on.

                    FLEABAG
Ok... An eleven-year-old boy was put in juvenile prison
for repeatedly sticking rubber-ended pencils up the
school hamster's arsehole.

Boo looks distraught.

                      BOO
What?!

                    FLEABAG
Yeah.

                      BOO
Why would they do that?

                    FLEABAG
Apparently he liked it when their eyes popped out.

                      BOO
          (genuinely upset for the boy)
No! Why would they send him away?! He needs help!

INT. ARSEHOLE GUY'S BEDROOM — DAY

Fleabag smiles with a slight sadness.

                    FLEABAG
          (to camera, with a sadness)
She was a surprising person.

INT. FLASHBACK, CAFÉ — DAY

Fleabag and Boo sit as before. Boo is as distraught.

                      BOO
They shouldn't have just locked him up.

                    FLEABAG
He pencil-fucked a hamster!

                      BOO
Yeah, but, he's obviously not happy. Happy people
wouldn't do things like that.

                          FLEABAG
     Fair point.

                            BOO
     And anyway. That's the very reason why they put rubbers
     on the end of pencils.

                          FLEABAG
     What, to fuck hamsters?

                            BOO
     No, because people make mistakes.

Beat. Boo looks innocently at Fleabag. She means that.

INT. ARSEHOLE GUY'S BEDROOM — DAY

Fleabag lies in bed thinking about this.

                     ARSEHOLE GUY (O.S.)
     Hey.

She turns to find Arsehole Guy is sitting on the edge of the
bed gazing at her.

                       ARSEHOLE GUY
     Hey.

                          FLEABAG
     Hey.

                       ARSEHOLE GUY
     Look, about last night.

                          FLEABAG
                        (to camera)
     Uh oh.

                       ARSEHOLE GUY
     I don't usually connect with women...

                          FLEABAG
     I know. That's what I like about you.

Beat.
                       ARSEHOLE GUY
     Yeah — Ok, erm — I —
                       (breathes out)
     Wow, this must be what insecure feels like.
                          (beat)
     Actually — can we speak about this later? I want to find
     the right words for you. I'll see you at the sexhibi-
     tion?

                         FLEABAG
Yeah, see you there.

                      ARSEHOLE GUY
I'm gonna go to yoga.

                         FLEABAG
Ok.

He kisses his fingers and places them on Fleabag's lips; she
kisses them awkwardly. He leaves.

INT. SEXHIBITION ENTRANCE — DAY

Fleabag and Arsehole Guy enter the sexhibition. There are lots
of pretentious people being greeted by Godmother and Dad.

They spot Fleabag.

                           DAD
   Marvellous!

                        GODMOTHER
I'm so relieved you are here.

                         FLEABAG
Hi!

Godmother kisses Fleabag on the cheek then moves on to
Arsehole Guy.

                        GODMOTHER
   And hello good-looking.

Godmother kisses him on the cheek while Dad and Fleabag
greet each other.

                        GODMOTHER
                       (to Fleabag)
   Well clung to.

                         FLEABAG
Thank you.

Beat.

Godmother looks at Arsehole Guy for a beat.

                        GODMOTHER
   Does it get very boring? Everybody telling you how
   gorgeous you are all the time.

He laughs charmingly.

                    ARSEHOLE GUY
                     (meaning it)
Er — a little.

                        DAD
Should we —

                     GODMOTHER
Ah yes.
                     (to Fleabag)
I won't forget this, I promise.

                     FLEABAG
Oh sure, is Claire here yet?

                     GODMOTHER
No, not yet. You're an angel for being here. Would you
just —

Godmother places a tray of champagne glasses in Fleabag's
hands. Fleabag looks confused.

                     GODMOTHER
Hold on to that. And there are bottles for topping up
on the little bar just inside. I am the luckiest thing
to have you.
                 (remembers something)
And um —

She puts a sticky badge on Fleabag that says 'Here to
help'.

Godmother takes a drink off the tray.

                     GODMOTHER
You're a natural.

Fleabag looks at Arsehole Guy, not sure how to handle the
situation.

Arsehole Guy takes a drink and leaves her.

INT. SEXHIBITION. MAIN GALLERY — DAY

There is a roar of laughter. A crowd of 'interesting'-looking people with eccentric outfits stand around
Godmother, who is introducing her event.

                     GODMOTHER
                 (so sweet, so humbled)
Now really though, this sexhibition isn't about me
trying to get you all aroused. It's about the beauty of
sex. And how it brings us all together.

                    (looks at Dad)
How it excites and connects, how it opens people's
minds. After all, sex got us all here. Sex...
brings... life.

INT. FLASHBACK, CAFÉ — DAY

Boo is crying.

INT. SEXHIBITION. MAIN GALLERY — DAY — CONT.

Fleabag shakes the memory out of her head and focuses back
on Godmother.

                    GODMOTHER
I've been building this sexhibition since I was eleven
and a quarter, which is when I first climaxed, by accident, on a bidet. The bidet is, of course, exhibited,
as are all the pieces from my first ever sexhibition.
All apart from one.

She gestures to an empty pedestal.

                    GODMOTHER (CONT'D)
A few weeks ago, one of my most delicate pieces was
stolen from my studio.

There is an audible gasp.

Fleabag glances at the camera, tries not to laugh.

                    GODMOTHER (CONT'D)
But in a sense, it was a blessing.

Fleabag looks annoyed.

                    GODMOTHER (CONT'D)
In fact her brutal snatching made me think of all the
women of the world who have been robbed of their
freedom, of their happiness and, in the saddest of
cases, of their bodies. So in many ways, I have to thank
the thief, for creating my most profound piece of work
to date. *A Woman Robbed*.

The crowd applaud lightly in a very British way. So
impressed and moved. Fleabag looks around, annoyed.

                    GODMOTHER (CONT'D)
Now, I would ask you all to leave your genitals at the
door and bring your minds to these pieces. I don't
believe people always think about sex when they see a
naked body. I believe they think about their own minds,

their own bodies and their own power. And that's what
this show is really about.
                    (she looks at Fleabag)
It's about power. Thank you.

Godmother gives a little smile to Fleabag. More
applause.

Godmother holds out her hand to Dad, who joins her, kissing
her on the cheek. Dad raises a glass to the room.

INT. SEXHIBITION. WALL OF COCKS — DAY

Fleabag is leaving a voicemail for Claire while walking
through the room with her tray. Godmother is discussing a
piece of her art with a guest in the background.

                        FLEABAG
                    (into phone)
    Claire, it's me. Just wondering where you are, I am very
    much here, and waiting... for you. Ok, bye.

She hangs up.

                        FLEABAG
    Dammit Claire.

She approaches Arsehole Guy, who is staring at something.

                        FLEABAG
    Have you seen a sort of stressed-out version of me
    anywhere?

Arsehole Guy is entranced by what he is looking at.

                    ARSEHOLE GUY
                    (looking at the wall)
    Is it weird that my mouth's watering?

Fleabag frowns. REVEAL: the art piece is a wall of cocks.

Godmother appears.

                    ARSEHOLE GUY
    Really fantastic work, honestly, it's amazing.

                    GODMOTHER
    Thank you so much.

She looks at Fleabag, awaiting her review.

                        FLEABAG
    Yes. Extraordinary. Really, really moving. And

present... I'd love one of these on my floor... Like a
rug with perks.

                    GODMOTHER
I'm sure you would. But it's very securely nailed to
the wall this evening.
          (she smiles, they all giggle. Beat)
Have you found your father yet?

                    FLEABAG
Oh yes, I think he's by the coats.

                    GODMOTHER
                    (laughs)
Oh! No no!
          (she gestures to the wall of cocks)
Have you found your father yet?

Fleabag looks unnerved.

                    GODMOTHER
It's just so very obvious to me.

Long pause. Fleabag looks at the entire wall of cocks. She
points to one randomly.

Godmother looks disturbed.

Long pause.

                    GODMOTHER
  Yeah.

Godmother leaves, noticing a man she immediately starts a
new conversation with.

                    GODMOTHER
  Oh, Conor!

Fleabag looks disturbed.

                    FLEABAG
                    (to camera)
  Whoops.

EXT. SEXHIBITION — EVENING

Outside the gallery Fleabag and Arsehole Guy smoke and drink
champagne.

                    ARSEHOLE GUY
  Look, about this morning —
                    (beat)
  Listen, what I was trying to say is...

                    FLEABAG
                   (to camera)
Here we go.

                  ARSEHOLE GUY
I didn't realise this until we were having sex earlier
and I — lost my —

                    FLEABAG
Erection.

                  ARSEHOLE GUY
Erection.

                    FLEABAG
One more time.

                  ARSEHOLE GUY
                   (deadpan)
Erection.

Fleabag looks at the camera, excited by him saying that.

                  ARSEHOLE GUY
But — it um, it made me realise... I'm in love.

She is stunned. He just said it.

                    FLEABAG
                     (coy)
Oh... Ok, I mean I don't really know what to —

He takes a drag of his cigarette. He looks stressed out.

                  ARSEHOLE GUY
And I don't want to have sex with anyone else. And
that's never happened to me before.

He puts his hands on her face.

                  ARSEHOLE GUY
I'm in love... And I... Need to tell her.

Fleabag looks confused.

                    FLEABAG
Her?

                  ARSEHOLE GUY
Yeah, we've been together for a couple of months and
physically she just never satisfied me — she has
these... really massive, bouncy tits, that really don't
do anything for me and you just kept turning up like
this sexy... plank... and, uh — it confused me but — I

just don't think I should be fucking around behind her
back any more. I just thought I should say that I am
sorry, if I have led you on...

Fleabag is stunned.

> **FLEABAG**
> Oh, no... God no, my erm — my ex is due back any day
> now anyway, so it's — I'm happy for you.

She pats him on the back. He smiles.

> **ARSEHOLE GUY**
> (laughing gently)
> I knew you wouldn't give a shit.

> **FLEABAG**
> Well, what can I say? I'm sorry! I don't... Give a
> shit...

He touches her hair and holds her face. He kisses her
passionately.

> **ARSEHOLE GUY**
> Cool...
> (charming as hell)
> Never wear padding, Ok?

She smiles. And she nods.

Fleabag is embarrassed and stung. She glances at the camera.
She tries to laugh it off.

INT. SEXHIBITION. MAIN GALLERY — EVENING

Fleabag is walking while talking into her phone to Claire's
answer machine.

> **FLEABAG**
> (into phone)
> Claire. Where are you? I can't survive much longer in
> this sea of penises and I don't know anyone — and —
> so...

Fleabag approaches a model of Harry. It is life size and has
no genitals.

> **FLEABAG**
> (to model)
> Harry?

She stares at it. She stares at the camera.

                              FLEABAG
                          (to camera)
    Harry?

Harry comes round the back of the statue.

                                HARRY
    Hi.

She is startled.

                              FLEABAG
    Hi.

They both look at the statue.

                              FLEABAG
    What did she do to you?

                                HARRY
    Oh, just covered me in plaster-cast and left me in the
    garden for a couple of hours.

She goes to hug him.

                              FLEABAG
    Oh God, hi! It's so good to see you-

As she breaks away we see his new girlfriend, ELAINE,
approach.

She looks like the sweetest person in the world and is
wearing a lovely, floaty dress.

Harry puts his arm around her.

                                ELAINE
    Hi.

                              FLEABAG
    Hi.

                                ELAINE
    Hi.

                              FLEABAG
                          (to camera, sweetly)
    Hi.

                                HARRY
    Um...

Beat.

                        ELAINE
I'm just gonna go and browse around. It was really nice
to meet you.

                        FLEABAG
You too.

Fleabag giggles awkwardly. Harry gestures to Elaine, who is
being floaty around Godmother.

                        HARRY
That's... Elaine.

                      GODMOTHER
                      (to Elaine)
Hello darling.

Fleabag nods and smiles. Trying to hide that she is actually
hurt by this.

                        HARRY
We're—

                        FLEABAG
Hey — did you see that really good-looking guy that came
in with me?

                        HARRY
No. But I saw a really good-looking guy on his motorbike outside. Why?

                        FLEABAG
Oh yeah, that's, he erm — Well, he and I are...

                        HARRY
Oh, great—

                        FLEABAG
                        (proud)
Yeah, he just dumped me.

                        HARRY
Oh! Hm — I'm sorry.

                        FLEABAG
                   (about the statue)
This is very... you.

                        HARRY
Yes! She uh — she said you were cool with us doing...
that...

Fleabag frowns. She looks around the room for Godmother, who
is still with Elaine but looks at them shiftily. Fleabag

smiles at Harry, clearly not cool with this. She looks back at the statue.

> **HARRY**
> I don't know why she— Where's my penis?

> **FLEABAG**
> Oh it's on the wall over there.
> (looking to the wall of cocks)
> Second from the left.

She smiles. He tries to smile.

> **HARRY**
> I should probably go and find Elaine. She doesn't like being left on her own... so—

> **FLEABAG**
> You've still got some stuff at the flat.
> (flirty)
> I've been rolling around in my lingerie all over it waiting for you to come and collect it...

> **HARRY**
> Yeah I—

> **FLEABAG**
> Your Tupperware, and your TV, and your dinosaur plate.

> **HARRY**
> Oh, I got a new dinosaur plate. But, um, thank you, but you um, you can keep those.

They look at each other for a moment.

> **FLEABAG**
> (cheeky)
> Hey, do you still wank about me sometimes?

Beat.

> **HARRY**
> (gently)
> No.

He walks off. Fleabag is embarrassed. Harry greets Godmother. Fleabag turns to camera.

> **FLEABAG**
> (to camera)
> Elaainneee.

INT. SEXHIBITION. MAIN GALLERY — EVENING

Fleabag is pouring a drink for a male guest. He smiles at her, she smiles back, he leaves.

Fleabag turns and sees Claire. She rushes towards her.

                    FLEABAG
     Claire! My God it's been hell, where have you been?

                    CLAIRE
     I uh... Hm...

Martin arrives next to Claire. He puts his arm on her shoulder. Claire is awkward but being strong.

                    MARTIN
     All parked up.
                         (to Fleabag)
     Hello you.

They stand awkwardly.

                    FLEABAG
     Erm...

                    CLAIRE
     We almost didn't make it, but... Um...

                    MARTIN
     We didn't want to let the old boy down.

                    FLEABAG
     But I thought that—

                    CLAIRE
     We're just gonna do a quick whizz around to show our faces.

She looks at Claire.

                    FLEABAG
     Ok, I—

                    CLAIRE
     We're just gonna do a quick whizz around.

She moves off. Martin follows her. Fleabag looks like she has been hit by a train. They go to greet Godmother, who then brings a tray full of champagne to Fleabag.

                    GODMOTHER
     Sorry, could you just — could you just do something with those.

She hands Fleabag the tray.

> **GODMOTHER**
> Thank you darling.

Godmother leaves. Fleabag looks at the camera angrily and walks away with the tray.

INT. SERVICE AREA — EVENING — CONT.

Fleabag takes her tray through to the service area and begins downing the champagne. She takes off her badge.

INT. FLASHBACK, CAFÉ — NIGHT

Fleabag and Boo drink wine and smoke in the café, happily.

INT. SERVICE AREA — EVENING

Fleabag tops up all the glasses.

INT. FLASHBACK, CAFÉ — NIGHT

Fleabag smokes while Boo dances, topping up their glasses.

INT. SERVICE AREA — EVENING

Fleabag downs another glass of champagne and heads back to the main gallery.

INT. SEXHIBITION — NIGHT

Fleabag holds her tray and downs another glass. She looks over and sees Godmother talking to Dad.

Godmother turns, looking for Fleabag, and clicks her fingers for her to come over. Dad looks embarrassed.

Fleabag lifts a glass off the tray, gesturing 'This is what you want?'

Godmother nods and beckons her.

Fleabag drops the glass to the floor.

Lots of people turn, an amused murmur.

Fleabag and Godmother stare at each other.

Fleabag holds up another glass. Dad sees her. He subtly gestures to her commandingly.

>   **DAD**
>   (whispered)
> Don't.

She stares at them and raises the glass.

>   **DAD**
>   (loudly, firmly)
> DON'T.

People have stopped talking and are looking.

Beat.

Fleabag holds up the single glass in her right hand. Then drops the entire tray with the other hand.

She takes a sip from the champagne glass she is still holding.

Godmother and Dad approach, laughing like it was a mistake.

>   **GODMOTHER**
>   (for the crowd)
>   The joys of butter-fingered staff!

Everyone laughs.

>   **DAD**
> Will you stop making a spectacle of yourself and clean that up.

>   **FLEABAG**
> You clean that up.

He looks down in despair. Godmother stands beside him.

>   **DAD**
> Apologise.

>   **FLEABAG**
> I'm sorry. Turns out I'm not such a natural after all...

She takes another sip of champagne. Godmother looks at her, steely. Then decides to play another card. She gets weepy. Her bottom lip shakes a little.

>   **FLEABAG**
> Oh, fuck off!

Dad turns to Fleabag, incensed.

> **DAD**
> I'm just going to say this once. I deserve to be happy.
> I am allowed to move on. I have a good life and I am
> happy, alright?
> (beat)
> Alright? If you don't mind. I'm going to go and get my
> cardie from the car. It's a little chilly.

He exits. Claire and Martin watch him go, then turn to look
at Fleabag.

Godmother's eyes harden.

> **GODMOTHER**
> (gently to the end)
> I'm sorry you had to hear that. But you did have to hear
> it.

An USHER has started to clear up.

> **GODMOTHER**
> (pointing at Fleabag)
> No, no. She'll do it.

Fleabag stares at Godmother as she leaves, then takes the
tray from the usher.

INT. SERVICE AREA — EVENING

Fleabag walks through the service area. Claire comes up to
her.

> **CLAIRE**
> WHAT THE FUCK WAS THAT?

> **FLEABAG**
> What is he doing here? You're not going to Finland?

Claire shakes her head. Martin enters.

> **FLEABAG**
> Oh, God. What are you doing here?

> **MARTIN**
> I'm helping.

Fleabag laughs, exasperated.

> **FLEABAG**
> He is—

                    CLAIRE
                    (gently)
He didn't try to kiss you.

                    FLEABAG
He did.

                    CLAIRE
He says it was more like the other way around.

Beat. Fleabag looks at Martin.

                    FLEABAG
What?! But that's just not true.

Martin exhales a laugh.

                    FLEABAG
No. Fuck you. Claire, no —

This is not easy for Claire. Fleabag is crying.

                    CLAIRE
Please don't—

                    FLEABAG
Claire, he came out into the garden—

                    CLAIRE
Please, I don't wanna hear it.

                    FLEABAG
Claire, you have to believe me.

                    CLAIRE
How can I believe you?

                    FLEABAG
Because I'm your sister!

                    CLAIRE
After what you did to Boo.

Beat. We stay on Fleabag. She can't believe Claire just said
that.

Beat. Fleabag's breathing picks up. She looks at the camera.

INT. FLASHBACK, FLEABAG'S BEDROOM — NIGHT

Close-up on hands undoing a man's belt buckle.

INT. SERVICE AREA — EVENING

Fleabag looks at the camera.

INT. FLASHBACK, CAFÉ — DAY

Boo's crying face.

INT. SERVICE AREA — EVENING

Fleabag turns away from Claire and Martin. She tries to avoid the camera, then turns back and looks straight into it, glancing between the camera and Claire.

INT. FLASHBACK, CAFÉ — DAY

Boo's crying face.

> **BOO**
> (weakly)
> He slept with someone else. He told me he — fucked someone else.

INT. SERVICE AREA — EVENING

Fleabag looks at the camera and then at Claire.

> **CLAIRE**
> I'm sorry, but you just have to see it from my point of view.

INT. FLASHBACK, SHOP — DAY

Fleabag sees Jack putting on a woman's shoe. He smiles at her.

INT. SERVICE AREA — EVENING

Fleabag, still crying, smiles and nods at Claire. Martin approaches Claire.

> **MARTIN**
> (putting his hand on Claire's shoulder)
> Come on.

Claire turns and walks away, Martin follows, looking back at Fleabag.

Fleabag turns and tries to back away from the camera but it follows her as she backs into the coat rail.

INT. FLASHBACK, CLUB — NIGHT

Fleabag watches, smiling, as Boo and Jack kiss.

INT. SERVICE AREA — EVENING

Fleabag tries to escape. The camera follows her.

INT. FLASHBACK, CAFÉ — NIGHT

Jack strokes Boo's hair affectionately while she holds Hilary.

INT. SERVICE AREA — EVENING

Fleabag still tries to escape. The camera still follows her.

INT. FLASHBACK, FLEABAG'S BEDROOM — EVENING

Fleabag and Boo sit on the bed.

                         BOO
    I think I love him.

INT. SERVICE AREA — EVENING

Fleabag walks down a corridor. The camera follows her from behind.

INT. FLASHBACK, FLEABAG'S BEDROOM — NIGHT

Fleabag downs a glass of wine. Jack strokes her arm. She looks at his hand on her shoulder. He looks into her eyes.

INT. SERVICE AREA — EVENING

The camera is coming right up close to Fleabag's face.

INT. FLASHBACK, FLEABAG'S BEDROOM — NIGHT

Jack is looking at Fleabag, licking his lips. There is want in his eyes.

We see the same shot as earlier and realise it is Fleabag undoing Jack's belt buckle.

They kiss.

INT. SERVICE AREA — EVENING

The camera is close on Fleabag's face.

>   **BOO (O.S.)**
>   I'm gonna hurt myself —

INT. FLASHBACK, CAFÉ — DAY

Boo is crying. She is trying not to get angry. She wouldn't get angry.

>   **BOO**
>   (beat)
>   — I'm gonna get hit by a bike and then...

EXT. FLASHBACK, STREET — DAY

Wide shot of Boo as a bicycle whizzes past her.

INT. FLASHBACK, CAFÉ — DAY

Back with Boo.
>   **BOO**
>   — hurt my finger, and then —

EXT. FLASHBACK, STREET — DAY

The bicycle whizzing past Boo again.

>   **BOO (O.S.)**
>   — he's gonna have to come and —

INT. SERVICE AREA — EVENING

Fleabag is slumped on the floor.

>   **BOO (O.S.)**
>   — see me in —

INT. FLASHBACK, FLEABAG'S BEDROOM — NIGHT

Fleabag and Jack kiss, passionately.

                    BOO (O.S.)
      — hospital, and be —

INT. FLASHBACK, CAFÉ — DAY

Boo crying.
                      BOO
      — really sorry for what —

EXT. FLASHBACK, STREET — DAY

Boo standing on the pavement, the traffic speeding past.

                    BOO (O.S.)
      — he did.

Profile shot of Boo. We see her step out of frame.

EXT. SEXHIBITION — NIGHT

Fleabag is walking down the road, exhausted. She looks to
the end of the road. She makes out a figure, hunched over a
car with his back to her.

It's Dad. He is crying.

She watches him.

Fleabag walks towards Dad.

He looks up, sees her coming, looks slightly afraid, but
he's been rumbled so there is no point running.

They lean on the car together. Fleabag smokes.

                      DAD
      I don't know where you came from.

                    FLEABAG
      What, you don't think we're the same?

                      DAD
      You've got the same lines on your forehead as me.

                    FLEABAG
      Thank you for fixating on them.

                              DAD
And you're stubborn.

                              FLEABAG
Snap. And sad.

                              DAD
You're not born sad.

                              FLEABAG
Some people are.

                              DAD
You weren't.

                              FLEABAG
No, I guess not.

They both wipe their noses on their sleeves at the same
time.

                              DAD
Jesus... Why do daughters get to say they are fucked up
by their fathers when it's so often the other way round.

Dad laughs. Fleabag laughs.

Beat.

She gives him the cigarette.

                              DAD
                    (referring to the cigarette)
Why do you do that to yourself?

He drops the cigarette.

                              FLEABAG
Looks cool.

Dad laughs softly.

                              DAD
I think your mother would have admired your little
performance up there.

Beat.

                              FLEABAG
Do you ever think about her?

He nods.

                    DAD
Yeah... Do you think about your friend?

                  FLEABAG
All the time.

                    DAD
Well.

Beat. They connect for a moment.

                  FLEABAG
I'm sorry.

                    DAD
I—

Dad sees Godmother walking down the street.

Dad looks at Fleabag.

                    DAD
                  (weakly)
I think you should go.

Fleabag sees Godmother. She looks at Dad. So disappointed.
He can't look her in the eye.

She walks away down the street.

EXT. STREET — NIGHT

Fleabag walks down the street.

We hear the audio of Boo's voice recording.

                  BOO (O.S)
Hi, this is Boo. I can't come to the phone right now
but please leave me a messiagio and I will get back to
you.

CUT TO: EXT. A DIFFERENT STREET — DAWN

Fleabag is in the same clothes. She is tear-stained.

                  BOO (O.S)
Hi, this is Boo. I can't come to the phone right now
but please leave me a messiagio and I will get back to
you.

INT. CAFÉ — MORNING

We watch Hilary in her cage. Fleabag's hand reaches in and drops a huge pile of cucumber into her bowl. She strokes Hilary.

Fleabag sits in the same clothes. She is tear-stained.

She looks around the café and then gets up.

EXT. STREET OUTSIDE CAFÉ — MORNING

Fleabag is standing on the kerb looking into the road. The flash of a car passing her, echoing the memory of Boo.

We flash between Fleabag standing there, and Boo standing there.

She builds herself up. She steps towards the kerb. She builds her confidence. Another few cars flash past her. A car drives up.

She builds her confidence but the car slowly parks.

She looks disappointed.

Then she looks at the driver. It's Bank Manager.

> **BANK MANAGER**
> You Ok?

He looks earnestly up at her through the car window.

INT. CAFÉ — DAY

Fleabag sits at a table.

> **BANK MANAGER (O.S.)**
> Big night then?

Fleabag nods. Bank Manager is standing awkwardly in the café. He looks at all the guinea-pig pictures.

> **BANK MANAGER**
> (realising)
> Mmmm!

> **FLEABAG**
> What?

                    BANK MANAGER
I thought in the application for your loan it said you
ran a café FOR guinea pigs.

Pause. He laughs again.

                BANK MANAGER (CONT'D)
That's why I thought it was funny. I never thought
guinea pigs needed...

                        FLEABAG
It's guinea-pig themed —

                    BANK MANAGER
Ok.

                        FLEABAG
Yeah.

                    BANK MANAGER
That makes sense.

                        FLEABAG
Yeah.

Beat.

                    BANK MANAGER
Can I get you a... cup of tea?

                        FLEABAG
Run out.

                    BANK MANAGER
Coffee?

                        FLEABAG
Run out.

                    BANK MANAGER
Well I should probably be heading back to the office.
                        (beat)
Cafés are a very... difficult business. You certainly
made this one very... Unique.

                        FLEABAG
I also fucked it into liquidation.

                    BANK MANAGER
Ok.

                        FLEABAG
And I fucked up my family.

Beat.

BANK MANAGER
Did you?

FLEABAG
And I fucked my friend by fucking her boyfriend.

Fleabag laughs.

Beat.

BANK MANAGER
Right.

FLEABAG
(starting to cry)
And sometimes I wish I didn't even know that 'fucking'
existed. And that I know that my body, as it is now,
really is the only thing I have left and when that gets
old and unfuckable I might as well just kill it.

Beat.

FLEABAG (CONT'D)
And somehow there isn't anything worse than someone who
doesn't want to fuck me... That I fuck everything,
except for when I was, in your office — I really wasn't
trying to — I was —
(beat)
Either everyone feels like this a little bit and they're
just not talking about it... Or I am completely fucking
alone. Which isn't fucking funny.

Beat. He doesn't know how to deal with this.

BANK MANAGER
Right, well uh — I should probably, erm... I should
probably um... I should —

He walks to the door and goes out, towards his car.

Then he comes back in with his folder.

BANK MANAGER
People make mistakes.

He sits down in the chair opposite Fleabag. He is now being
very official.

FLEABAG
That's why they put rubbers on the ends of pencils.

> **BANK MANAGER**
> Is that a joke?

> **FLEABAG**
> I don't know.

Pause. He looks at her.

> **BANK MANAGER**
> I think we should start your interview again.

> **FLEABAG**
> Here?

> **BANK MANAGER**
> Yeah. Go on.

> **FLEABAG**
> Ok.

She sits up.

> **BANK MANAGER**
> Well, thank you for coming in.

He nods. She nods.

> **FLEABAG**
> No problem.

> **BANK MANAGER**
> I've uh, read through your application form. Says you run a café for guinea pigs.

Beat.

She laughs.

> **BANK MANAGER**
> Told you it was funny.

Fleabag looks at him. He looks at her. They smile at each other.

END OF SERIES ONE

SERIES
TWO

EPISODE 1

INT. COOL RESTAURANT. BATHROOM — NIGHT

Frank Sinatra's 'Strangers in the Night' plays.

Wide shot of FLEABAG from behind as she stands at a sink.
Her head is bowed down as she is washing her hands. We can't
see her face.

She looks up into the mirror. We see that there is blood all
over her mouth. She takes a damp towel and wipes most of the
blood off her mouth and nose. There is a bang on the door.
She ignores it.

                    MAN (O.S.)
    Can I do anything?

                    FLEABAG
    No, thank you.

                    MAN (O.S.)
    They've gone, so...

She grabs a few tissues and hands them casually to a NEEDY
WAITRESS, who, we discover, is sitting, slumped on the floor
with blood on her face and a bruised eye.

                 NEEDY WAITRESS
                 (grateful, sweet)
    Thank you.

Fleabag smiles at her. She checks her hair in the mirror.
Takes a breath.

                    FLEABAG
                  (to camera)
    This is a love story.

              TITLES: FLEABAG

Soaring choral music over titles and perhaps next scene,
rather than the discordance of last series.

INT. RESTAURANT — NIGHT

Earlier that evening.

Close-up of Fleabag. She is sat at a restaurant table
holding a glass of champagne. She looks well.

We can't see who else is at the table. We can only see the
restaurant glittering and bustling behind her.

>   **FLEABAG**
>   (to camera)
>   You know when you've done... everything.
>   (beat)
>   When you've been all—

EXT. FLASHBACK, PARK — DAY

Fleabag is doing squats in a park with a DRILL SERGEANT kind
of guy. He is shouting at her.

>   **DRILL SERGEANT**
>   SQUAT. SQUAT.

INT. RESTAURANT — NIGHT

Back at the table with Fleabag.

>   **FLEABAG**
>   (to camera)
>   And—

INT. FLASHBACK, CAFÉ — DAY

Shot of a piece of rye bread/pumpernickel with sliced
avocado and feta cheese and chopped baby tomato on it.

Fleabag chops it in half and looks at the camera very seriously.

INT. RESTAURANT — NIGHT

Back at the table with Fleabag.

>   **FLEABAG**
>   You've even—

EXT. FLASHBACK, ARSEHOLE GUY'S FLAT — EVENING

Close on ARSEHOLE GUY looking seductively at Fleabag.

>   **ARSEHOLE GUY**
>   Wanna have sex?

Beat.

Fleabag is conflicted.

>   **FLEABAG**
> No.

She turns and runs away down the street.

>   **ARSEHOLE GUY**
>   (calling after her, desperate)
>   Can I at least go down on you?!

>   **FLEABAG**
> NO!

INT. RESTAURANT — NIGHT

Back at the table with Fleabag.

>   **FLEABAG**
>   You've done everything. And you feel great.

INT. FLASHBACK, PUB — EVENING

Fleabag laughing with a bunch of 'friends' we've never seen
before and will never see again.

INT. RESTAURANT — NIGHT

Back at the table with Fleabag.

>   **FLEABAG**
>   You're not even thinking about—

EXT. FLASHBACK, PARK — DAY

BOO putting a tiny hat on Hilary's head and looking up at
us, very pleased with it. Fleabag's dialogue cuts it off
again.

INT. RESTAURANT — NIGHT

Back at the table with Fleabag.

>   **FLEABAG**
>   You don't even think about—

EXT. FLASHBACK FROM LAST SERIES: CLAIRE'S HOUSE — NIGHT

MARTIN kissing Fleabag on CLAIRE's birthday from the last series.

INT. RESTAURANT — NIGHT

Fleabag passes bread across to her left —

> **FLEABAG**
> (to camera)
> And even though your sister still hates you.

We reveal Claire eyeing Fleabag. She gives a tight smile as she accepts the bread.

> **CLAIRE**
> Thank you.

> **FLEABAG**
> (to camera)
> You're pretending to be friends because your dad is—

EXT. GRAVESIDE — DAY

Fleabag and Claire are standing by a grave.

INT. RESTAURANT — NIGHT

Back at the table with Fleabag and Claire.

> **FLEABAG**
> (to camera)
> I'm joking, he's just there.

We reveal DAD sitting next to GODMOTHER, with her hand on his.

> **GODMOTHER**
> (holding up her glass)
> Here's to love!

> **FLEABAG**
> And engaged.

They all cheer.

> **FLEABAG**
> To love!

                              EVERYONE
     To love!

Suddenly Martin arrives.

                               MARTIN
     HEEEEEY!

                              FLEABAG
                            (to camera)
     Ugh.

                               MARTIN
                     (to Dad and Godmother)
     CONGRATULATIONS YOU ASSHOLES!

He kisses a smiling Claire from behind as he speaks.

Dad and Godmother laugh happily. Everyone laughs happily.

Fleabag looks to camera. Ugh.

INT. RESTAURANT — NIGHT

Later. Dad holds his glass mid-toast. Fleabag is now holding
a tequila shot.

Godmother, Martin and Claire listen to Dad speak.

We reveal there's also an UNFAMILIAR MAN at the table, also
listening. He is dressed in a regular shirt and trousers,
but we will later find out that this is PRIEST.

                                DAD
     It means a great deal to both of us that you... that
     we...
                        (gets a little emotional)
     Are all here together... for this very special
     family... gang bang...

Fleabag looks, confused, at Priest.

                                DAD
     Just... being here... I know we've had our... I
     just... The feeling that I have... is... right in...
     I just want to say I... Very much. And... That's it.

                              GODMOTHER
                               (moved)
     Oh darling.

                               CLAIRE
     Congratulations Dad.

>   MARTIN
> Congratulations!

>   DAD
> Thank you!

>   PRIEST
>   (raising a glass)
> May these be the worst of our days!

>   FLEABAG
>   (to camera)
> Don't know who this guy is.

>   MARTIN
> Happy for you, old boy. Best decision a man can
> make.

Martin and Claire smile smugly at each other.

>   FLEABAG
>   (to camera)
> Ugh.

>   MARTIN
>   (to Fleabag)
> You look well.

>   FLEABAG
> Thank you.

Claire and Fleabag share a fleeting look.

>   DAD
> Wine everyone?

>   PRIEST
> Yes please! I'd love some wine.

>   GODMOTHER
> You'll adore it, I chose it.

>   CLAIRE
> Not for us, thanks.

>   MARTIN
> Off the sauce.

>   CLAIRE
> Six months and counting.

Everyone falls silent. In shock.

> PRIEST

Why... would you do that?

> CLAIRE

We just enjoy each other more this way.

> MARTIN
> (looking at Claire)

Just don't want to miss a thing.

Claire flicks her eyes at Fleabag.

> FLEABAG
> (to camera)

Haven't seen her since—

FLASHBACK FROM SERIES ONE INT. GALLERY — NIGHT

Claire and Fleabag in the back room at the Tate at the end of the last series. Both with tears in their eyes.

> CLAIRE

I'm sorry.

She turns sadly and walks away.

INT. RESTAURANT — NIGHT

Back at the table.

> FLEABAG

Except for—

INT. RESTAURANT. A DIFFERENT AREA — NIGHT

Earlier in the evening. Fleabag and Claire have both just arrived. They have their coats over their arms before heading off to the table.

> CLAIRE
> (spiky)

Nice jumpsuit.

> FLEABAG
> (spiky)

Thank you.

> CLAIRE
> (spiky)

You look well, where have you been?

> **FLEABAG**
> Boots. Lovely there this time of year.

Claire is not amused.

INT. RESTAURANT — NIGHT

We return to Fleabag, Claire, Godmother, Dad, Martin and Priest at the table.

> **DAD**
> Well you look fantastic.

> **CLAIRE**
> (to Dad and Godmother)
> You both look gorgeous.

> **GODMOTHER**
> Thank you!

> **CLAIRE**
> Is that fur?

> **GODMOTHER**
> Yes, but it's Ok because it had a stroke.

> **CLAIRE**
> Oh, lovely.

> **GODMOTHER**
> (joking to Priest)
> I can't go to hell for that can I, Father?

> **PRIEST**
> No, no, as long as you confess —

> **FLEABAG**
> (to camera)
> Oh God, he's their priest.

> **PRIEST**
> — you've got nothing to fucking worry about.

> **FLEABAG**
> (to camera)
> Their cool, sweary priest.

> **GODMOTHER**
> Love the Catholics. You can get away with anything.

> **MARTIN**
> (laughing)
> A lot of them did.

PRIEST
(to Godmother)
It's an honour to be marrying you two. Thank you.

GODMOTHER
But I didn't realise you were allowed out without your
little —

She gestures to her neck i.e. his dog collar.

PRIEST
(joking)
Oh no, have I disappointed you?

GODMOTHER
(disappointed)
Of course not.

FLEABAG
(to camera)
Devastated.

The Needy Waitress appears. She points at the champagne
bottle.

NEEDY WAITRESS
Can I get you another bottle?

FLEABAG
(to camera)
Needy waitress.

GODMOTHER
No it's alright, we've already ordered wine.

NEEDY WAITRESS
(so gutted)
Oh no. Really?

FLEABAG
(kindly)
I'll have another tequila.

PRIEST
I'll have a tequila!

Fleabag looks at him. He smiles.

NEEDY WAITRESS
Oh great! Thank you so much!

MARTIN
Can I have a sparkling water with a dash of lime,
please?

>   **CLAIRE**
> I'll have the same.

>   **MARTIN**
> Dream team.

They do a little high five at the table. Fleabag notices.
Ugh.

>   **GODMOTHER**
>   (about Priest)
> Now the most FASCINATING thing about Father here is that
> his mother was originally a lesbia—

HARD CUT TO: EXT. BACK OF RESTAURANT — NIGHT

Fleabag is leaning, head against a wall. One hand has a
cigarette in it. She exhales deeply.

INT. RESTAURANT — NIGHT

Fleabag is back at the table with Claire, Godmother, Dad,
Martin and Priest. Their starter plates are being cleared
away by the Needy Waitress.

>   **GODMOTHER**
> You do look tired.

>   **CLAIRE**
> It's not as exhausting as I thought it would be actu-
> ally.

>   **FLEABAG**
>   (to camera)
> She's commuting from Finland.

>   **MARTIN**
> She has got her packing down to a ten-minute turnaround.

>   **CLAIRE**
>   (laughing)
> It's fine.

>   **GODMOTHER**
> Fabulous!

>   **MARTIN**
> It's all about—

>   **CLAIRE**
> Rolling it up rather than—

                         MARTIN
Folding it.

                          DAD
Yes, I've read about that. Sure you don't want wine?

                     MARTIN/CLAIRE
No, thank you.

                       GODMOTHER
                      (sipping wine)
It really is delicious. I admire you both so much.

                         MARTIN
It's really turned us around hasn't it, honey?

                         CLAIRE
So much more energy. You know, in Finland they—

                         PRIEST
Is there a reason you're not? Or is that...?

                         CLAIRE
He's an alcoholic.

                         PRIEST
Oh fun! My parents were alcoholics!

                         CLAIRE
Oh, great. Well, we found it's easier if we do it
together. I don't really like the taste any—

                         MARTIN
And we're trying for a baby.

Beat. Claire and Fleabag look at each other.

                       GODMOTHER
Oh Claire. We thought you couldn't have them.

                         CLAIRE
What? Why?

                       GODMOTHER
You just seem a little—

                         MARTIN
They say a lifestyle change can help so here we go!

                          DAD
That's SO exciting darling! Good luck.

                         PRIEST
That's wonderful!

Everyone sort of smiles. Fleabag eyes Claire.

> **FLEABAG**
> (to camera)
>
> Something's up.

> **GODMOTHER**
>
> And now you have money for proper help! Ghastly without help I imagine. Tell us about Finland!

> **CLAIRE**
>
> Well, it's um — cold and beautiful and dark.

> **FLEABAG**
> (bemused)
>
> I think she might be happy.

> **CLAIRE**
>
> It's a lot of pressure, but I love it. I have an amazing new partner out there who's really pushed the company forward with—

> **GODMOTHER**
>
> You know, I can't remember the last time we went away!

> **MARTIN**
>
> Weren't you both in Japan recently?

> **PRIEST**
> (amazed)
>
> JAPAN?! Wow!

> **GODMOTHER**
>
> Oh yes! But that was just a little fortnight.

> **FLEABAG**
> (to camera)
>
> Don't ask her—

> **PRIEST**
>
> Why were you in Japan?

> **DAD**
>
> Well, she—

> **GODMOTHER**
>
> I was — oh sorry darling.

> **DAD**
>
> No, no you—

> **GODMOTHER**
>
> Oh thank you. Well they flew us out with the sexhibition.

                              DAD
It really made an impa—

                           GODMOTHER
                      (sweetly to Dad)
Sorry darling, do you want to — no?
                      (to the table)
You see you think of the Japanese as very prudish
people.

                              DAD
Well not to generali—

                           GODMOTHER
But really they have a deep interest in sex in their
culture. It's just hidden in the underbelly. It's not
allowed to the surface.

                            CLAIRE
Fair enough.

                              DAD
They really appreciated—

                           GODMOTHER
The honesty of the sexhibition. Whereas of course the—

                              DAD
Americans! Now they—

                           GODMOTHER
The Americans! Just took me in their stride. The
Japanese were really quite moved by my work, weren't
they darling?

                              DAD
Yes.

                           GODMOTHER
It caused quite a cultural—

                              DAD
Ripple.

                           GODMOTHER
Wave.

Beat.

                              DAD
Wave.

Beat.

                              FLEABAG
                            (to camera)
No one's asked me a question in forty-five min—

                           PRIEST
                         (to Fleabag)
So what do you do?

Everyone stops and stares at Fleabag. She's shocked. She
looks at him.

                              FLEABAG
I run a café.

                            PRIEST
Oh, cool!

Beat.

                                       DAD
It's going well, is it?

                              FLEABAG
Yes. It is. It really is.
                            (to camera)
It actually is.

They smile sympathetically, not believing her.

                              FLEABAG
It is.

Beat.

No one knows what to say. Needy Waitress appears.

                        NEEDY WAITRESS
Can I get anyone any... ice?

EXT. BACK OF RESTAURANT — NIGHT

Fleabag now has her forehead against the brick wall. She
exhales cigarette smoke.

The Priest appears.

                            PRIEST
Fellow smoker.

She smiles.

                            PRIEST
Do you have a spare one?

FLEABAG
Sure.

She hands him one and a lighter. He lights it.

Beat.

PRIEST
So, do your family get together much or—

Fleabag puts her cigarette out and exits.

PRIEST
(lightly)
Fuck you, then.

She stops and turns to look at him. Incredulous.

He smiles. She smiles back. She exits...

INT. RESTAURANT — NIGHT

Fleabag, Claire, Godmother, Dad, Martin. The main meal has arrived. The Priest has not arrived yet. Martin starts to eat.

CLAIRE
(quietly)
We should wait.

He puts his cutlery down. Awkward silence. In the absence of the Priest, they have nothing to talk about.

GODMOTHER
(referring to Priest's seat)
He's such a lovely man.

Everyone answers at the same time, relieved to have something to talk about.

DAD
We're so lucky to have him.

GODMOTHER
(to Fleabag)
Did you have a cigarette?

CLAIRE
He's going to be perfect.

MARTIN
Why be a priest?

                          GODMOTHER
                    (gestures to collar)
I wish you'd seen him in his little—

                          MARTIN
You know they can't even masturbate! Shit life, man.

The Priest enters and sits down, seeing the food has
arrived.

                          PRIEST
Oh, sorry.

                          GODMOTHER
We were just saying it's so fascinating, this notion of
a 'calling'.

                          PRIEST
Yes, well, marriage is a calling too, of course.

                          DAD
Did you always want to join the priesthood?

                          PRIEST
Fuck no.

Everyone laughs. Loving that he is a 'cool sweary priest'.

                          PRIEST
Sorry — no, I came quite late to it actually. But it's
been a good life to me. I've really found peace in it.

Fleabag eyes him.

                          CLAIRE
Is anyone in your family in the church?

                          PRIEST
Actually both my parents are lawyers and my brother is
a long-distance lorry driver.

                          GODMOTHER
How unusual. Were your parents successful?

                          PRIEST
They were very successful alcoholics, yes!
                       (to Martin)
Better than you anyway! But, beyond them my family is
crawling with nuns, so it wasn't too much of a leap.

He smiles at Fleabag again.

                          MARTIN
Must be hard on the balls.

                          CLAIRE
    Martin.

Priest laughs.

                          PRIEST
    Not as hard on them as trying to make a baby for five
    months, I imagine.

He laughs. Martin is put in his place a little. Priest and
Fleabag catch each other's eyes.

                          DAD
    Food good?

                          CLAIRE
                    (taking a bite)
    This sauce is disgusting.

The Needy Waitress appears.

                       NEEDY WAITRESS
    Is everything Ok?

                          CLAIRE
    Delicious thank you!

Needy Waitress pours Godmother's wine.

                        GODMOTHER
                    (prompting Dad)
    Darling.

                          DAD
    Uh no... we'd like to pour our own wine please.

                       NEEDY WAITRESS
                    (so enthusiastic)
    Oh. But I actually love doing the—

                        GODMOTHER
                        (stern)
    Thank you.

                          PRIEST
    You can pour me some.

                       NEEDY WAITRESS
                      (relieved)
    Oh thank you.

                        GODMOTHER
    (suddenly warmly to waitress in front of Priest)
    Ah!

                           MARTIN
                      (to the Priest)
        Have you done a lot of older weddings?

                         GODMOTHER
        I don't think that's how we'd—

                           PRIEST
        This is my first wedding ever actually!

Everyone reacts with polite surprise and cheer.

                         GODMOTHER
        You know I've always been very suspicious of
        religion, but I have to say I do think there is some-
        thing rather chic about having a real priest at a
        wedding.

                          FLEABAG
        Are you a real priest?

Beat.

                           PRIEST
                      (bit bemused)
        Yes.

                         GODMOTHER
                    (touching his arm)
        It's so nice spending time getting to know the man who's
        going to marry us!

                           MARTIN
        Is that usual?

                           PRIEST
        Well, no...! But I'm new to the parish and well I guess
        I'm just...
                          (laughing)
        Really fucking lonely! So I appreciate this, thank you
        very much.

Fleabag looks at him.

                            DAD
        New to the parish?

                           PRIEST
        Yes. Father Patrick sadly died so I got the gig.

                           CLAIRE
        What did he die of?

                              PRIEST
Just... time. He was a dedicated man. A brilliant
priest.

                            FLEABAG
Sounds like a riot.

                              PRIEST
                             (light)
He was actually.

Godmother doesn't like them interacting. She interrupts.

                           GODMOTHER
Do you know how we met?

                            FLEABAG
No.

                             CLAIRE
Through Jake.

                            FLEABAG
                          (to camera)
Creepy stepson.

                           GODMOTHER
He plays the flute—

                         MARTIN/CLAIRE
The bassoon.

                           GODMOTHER
In the church band. Just adorable. Claire introduced us
and we just hit it off. Didn't we?

                              PRIEST
We did!

They laugh.

                               DAD
They did!

                              PRIEST
She's donating a painting to the fête. It's going to
cause quite a stir.

                           GODMOTHER
Oh it's just an old one. But, now, listen. We don't want
gifts at the wedding. It's enough that people slog it
over, but to then expect a gift...

Claire forces a smile.

                              GODMOTHER
So we have decided to ask people to make a small
donation to a charity of their choosing, in our
name.

                               FLEABAG
                    (charming, to Godmother)
That sounds lovely.

Godmother smiles at her. Dad looks at her suspiciously.

                              GODMOTHER
Can I tell you about the gift I am giving your
father?

                               FLEABAG
                         (to camera)
Oh God.

                              GODMOTHER
It's a portrait.

                               FLEABAG
                         (to camera)
Oh God.

                              GODMOTHER
Of you girls.

Both girls look mortified.

                               CLAIRE
Oh, God. Um...

                               FLEABAG
You mean—

                               CLAIRE
Together or um...

                              GODMOTHER
I'd only need a couple of sittings.

                               CLAIRE
Right. Can't you use photos?

                              GODMOTHER
No. Because the lighting's never good enough and —
                    (gestures lightly to Fleabag)
— if you're not photogenic it does you no favours. Plus,
the only photos of you two together are from when you
were children.
                         (to Fleabag)
And you looked like a boy, so.

PRIEST

I had no idea you had a sister, Claire.

CLAIRE

Oh well, we um — we don't get to see each other much.

DAD

Do you see your brother?

PRIEST

I don't really speak to my brother.

GODMOTHER
(over-devastated for him)
Oh no! That's desperately sad.

Fleabag looks at Claire.

GODMOTHER

Why is that?

PRIEST

Oh. Um... Well it's a bit...

DAD

You don't have to—

PRIEST

No, no, that's Ok.

GODMOTHER

Does he not approve of what you do? Of your choices or...

PRIEST

Um... No it's not that, it's not—

GODMOTHER

Is he not in the church?

PRIEST

No he's not in the church—

GODMOTHER

Oh, it must be so hard.

PRIEST

Well no it's mainly hard becau—

GODMOTHER

Is it because he's Mummy's favourite?

PRIEST

Because he's a paedophile.

There is an enormous silence.

GODMOTHER
Oh.

Fleabag looks to camera. Whoa.

PRIEST
I'm aware of the irony of that.

Everyone laughs with relief.

HARD CUT TO: EXT. BACK OF RESTAURANT — NIGHT

Fleabag is outside again having a cigarette. She stares at the camera for a second.

Dad comes out.

DAD
Just a breath of air.

Fleabag smiles. They stand outside. They don't know what to say to each other.

DAD
Interesting man.

Fleabag nods. She offers him a drag of her cigarette.

DAD
No, thanks.

Dad is clearly desperate to say something.

DAD
Darling. I — I missed your birthday.

FLEABAG
That's Ok.

DAD
I just. I got you —

He holds out an envelope.

DAD
In case you were struggling.

FLEABAG
The café's good Dad, I don't—

DAD
Oh no just — That's not for work or — It's just for you.

She smiles. Takes the envelope.

                    FLEABAG
    Thanks.

                      DAD
    You look... strong.

                    FLEABAG
    Thanks.

                      DAD
    Are you?

                    FLEABAG
    Are we going to have a fight?

                      DAD
    No, it's just I wanted to check that you were — That
    you and I were — You're being very...
                     (beat)
    You're not being naughty.

                    FLEABAG
                   (laughing)
    No.
                      DAD
              (laughing nervously)
    Why?

                    FLEABAG
                  (genuinely)
    Because... I guess...

                      DAD
                   (laughing)
    Yes?

                    FLEABAG
    It doesn't matter.

He looks at her. Hurt.

                      DAD
    Oh. Well... I —
                     (beat)
    Is that right?
                     (beat)

                    FLEABAG
    I'm happy for you, Dad.

Beat.

                                    DAD
        Thank you.

Dad exits.

INT. RESTAURANT. DIFFERENT AREA — NIGHT

Fleabag approaches Martin, as he necks a whisky and hands
the empty glass to the Needy Waitress.

                          MARTIN
        Thank you. You're an exceptional waitress.

Fleabag passes. He's aware she has caught him.

                          FLEABAG
        Apple juice?

                          MARTIN
        Yeah.

She passes him. He stops her.

                          MARTIN
        I — I just wanted to say.
                    (beat)
        I'm so intrigued to see how you're going to make this
        whole evening about you.

He smiles. They move off at the same time. He touches her
shoulder.

                          MARTIN
        No, no. We probably shouldn't arrive at the table
        together.

He walks ahead of her. Fleabag looks at us with cold fury.

INT. RESTAURANT — NIGHT

Back at the table with Claire, Priest, Dad and Godmother.
Godmother is mid-flow with the Priest, as Martin and Fleabag
come in. Claire notices them arrive together.

                          GODMOTHER
                    (to Priest)
        A lot of people would say praying is just talking to
        yourself in the dark.

                          PRIEST
                    (he laughs)
        Prayer is just more about connecting with yourself at

the end of the day. It takes a bit of effort, but it's
a positive way to—

CLAIRE
Yes, I completely agree. Positive energy takes work. In
the last six months I have excelled. I just take all
the negative feelings and just bottle them and bury
them. And they never come out.

PRIEST
That's not really how I would—

CLAIRE
I've basically never been better!

She looks at Fleabag.

GODMOTHER
Us neither.

MARTIN
I feel fantastic.

PRIEST
You're a very positive family, I have to say.

DAD
Absolutely.

CLAIRE
I think it's all about positivity. It takes real commit-
ment to be this happy. It's not just drinking and eating
well either. Putting pine nuts in your salad doesn't
make you a grown-up.

FLEABAG
(to camera)
Fucking does.

CLAIRE
It's about — It's about — Well, in Finland they have a
saying that I can't quite remember now, but it's about
being open to the people who want to love you.

MARTIN
And she is wide open these days.

PRIEST
What do you do?

CLAIRE
I work in finance.

DAD
What?

FLEABAG
(to camera)
What?

CLAIRE
Across two firms. One in Finland and one here.

FLEABAG
(to camera)
No, no, she's a lawyer.

GODMOTHER
I thought you were a lawyer?

CLAIRE
No.

MARTIN
What?

CLAIRE
I work WITH lawyers. I am not a lawyer.

DAD
Darling you're a solicitor.

CLAIRE
I went to business school.
(suddenly to Fleabag)
You're being SO quiet. Why aren't you saying anything?!

Pause. They look at each other.

FLEABAG
(gently)
What do you want me to say?

CLAIRE
Anything — What's that in your hand?

DAD
Um... she doesn't have to...

FLEABAG
Birthday present from Dad.

GODMOTHER
It's a nice thing, Claire.

MARTIN
Chunk of change?

                              DAD
No. It's . . .

                             CLAIRE
What is it?

                            FLEABAG
I don't know.

She starts opening it.

                              DAD
Um. . . No you don't need to . . .

                             PRIEST
Love presents. Never get presents.

She pulls out the piece of paper and reads it.

                              DAD
It's just because you . . . you're — Um.

                            FLEABAG
It's a voucher for a counselling session.
                             (beat)
Thanks, Dad.

Everyone feels a bit weird about this. Martin can't help but
laugh.

                          GODMOTHER
So thoughtful.

                             PRIEST
                            (laughing)
I'd kill for one of those.

                             CLAIRE
No, I don't believe you can pay your problems away. I
think you have to face who you are and suffer the conse-
quences. It's the only road to happiness.

                            FLEABAG
Maybe happiness isn't in what you believe, but who you
believe.

Claire gives her a look. The Priest looks at Fleabag. Martin
looks at Fleabag. There is a beat of tension.

                             CLAIRE
                   (almost under her breath)
Fuck.
                             (beat)
Excuse me.

Claire suddenly gets up and leaves the table.

Needy Waitress appears immediately.

> **NEEDY WAITRESS**
> Oh! Do you think she needs anything?

> **EVERYONE**
> No.

> **DAD**
> That was meant to be a bedroom present.

> **PRIEST**
> A what?

> **DAD**
> A present you open in your bedroom, alone.

> **GODMOTHER**
> (to Dad)
> All my presents are bedroom presents, aren't they?

Dad laughs cheekily.

> **PRIEST**
> Want some more wine?

> **DAD**
> Oh yes.

> **GODMOTHER**
> No.

Fleabag frowns and looks towards the bathroom.

INT. COOL RESTAURANT. BATHROOM — NIGHT

Moments later. Fleabag enters.

> **FLEABAG**
> Claire? You've been ages. Are you pissed off or are you
> doing a poo?

She stands by the sinks for a second. She thinks about
knocking on the cubicle.

Then she hears...

> **CLAIRE (O.S.)**
> (whispered)
> Fuck.
> (beat)
> Fuck it.

                              (beat)
                         FLEABAG
Claire? Can we just—

                         CLAIRE (O.S.)
Have you got a — sanitary towel?

                         FLEABAG
Um, no, but I know a waitress who would jump on that
request.
                              (beat)
You want me to ask her?

                         CLAIRE (O.S.)
No.
                              (sighs)
Fuck.

                         FLEABAG
Or there are some sturdy hand towels here. We can
fashion something with wings out of these...

                         CLAIRE (O.S.)
Yes. Fine.

Fleabag gets the towels.

                         FLEABAG
Open the door.

We hear Claire click the door open.

Fleabag swings the door open.

                         CLAIRE
FUCK. GIVE IT TO ME. DON'T COME IN.

                         FLEABAG
Jesus, it's a period, it's not going to bite me.

She pushes the door.

                         CLAIRE
DON'T LOOK AT IT.

                         FLEABAG
I'm not looking at your period. Just take this—

The door opens and Fleabag sees Claire, who has blood down
her legs and on the loo seat. (We do not need to show this.)

                         FLEABAG
Oh God...

> CLAIRE
>
> It's not a period, it's a fucking miscarriage, Ok?

Beat.

Fleabag is shocked.

> FLEABAG
>
> Jesus Claire.

> CLAIRE
>
> It's Ok.

> FLEABAG
>
> No, it's not Ok! What the — we need to get you to a hospital.

> CLAIRE
>
> It's fine. I just need—

Fleabag leans forward with the towels to help Claire.

> CLAIRE
>
> No—

> FLEABAG
>
> There's so much — Let me—

> CLAIRE
> (hard)
>
> Get your hands — off —
> (beat)
> — my miscarriage!

Pause.

> CLAIRE
>
> It's mine.

Claire is crouched over herself. She rests an arm on the cubicle wall and breathes.

> CLAIRE
> (quiet)
>
> It's mine.

Emotion comes to the surface for a split second as she shuts the door to sort herself out.

Beat.

Fleabag waits.

Claire comes out. All sorted.

CLAIRE

Ok.

FLEABAG

CLAIRE.

CLAIRE

Ok. It's Ok.

FLEABAG

We need to get to a hospital. Now.
(beat, gently)
Now.

Claire nods and takes a deep sigh.

CLAIRE

Yes. Ok.

She washes her hands in the sink and fixes her face.

FLEABAG

Ok.

CLAIRE

Ok.

FLEABAG

Come on.

They move to the door. Fleabag almost puts her hand on
Claire's back. Claire gently bats it away.

CLAIRE

All good.

They leave the room together.

INT. RESTAURANT — NIGHT

Moments later. Fleabag follows Claire towards the table.

CLAIRE

Don't tell anyone.

FLEABAG

Ok. Just grab your coat. I'll get a taxi.

CLAIRE

I'll tell them I don't feel right.

FLEABAG

Ok.

                              CLAIRE
       Thank you.

Fleabag nods.

They get to the table to join Martin, Godmother, Dad and
Priest, who are talking generally about Venice.

Claire moves behind her chair and puts her hand on her coat.

Then she suddenly sits down and lunges for the bottle of
wine.

                              CLAIRE
       Fuck it, I'm having some.
                         (to Martin)
       Sorry, darling.

                            GODMOTHER
       Good girl! One night off!

Claire pours herself some wine.

                             MARTIN
       Um... wow, what did you say to her?!

Fleabag stands stunned at the side of the table.

                            FLEABAG
       No. Um.

                             CLAIRE
       Nothing! I just — just sit down. Come on, it's a party.

Fleabag doesn't sit.

                             MARTIN
       Can I have some?

                               DAD
       Well someone suddenly got in the party spirit!

                             CLAIRE
       SIT DOWN!

Fleabag does. Shocked.

                             PRIEST
       Wow, what did you take in there?!

                             MARTIN
       Your sister is finally a good influence on you!

They all laugh.

                         CLAIRE
We just suddenly realised what a monumental fucking day
this is!
                    (to Fleabag)
Drink.

                          DAD
Honestly, leave them in there for two minutes and they
are teenagers again!

Everyone laughs.

                         PRIEST
Shall I order another bottle?

                         CLAIRE
Yes!

                         MARTIN
Ok!

He gestures for the waitress. Fleabag looks at Claire in
shock.

                        GODMOTHER
We were just talking about Venice and this wonderful
little trip we had—

                         MARTIN
                    (to Claire)
How many times have we said that we have to go to
Venice?

                         CLAIRE
                      (tense)
I've always wanted to go! Top of my list.

The conversation builds round the table until —

                        FLEABAG
                    (to Claire)
Oh for fuck's sake, STOP IT!

Everyone looks at her, shocked.

Pause.

Claire glares at her. No one says anything. They just look
at Fleabag, confused.

                         PRIEST
Are you Ok?

                                    FLEABAG
     Yeah I'm uh...

Claire shakes her head at Fleabag.

                                      DAD
     Is — um — is...?

                                    FLEABAG
     Sorry, I — Sorry — it's...

She starts getting emotional.

                                    MARTIN
     Here we go.

                                    FLEABAG
                               (to Claire)
     Sorry I—

                                    PRIEST
     No, come on, what's happened?

                                    CLAIRE
     Nothing's happened.

                                   GODMOTHER
     What's happened?

                                    FLEABAG
                           (to Claire, pointed)
     Something's happened.

                                    MARTIN
                              (simultaneously)
     Come on.

                                   GODMOTHER
                              (simultaneously)
     Spit it out—

                                      DAD
                              (simultaneously)
     It's alright—

                                    MARTIN
                              (simultaneously)
     No secrets here.

                                   GODMOTHER
                              (simultaneously)
     This is a safe space.

FLEABAG
(to Claire)

I — just had a...

Claire gives her a look... 'don't you dare.'

MARTIN

Come on!

FLEABAG
(panicking)

I just... Had a...

GODMOTHER

WHAT?

FLEABAG

A little—

DAD

What darling?

FLEABAG
(beat. She can't think of anything)

Miscarriage.

Beat.

Claire looks at her in disbelief.

Fleabag is horrified at herself.

GODMOTHER

Oh my God.

They all look at Fleabag.

PRIEST

What?

FLEABAG

Um...

CLAIRE

What the fuck.

DAD

Um...

GODMOTHER

How far gone were you?

DAD

You should go to the hospital.

                        GODMOTHER
Whose was it?

                        DAD
Maybe save that for later?

                        GODMOTHER
Was it the tooth man?

                        DAD
Hospital now darling.

                        GODMOTHER
But the bill? Sit down.

                        PRIEST
I'll cover her. I'll cover you.

                        CLAIRE
She doesn't want to go.

                        MARTIN
Why?

                        FLEABAG
Because I'm stubborn and for some inexplicable reason I would rather stay here and have a passive-aggressive party.

                        GODMOTHER
But how far gone were you?

                        CLAIRE
It was very early stages.

                        MARTIN
                    (to Claire)
You knew?

                        PRIEST
               (shocked at Claire)
I really think... she should see a doctor.

                        FLEABAG
So do I.

                        MARTIN
I thought you hadn't spoken?

                        CLAIRE
She's fine. She's absolutely fine.

She pours Fleabag a glass of wine and pushes it across the table.

                         CLAIRE
Drink.
                         (beat)
If it's gone, it's gone.

Pause.

                         PRIEST
Claire...

                         FLEABAG
But what if it's not gone.

Beat.

                         CLAIRE
It's gone.

                         DAD
Darling please...

                       GODMOTHER
                         (sadly)
It was probably ectopic.
                      (beat, serious)
Awful.

She pours herself some wine. Fleabag stands up.

                        FLEABAG
                       (to Priest)
I'll pay you back.

                         PRIEST
Do you need someone to go with you?

                        FLEABAG
No. Thank you. I'll just deal with this in my own
insane, irrational, anal way if that's Ok.

                        MARTIN
                    (under his breath)
It's probably for the best.

                         PRIEST
What did you say?

                        FLEABAG
Ignore him. He's been drinking.

                         CLAIRE

What?

                              MARTIN
Just — you know. It's like a goldfish out the bowl sort
of thing.
                    (he mimes a jumping fish)
If it didn't want to be in there, it didn't want to be
in there. Something wasn't right.
                         (beat)
WHAT? It's the kid's choice if it wants to jump ship
right?

                                DAD
Now, Martin.

                              MARTIN
Either way, she got her spotlight.

Fleabag turns to Martin and punches him square in the face.

There is a scream from Dad and Claire. Priest stands up.

                              MARTIN
WHAT THE FUCK?! FUCK.

Fleabag goes to hit him again. Martin blocks it and accidentally hits her. The Priest moves forward to stop her falling
but gets hit in the face by the back of her head.

                              PRIEST
JESUS CHRIST.

More people turn and gasp.

Needy Waitress is approaching. Martin is doubled over.

                          NEEDY WAITRESS
Oh God, is there anything I can do—

She touches Martin's back, which makes him jump, and he
turns, whacking the Needy Waitress in the face.

                          NEEDY WAITRESS
Agh!

                            GODMOTHER
Oh for God's sake!

INT. COOL RESTAURANT. BATHROOM — NIGHT

The same moment as the opening.

Wide shot of the back of Fleabag as she stands at a sink.
Her head is bowed down as she is washing her hands. We can't
see her face.

She looks up. We see that there is blood all over her mouth.

She holds up a damp towel and wipes most of the blood off her mouth and nose.

There is a bang on the door. She ignores it.

> **PRIEST (O.S.)**
> Can I do anything?

> **FLEABAG**
> No, thank you.

> **PRIEST (O.S.)**
> They've gone so...

She grabs a few tissues and hands them casually to the Needy Waitress, who we discover is sitting, slumped on the floor with blood on her face and a bruised eye.

> **NEEDY WAITRESS**
> (grateful, sweet)
> Thank you.

INT. OUTSIDE COOL RESTAURANT BATHROOM — NIGHT

Fleabag opens the door and sees the Priest.

He is nursing his punched eye, holding her bag and coat.

> **PRIEST**
> Oh hey. I got your stuff. You Ok?

> **FLEABAG**
> Yeah, you Ok?

> **PRIEST**
> Yeah...

She moves off. He stops her and hands her a napkin with his details written on it.

> **PRIEST**
> If you ever need someone. To talk to or uh — I'll be there. I'm always... there.

She stares at him for a second. Then walks past him. Through the corridor and out into the London streets.

EXT. LONDON STREETS (VARIOUS) — NIGHT

Jump cuts of Fleabag walking through the busy city streets with her bloody nose. Soaring score.

She walks over a bridge. London looks resplendent.

Fleabag is defiant, but emotionally lost when—

                    CLAIRE (O.S.)
     HEY!

Fleabag turns her head. No one.

Beat.

Then through the noise of London again...

                    CLAIRE (O.S.)
     HEY!

Fleabag turns again and sees Claire in the distance, leaning out of the open door of a cab.

She beckons to Fleabag.

Fleabag walks towards her. We stay with her all the way.

INT. CAB — NIGHT

Fleabag climbs into the cab and closes the door.

Beat.

                    FLEABAG
     Thank you.

Claire nods.

                    CLAIRE
     Just tell him where you live and we'll talk about this
     tomorrow.

Fleabag nods. She leans forward to speak to the CABBIE.

                    FLEABAG
     Can you take us to the nearest hospital please.

The Cabbie nods. Fleabag sits back, next to her sister. They share a look.

Claire accepts it and the cab moves off.

They sit in sisterly silence.

They both look out their windows.

Long pause.

                              CLAIRE
        The priest was quite hot.

                              FLEABAG
        So hot.

An imperceptible smile on each of their lips.

Fleabag looks to camera. She's back.

                    END OF EPISODE 1

EPISODE 2

INT. CHURCH — DAY

Fleabag is shaking hands with CONGREGANTS. We hear murmurs of 'peace be with you' and the response 'and also with you' said between them.

We do not see the Priest yet, although he is standing at the pulpit.

> **FLEABAG**
> (shaking a hand)
> Peace be with you. Yeah, you too. Thank you.
> (shaking a hand)
> Peace be with you.
> (shaking a hand)
> Peace be with you.
> (shaking a hand)
> Peace be with you.

A KIND OLD MAN nearby—

> **KIND OLD MAN**
> Peace be with you.

> **FLEABAG**
> And also with you.

> **PRIEST**
> Let us pray.

Everyone kneels, so does Fleabag.

She looks at the Priest as he starts to pray. He has a light bruise under his left eye.

During the prayer, Fleabag looks around the church. The following action happens while the prayer is recited.

> **PRIEST / CONGREGANTS / FLEABAG**
> Our Father, who art in heaven, hallowed be thy name.
> Thy Kingdom come. Thy will be done on earth, as it is
> in heaven. Give us this day our daily bread, and forgive
> us our trespasses, as we forgive those who trespass
> against us. And lead us not into temptation, but deliver
> us from evil.

She sees an oil painting of Jesus in a gilded frame. He is semi-nude except for a loose toga wrapped around his body. A woman kneels before him, gazing adoringly at his form.

She looks across to another picture of Jesus. This time he's wearing nothing but a loin cloth, lounging over two fully dressed women who are kissing his hand and bathing his body. And finally, she sees an ornate wooden carving of

Jesus on the cross. The tiny loin cloth draped around his waist, his torso exposed, his carved muscles glistening in the light, the blood dripping down his chiselled face... Fleabag looks at the camera just as everyone in the congregation says—

                              FLEABAG
                           (to camera)
Amen.

                    TITLES: FLEABAG

INT. CHURCH — DAY

As before with Fleabag, Priest and the Congregation. The congregation finish singing Bread of Heaven.

                              PRIEST
          Please be seated.

They start to sit.

                              FLEABAG
                          (by accident)
          And also with you.

Her voice echoes through the church.

The Priest looks up at her.

They hold eye contact for a second.

He smiles.

She smiles back.

Beat. He looks back down to his bible, a little thrown.

                              PRIEST
          Erm — sorry... yes. Today's — erm. Today's notices!
          There's a raffle at tomorrow's fête to raise funds for
          the, erm... sorry. The diocesan pilgrimage to Lourdes.
          Congratulations to St Ethelred's football club.

A whoop of joy from a congregant.

                              PRIEST
          3—1 victory. Next Friday is a first Friday and I'm going
          to be making my usual sick calls to the housebound with

the Eucharist. And finally on Thursday I am going to
begin holy communion preparation classes — and there
are more details of that in the parish newsletter along
with my latest review.

On 'review' he smiles and nods to his congregation while
appreciative laughter ripples around the room.

> **PRIEST**
> That's all folks. Please stand for God's Blessing.

The Congregation and Fleabag stand.

INT. CHURCH — LATER

People are filing out of the church shaking the Priest's
hand saying 'thank you Father'. He replies with 'you're
welcome, all the best, see you next week' etc. One elderly
woman, GINA, stops.

> **GINA**
> Really good one, Father.

> **PRIEST**
> (to Gina)
> Nice to see you Gina.

> **GINA**
> Loved the story about your eye.

> **PRIEST**
> (laughing)
> Yes. Off you go. Give my regards to those budgies.

Gina moves on. Fleabag comes up to him.

> **PRIEST**
> Hello.

> **FLEABAG**
> Hi.
> (gestures to his outfit)
> This is lovely.

> **PRIEST**
> Thank you. Thank you. I thought you'd be in prison by
> now!

> **FLEABAG**
> (laughing)
> Oh well, I keep trying, but they just won't have me.

He laughs.

FLEABAG
I'm sorry about your eye —

PRIEST
That's Ok, it gives me some edge. I've told them some
heroic bullshit.

A woman, SANDY, passes.

PRIEST
(recovering quickly)
Erm, bless you Sandy.

SANDY
Thank you, Father.

PRIEST
Bless you, Sandy.

Beat. Sandy leaves, the rest of the congregation file out
slowly each saying goodbye to the Priest as Fleabag stands
with him. She waits for the last to leave before she says—

FLEABAG
I just wanted to pay you back for dinner.

She thrusts a wad of notes towards him. He pushes them away.

A battle of politeness ensues.

PRIEST
Oh no, no—

FLEABAG
No really I insist—

PRIEST
No, I don't want it—

FLEABAG
It'll have to be in instalments, but I insist.

PRIEST
(indicating his vestments)
I've got no pockets.

They laugh together, suddenly a woman, PAM, approaches.

PAM
I'm going to knife the candles Father, they're a bit
clogged up.

PRIEST
Ok, Pam.

A beat as Pam nods enthusiastically.

> **PRIEST**
> Well, the um, hair dryer is in the drawer, under the—

> **PAM**
> Under the wonky drawer, yes I know.
> (to Fleabag, kindly)
> Hello love.

> **FLEABAG**
> Hi.

Pam sees the wad of cash in Fleabag's hand.

> **PAM**
> Oh, is that for the collection? Oh how sweet.
> (she takes the cash)
> How kind. Thank you.

Pam leaves.

> **PRIEST**
> That's Pam.
> (beat)
> Do you like tea?

HARD CUT: INT. CHURCH. BACK ROOM — DAY

Fleabag is sitting in the back room looking around. It's filled with bric-a-brac for the garden-party the next day.

She looks around the room. There is another painting of Jesus, scantily clad in a loin cloth, another fully dressed woman kneeling at his feet, touching his thigh.

> **FLEABAG**
> (to camera, slightly aroused and shocked)
> Jesus.

There is a bible on the table. She picks it up, she smells the pages. The Priest comes in with the tea.

> **PRIEST**
> Tea!

Fleabag puts the bible down quickly.

> **FLEABAG**
> Great.

> **PRIEST**
> I don't want to boast, but I make a cracking —

He puts down the tray but nervously spills it.

                    PRIEST
    Oh! BASTARD. Sorry.

                    FLEABAG
    Um.

                    PRIEST
    BASTARD.

He smiles as he mops up the tea.

                    PRIEST
    I — Let me — just get this —

He keeps mopping until it's all gone. He looks at the
material he just cleaned the tea up with. He sees it's an
official holy piece.

                    PRIEST
    Oh dear.

                    FLEABAG
    Oh, is that holy?

                    PRIEST
    A bit... Less than it was before I think. Shit. Oh
    well. He'll understand. He's an understanding sort.

He smiles. She smiles. He settles.

                    PRIEST
    Sorry about all the tat. It's for a fundraiser, garden-
    party thing tomorrow. So much stuff, absolutely no
    staff. You can volunteer if you want!

                    FLEABAG
                  (interested)
    Oh!

                    PRIEST
    I'm only joking.

                    FLEABAG
          (to camera, disappointed)
    Oh.

                    PRIEST
    You've probably got a life.
                  (beat)
    What's the time?

FLEABAG

Um.

PRIEST

Do you want a proper drink? I have cans of G&T, from M&S.

FLEABAG

Um... Well it's—

PRIEST

I will if you will.

FLEABAG

Ok!

PRIEST

Ok.

He gets two cans out of a cupboard. Hands her one. Pause. She cracks hers open, they drink.

FLEABAG

So, you're a cool priest are you?

PRIEST

A cool priest?

FLEABAG

Yeah.

PRIEST

No. I'm a big reader with no friends. Are you a cool person?

FLEABAG

No, I'm a pretty normal person.

PRIEST

A normal person?

FLEABAG

Yeah, a normal person.

PRIEST

Oh really, and what makes you a normal person?

FLEABAG

Well I don't believe in God—

In that moment the hot painting of Jesus falls off the wall. Fleabag jumps. She looks at the Priest.

He laughs.

PRIEST

I love it when He does that.

He drinks, Fleabag looks at him and then nervously at the
camera. He leans in.

PRIEST

You were in my prayers last night.

FLEABAG
(to camera)

Likewise.

PRIEST

I'm sorry for your loss.

FLEABAG

What?

PRIEST

Your baby.

FLEABAG

Oh yes, thank you. Thank you. Yes, I... am... Thank
you.

PRIEST

Is the father... alright?

FLEABAG

Well he, doesn't really... exist.

PRIEST

I understand.
(pause)
The funeral liturgy says that life is changed and not
ended. I've always loved that, if that's of any help.

FLEABAG

Thank you very much but I really am an atheist.

PRIEST

Yes I gathered that by the smelling of the bible.

Fleabag laughs, glances at the camera — caught out. She
looks at a pad on the table.

FLEABAG

New sermon?

PRIEST

Oh, no no no no. I write er, restaurant reviews for the
parish magazine. I was just finishing up the last one and I
actually just came up with a really good title.

                    FLEABAG
Ah! What is it?

                     PRIEST
No.

                    FLEABAG
What?

                     PRIEST
No... It's not cool.

                    FLEABAG
Well neither are we, so.

Beat.

                     PRIEST
I'd spend forty days and forty nights in THAT dessert.

Long pause. He looks slightly vulnerable.

                    FLEABAG
                (to camera, deadpan)
Oh God, I fancy a priest.

INT. FLEABAG'S FLAT. BEDROOM — NIGHT

Fleabag sitting up in bed on her laptop. She types into a
search engine — 'catholic priest sex'.

It brings up 'Celibacy'. She thinks again, glances at the
camera.

She types 'definition of celibacy'. She looks at the
results, glances at the camera again.

She types again: 'what happens when a priest has sex'. Her
eyes widen at the results.

She looks at the camera, an excited expression on her face.

EXT. HILARY'S CAFÉ — DAY

The café is rammed with CUSTOMERS. The door is open and
there are tables outside, all full.

Everyone there is talking to each other, almost as if it is
an event.

Fleabag is delivering a coffee to someone. Claire approaches,
taking in the buzzing café.

                              FLEABAG
Hey!

                               CLAIRE
Are you... having an event?

                              FLEABAG
No.

                               CLAIRE
What? Why are there so many people here?

                              FLEABAG
Well it's just erm, successful I guess.

                               CLAIRE
Why is everyone talking to each other?

                              FLEABAG
It's Chatty Wednesday. If you buy something, you have
to have a chat with someone you don't know.

                               CLAIRE
                             (horrified)
What?

                              FLEABAG
                              (shrugs)
Loneliness pays.

                               CLAIRE
Listen. Can we...?

                              FLEABAG
Sure.

Fleabag glances at the camera. They sit.

                               CLAIRE
I know you and I haven't—

                              FLEABAG
Have you had a check-up?

                               CLAIRE
Yes. It's fine. It's really not a big deal, it happens
all the—

An elderly man, CHATTY JOE, approaches.

                             CHATTY JOE
Hello!

                               CLAIRE
No.

CHATTY JOE

Where are you from?

CLAIRE

I — I'm not — this isn't — I'm not part of this. I
shouldn't have to. I don't want to tell you that. No.
Sorry. No.
>   (beat)

Tooting.

FLEABAG

She hasn't bought anything yet, Joe.

CHATTY JOE

Oh! Shit, I'm so sorry.

Chatty Joe walks away. Beat.

FLEABAG

Does Martin know—

CLAIRE

You're not supposed to tell anyone for the first twelve—

FLEABAG

I think you can tell the father.

CLAIRE

I just didn't tell him, Ok.

FLEABAG

So what does he know—

CLAIRE

I don't want to talk about it Ok and I never want anyone
to know about it.
>   (beat)

You have it. You're better at dealing with awful things
anyway.

FLEABAG

I don't want it.

CLAIRE

Well you took it and now everyone thinks you have it so
you have it.
>   (she sighs and crosses her legs)

Fleabag stares at Claire.

CLAIRE (CONT'D)

What?

FLEABAG
They're some pretty funky trainers.

CLAIRE
I said I'm fine. I just really, really don't want anyone to make a big deal out of this, Ok.

HARD CUT TO: EXT. DAD'S HOUSE. HALLWAY — DAY

Godmother hugging Fleabag intensely while Claire stands by.

GODMOTHER
Brutal. Just brutal. You must be feeling rotten.
(beat)
Do you feel rotten?

FLEABAG
I'd rather not talk about it if that's Ok.

GODMOTHER
Of course, Darling. Come on up. Claire get the door for God's sake.

Claire shuts the front door behind them.

GODMOTHER
(very caring, helping Fleabag with her coat)
Did you know who the father was?

FLEABAG
I'd rather not talk about it if that's Ok.

GODMOTHER
No, of course darling.

She dumps Fleabag's coat on to Claire.

INT. GODMOTHER'S STUDIO — DAY

Godmother, Fleabag and Claire enter. There is an easel set up and an upholstered bench, with no back to it, in front of it. Godmother ushers them over to the bench.

GODMOTHER
I've got a set up that I'm very excited about. It's going to be very striking.

FLEABAG
Cool.

GODMOTHER
So, Claire if you sit here, that's lovely and darling
if you could just sit beside her, that's lovely —

Claire sits. Godmother sits Fleabag next to Claire on the
end of the bench.

GODMOTHER
And actually if you could just . . .

She starts edging Fleabag around the bench.

GODMOTHER
That's it, that's it —

She does it a bit more.

GODMOTHER
Just a bit — There you are. Now there! Perfect!
Gorgeous, yes.

Fleabag is now facing the opposite direction from Claire
with her back to the easel.

Fleabag has a little frown and turns her head toward
Godmother.

GODMOTHER
Sorry, no if you could just —

Fleabag faces back to the back of the room.

GODMOTHER
That's it, thank you darling.

Godmother begins painting.

GODMOTHER
So, um —

FLEABAG
(to camera)
She can't not talk about it.

GODMOTHER
You know, I have six friends —

FLEABAG
(to camera)
A lie.

GODMOTHER
— who have had miscarriages. Five of them never actually managed to produce a child afterwards, but the

sixth one did and rather regretted it. So — I think you've probably done the right thing.

> **FLEABAG**
> Thank you.

> **CLAIRE**
> Did you never want them?

> **GODMOTHER**
> Oh, I'm still thinking about it.

Fleabag glances at the camera.

> **FLEABAG**
> Is Dad here? I texted him but—

> **GODMOTHER**
> Oh I saw that.

> **FLEABAG**
> Oh, so he is here.

> **GODMOTHER**
> Sorry, no. I've got his phone today.

Fleabag and Claire exchange a look.

> **FLEABAG**
> I love that colour.

> **GODMOTHER**
> Which one?

> **FLEABAG**
> That one.

> **GODMOTHER**
> Oh, that's three colours.

> **CLAIRE**
> Right.

> **GODMOTHER**
> I'm getting rid of it. But it was quite an Adventure Painting. I actually had an orgasm as I finished it.

We look at the painting. It has a large orgasmic splodge of colour on it.

> **FLEABAG**
> Well, let's hope we all get as much pleasure out of this one.

Fleabag turns to Godmother as she says this.

> **GODMOTHER**
> No no, could you turn—

> **CLAIRE**
> Um. I have a pretty full afternoon so—

> **GODMOTHER**
> Oh have you got to go back to Finland again?

> **CLAIRE**
> No, Finland are coming here.

> **GODMOTHER**
> Oh. Well, that's easier for you.

> **CLAIRE**
> Mm.

> **GODMOTHER**
> Are you still Ok to pick up the invitations?

> **CLAIRE**
> Yes, of course.

> **GODMOTHER**
> And did you find that ribbon thing for the flowers?

> **CLAIRE**
> Yes.

> **GODMOTHER**
> Great.
> (beat)
> And is Martin's nose on the mend?

> **CLAIRE**
> Yes.

Fleabag glances at the camera.

> **GODMOTHER**
> And how is the bassoon solo coming on?

> **CLAIRE**
> (looking at her phone)
> Yes. He's practising. Oh God and NOW I just have to—

> **FLEABAG**
> What?

> **GODMOTHER**
> Claire could you look up please. Thank you.

                              CLAIRE
— organise canapés for an awards ceremony.

                            GODMOTHER
Oh gosh you must be exhausted. Does the little café do
canapés?

                             FLEABAG
It totally could, yeah!

                            GODMOTHER
There you are. That's one off the list!

                              CLAIRE
                      (through her teeth)
Great.

Beat.

                            GODMOTHER
                        (to Fleabag)
Gosh. Haven't you got a lovely, thick neck.

Fleabag looks to camera.

EXT. DAD'S HOUSE — DAY

Claire and Fleabag are leaving Dad's.

                             FLEABAG
Well that was fun. I really can help with the
canapés—

                              CLAIRE
I'm going to say this quickly Ok.

                             FLEABAG
Ok.

                              CLAIRE
Martin wants to press charges against you for assault.
I've tried to talk him down but to be fair you did hit
him fucking hard.

Claire turns to go. Fleabag follows her.

                             FLEABAG
What?!

Claire holds up her hand and continues fast.

                        CLAIRE
I will provide you with exceptional legal advice if you
don't tell anyone that I am providing you with exceptional legal advice.

                        FLEABAG
What?!

                        CLAIRE
This is happening. I'm mortified. But this is happening,
Ok. I will hire this lawyer to scare him off and I will
hire you to do the canapés.

Beat.

                        FLEABAG
Who's the lawyer?

                        CLAIRE
He's a friend. He mainly defends rapists.

                        FLEABAG
He has a high success rate then.

                        CLAIRE
Undefeated. Come on.

INT. LAWYER'S OFFICE. CORRIDOR — DAY

Claire is walking with Fleabag.

                        CLAIRE
I've filled him in with the basics.

                        FLEABAG
That your husband is an animal?

                        CLAIRE
Be serious. Just do whatever he says — and don't flirt
with him.

                        FLEABAG
I'm not going to f—

Just then the door opens and a handsome, charming man opens
the door — this is HOT MISOGYNIST.

                        FLEABAG
                (to camera, impressed)
— fucking hell, Ok.

                        HOT MISOGYNIST
Claire!

> ### CLAIRE
> David thank you so much—

Claire goes to shake his hand but he's already moved
forwards and instead her outstretched hand hits him right on
the crotch.

> ### HOT MISOGYNIST
> Wow.

> ### CLAIRE
> Sorry.

> ### HOT MISOGYNIST
> (naughty grin)
> I could take you to court for that.
> (to Fleabag)
> This the little troublemaker then?
> (to both of them, seriously)
> Now listen, I just want to be clear that whatever
> happens, I don't sleep with people I work with, Ok?

He suddenly laughs. The girls laugh too. As he lets them
enter, off the cuff...

> ### HOT MISOGYNIST
> I'm joking. Slip on in ladies.

INT. LAWYER'S OFFICE — DAY

Hot Misogynist sits opposite Fleabag and Claire behind a
large oak desk.

He's eating his lunch messily. He's all 'powerful' in his
attitude. Loves himself.

> ### HOT MISOGYNIST
> Well... If you spit guilty, you'll have to swallow a
> short jail term. Or community service if you're lucky.

> ### FLEABAG
> Or?

> ### HOT MISOGYNIST
> You definitely started it?

> ### FLEABAG
> Yes.

> ### HOT MISOGYNIST
> Any witnesses?

                         FLEABAG
About ... thirty.

Claire holds her temples.

                      HOT MISOGYNIST
The most important thing, honey, is that you do not,
under any circumstances, apologise.

                         FLEABAG
Oh well I can do that—

                          CLAIRE
No that's not what we discussed—

                      HOT MISOGYNIST
Or that can be taken as an admission of guilt. I assume
you know the victim personally.

                         FLEABAG
Yes—

                          CLAIRE
                      (interrupting)
No. And let's not call him the victim yet, shall we?

He looks up with a glare.

                      HOT MISOGYNIST
Well that's what he is—

                          CLAIRE
Yes. Right.

                         FLEABAG
                      (to camera)
They've definitely fucked.

                          CLAIRE
We just want a letter to scare him off if he ends up
seeking proper action.

                      HOT MISOGYNIST
That really doesn't make sense, Claire.

                         FLEABAG
                      (to camera)
Actually maybe not.

                          CLAIRE
I think that makes perfect sense. I just want to be
ahead of the game.

> **FLEABAG**
> (to camera)

God I can't tell.

> **HOT MISOGYNIST**

That's a habit of yours, I've heard.

> **FLEABAG**
> (to camera)

Oh I've got it.

> **CLAIRE**

Is it?

> **FLEABAG**
> (to camera)

They haven't.

> **CLAIRE**

You're going to have to tell me who said that.

> **HOT MISOGYNIST**

Never.

> **FLEABAG**
> (to camera)

But they're going to.

> **CLAIRE**

David.

> **FLEABAG**
> (to camera)

Oh God, I've got to get out.

> **HOT MISOGYNIST**

Claire.

Fleabag gets up.

> **FLEABAG**

Excuse me.

> **HOT MISOGYNIST**

Where you off to, little lady?

> **FLEABAG**
> (leaving)

I'm just gonna... let this, er. Yeah.

EXT. LAWYER'S OFFICE — DAY

Fleabag waits outside for Claire. She looks up at the sky, the wind rustling through the trees.

Lost in her thoughts, she begins to hear a hymn from the church earlier.

Claire interrupts her reverie.

> CLAIRE
> You alright?

> FLEABAG
> Yeah. Just thought I'd leave you to it.

Claire holds a business card.

> CLAIRE
> Sorry.

> FLEABAG
> What?

> CLAIRE
> He says he'll only talk you through potential proceed-
> ings if you go for a drink with him.

> FLEABAG
> (thrilled/offended)
> What?

> CLAIRE
> I know.

> FLEABAG
> (to camera)
> Outrageous.

> CLAIRE
> Stop smiling.

> FLEABAG
> I thought he was going for you?

> CLAIRE
> So did I. But my hair isn't great at the moment. Either
> way, it's very inappropriate. Don't sleep with him.

> FLEABAG
> I won't.

> CLAIRE
> Don't.

                              FLEABAG
I won't! I don't do that anymore.

                         CLAIRE
What? Why? Are you ill?

                              FLEABAG
No!

                         CLAIRE
Then what?

                              FLEABAG
Well, I — just. Just—

                         CLAIRE
Oh my God. Have you met someone?

                              FLEABAG
Well, not really.

                         CLAIRE
Back with Harry?

                              FLEABAG
No, it's actually—

                         CLAIRE
Someone new?

                              FLEABAG
Well—

                         CLAIRE
Is he single?

                              FLEABAG
Sort of.

Claire gives her a look. Then hands her the business card
with a sigh.

                         CLAIRE
Take this. I'll try to talk Martin down but call him if
you need him. He's a very good lawyer. Surprisingly...
tender. Underneath it all.

                         FLEABAG
                        (to camera)
Knew it.

                         CLAIRE
What you did in the restaurant was unforgivable.

                        FLEABAG
I know.

                        CLAIRE
Thank you.

They smile.

                        CLAIRE
Ok, well I've got to—

                        FLEABAG
Look, I just wanted to give you this.

Fleabag reaches in her bag and produces the vouchers for the
counselling session Dad gave her in Episode 1.

                        FLEABAG
It's only one session but you've been through a lot so—

                        CLAIRE
I said I'm FINE. I'm weirdly fine. I'd rather have the
money.

She leaves. Fleabag looks at the voucher. Good point.

HARD CUT TO: INT. COUNSELLOR'S OFFICE — DAY

Fleabag sits opposite an inscrutable COUNSELLOR. She is
moisturising her forearms. She has a small notepad on the
table.

                        COUNSELLOR
Excuse me, I have dry forearms.

                        FLEABAG
Sure.

                        COUNSELLOR
So why have you come to this session?

                        FLEABAG
It was a birthday present from my father.

                        COUNSELLOR
Is that a joke?

                        FLEABAG
No.

The Counsellor reaches for her notepad quickly. She writes
it down.

                         COUNSELLOR
It would be good not to make jokes here in case anything
gets lost in humorous translation.

                         FLEABAG
    I don't know if I can do that.

The Counsellor looks at her.

                         COUNSELLOR
    Is that a joke?

                         FLEABAG
    No.

Beat.

                         COUNSELLOR
    Well. Just try not to. Or make it obvious.

                         FLEABAG
    Sure.

                         COUNSELLOR
    So why do you think your father suggested you come for
    counselling?

                         FLEABAG
Um. I think because my mother died and he can't talk
about it, because my sister and I haven't spoken in a
year because she thinks I tried to sleep with her
husband and because I spent most of my adult life using
sex to deflect from the screaming void inside my empty
heart.
                    (to camera)
    I'm good at this.
                    (back to the Counsellor)
    Although I don't really do that anymore.

Counsellor looks at Fleabag for a beat.

                         COUNSELLOR
    Are you close with your family?

Flashback of Fleabag punching Martin.

                         FLEABAG
    We get on with it.

                         COUNSELLOR
    Do you talk?

                         FLEABAG
    God no.

                    COUNSELLOR
Any friends?

                    FLEABAG
Sorry?

                    COUNSELLOR
Any friends.

Quick flashback of Boo eating a sandwich in the café.

                    FLEABAG
Well, I don't really have time for... I have a guinea
pig! But she blows hot and cold.
    (She laughs. Then turns to camera — seriously.)
Not a joke.

The Counsellor looks at Fleabag.

                    COUNSELLOR
Tell me about the sex.

                    FLEABAG
All of it?!

                    COUNSELLOR
You said you don't do that now.

                    FLEABAG
No, I just play tennis now.

Counsellor looks at her suspiciously.

                    FLEABAG
                (to camera)
Tough crowd.
                (to Counsellor)
Sex didn't... bring anything —

Quick flashback of Boo in tears, standing at the edge of the
road.

                    FLEABAG
— good. So I'm — trying not to um—

                    COUNSELLOR
And what have you found in your abstinence?

                    FLEABAG
Well I'm very horny and your little scarf isn't helping.

Beat. The Counsellor writes something down.

> **COUNSELLOR**
> So the impulse is still there?

> **FLEABAG**
> Oh —

Flashback of the Priest from that morning.

> **FLEABAG**
> Oh yes. The impulse is very much still there, but —
> (beat)
> — it's just — never the right person.

> **COUNSELLOR**
> So there is a particular person you're not having sex with?

> **FLEABAG**
> No — well nothing's happened, it's just — he's not available.

> **COUNSELLOR**
> In a relationship.

> **FLEABAG**
> Yes, a bad one.

> **COUNSELLOR**
> How so?

> **FLEABAG**
> It's the sort of relationship where one partner tells the other how to dress.

> **COUNSELLOR**
> Are you in love with him?

> **FLEABAG**
> (laughing)
> No.

> **COUNSELLOR**
> Why do you find that funny?

> **FLEABAG**
> Well I — I no — I — No.

> **COUNSELLOR**
> Not a romantic?

> **FLEABAG**
> No.

                    COUNSELLOR
Just a girl with no friends and an empty heart.

Fleabag looks at the Counsellor.

                    COUNSELLOR
By your own description.

                      FLEABAG
I have friends.

                    COUNSELLOR
Oh, so you do have someone to talk to.

                      FLEABAG
Yeah.

She winks at the camera.

                    COUNSELLOR
Do you see them a lot?

                      FLEABAG
                    (laughing)
Oh, yeah. They're always there. They're...
                    (to camera)
Always there.

                    COUNSELLOR
Why do you find that funny?

                      FLEABAG
I don't need to be analysed. I have a nice life, I just
wanted to exchange the voucher for the money.

                    COUNSELLOR
It's a bit late for that now.

                      FLEABAG
I've only been here five minutes —
                    (beat)
I want the money.

The Counsellor looks at her. Silence.

                      FLEABAG
I want to fuck a priest.

                    COUNSELLOR
Catholic?

                      FLEABAG
Yes.

                              COUNSELLOR
A good one?

                               FLEABAG
Yes.

                              COUNSELLOR
Looks good in the —

Gestures to the dog collar.

                               FLEABAG
Mm hm. Yes.

                              COUNSELLOR
I understand. Do you really want to fuck the priest or
do you want to fuck God?

                               FLEABAG
Can you fuck God?

                              COUNSELLOR
Oh yes.

                               FLEABAG
Just please — tell me how to not fuck a priest before I
get arrested.

                              COUNSELLOR
I don't think fucking a priest will make you feel as
powerful as you think it will.

                               FLEABAG
Can you just tell me what to do?

                              COUNSELLOR
You know.
                                (beat)
You already know what you're going to do. Everybody
does.

                               FLEABAG
What?

                              COUNSELLOR
You've already decided what you're going to do.

                               FLEABAG
So what's the point in you?

                              COUNSELLOR
You know what you're going to do.

                         FLEABAG
No I don't.

                         COUNSELLOR
Yes you do.

                         FLEABAG
I don't!

                         COUNSELLOR
You do.

                         FLEABAG
I don't!

                         COUNSELLOR
You do.

                         FLEABAG
I don—

HARD CUT TO: EXT. CHURCH FÊTE — DAY

The Priest laughing with a group of women. Fleabag is
helping out with the raffle tickets on a stall.

                         FLEABAG
                 (handing a raffle ticket)
Good luck!
                         (to camera)
Shut up.

                    HARRY (O.S.)
Can I have two raffle tickets please?

                         FLEABAG
Oh my God.

Harry appears with a BABY in a baby harness.

                         HARRY
Oh my God, hi.

                         FLEABAG
Hi! You're —

                         HARRY
Yeah!

                         FLEABAG
With child.

>   **HARRY**
> Yes.

>   **FLEABAG**
> Cool!

>   **HARRY**
> Yeah! You've got a fringe!

>   **FLEABAG**
> Yeah!

>   **HARRY**
> Cool!

>   **FLEABAG**
> You always wanted a baby!

>   **HARRY**
> You always wanted a fringe!

They laugh awkwardly.

>   **HARRY**
> Yeah. She is amazing. It's been tough. But amazing.

>   **FLEABAG**
> Oh yeah?

>   **HARRY**
> Yeah I mean, the birth really took its toll.

>   **FLEABAG**
> Oh really? Was it a tricky one?

>   **HARRY**
> I can't really remember it now. But the whole thing has
> just really changed me. I just don't feel — my emotions
> are up and down, my body just feels different. Elaine
> has been amazing. So supportive, but—

>   **FLEABAG**
>   (laughs)
> Sounds like you've got post-natal depression.

>   **HARRY**
> I do, yeah. But we're working through it.

Beat. Fleabag glances to camera.

>   **FLEABAG**
> Sure.

The Priest approaches them.

PRIEST
Just to let you know the band are going to start in a
couple of minutes —

HARRY
Hey Father! This is Suzie!

PRIEST
Aw — I don't know how to talk to babies, sorry. Do you
guys know each other?

FLEABAG
Yeah, well we used to—

HARRY
Uh yeah — I used to be her — girlfriend.

PRIEST
Cool! Good for you!

Harry smiles. Not realising what he said.

HARRY
(holding his baby)
I'm going to go show her the coconuts. She's really good
at counting.

Harry walks off. Pam appears in the crowd and shouts—

PAM
(loud)
Excuse me everyone, the Youthy band are about to play
the ode to something.

Fleabag and the Priest share a laugh.

PRIEST
You having fun?

FLEABAG
Oh yeah, I think so.

PRIEST
(looking at the stall)
Oh a puzzle! Love a puzzle.

Pam suddenly approaches them at pace. Does she sense a
flirtation?

PAM
The Youthy band are about to play.

PRIEST

Yes, I heard you Pam, thank you!

She walks off with a pointed smile to Fleabag.

The Priest notices Godmother's Orgasm painting propped up on Fleabag's raffle stall.

PRIEST

Ah, the main event.

FLEABAG

Yeah!

PRIEST

She's very talented.

FLEABAG

Yes ... she uh —
> (to camera)

Don't say it. She, uh —
> (to camera)

Just don't say it.
> (to Priest)

— she actually orgasmed ... when she finished it.
> (to camera)

Just said it.
> (to Priest)

Apparently.

PRIEST

Oh!
> (beat)

Well, whatever gets you there!

Fleabag smiles and briefly looks to camera. Not quite the reaction she expected.

PAM

FATHER THERE IS A CUPCAKE SITUATION OVER HERE.

PRIEST

THANK YOU, PAM! I WILL BE THERE TO CUPCAKE.
> (beat, to Fleabag)

Thank you so much for helping.

He touches her arm gently before walking away.

Fleabag looks to the camera.

FLEABAG
> (to camera, aroused)

Arm touch.

CUT TO: EXT. CHURCH FETE. ELSEWHERE — DAY

Minutes later. Fleabag is at the back of the semi-circle crowd watching the Youthy band play. She focuses on JAKE. Then she hears, behind her—

> **MARTIN (O.S.)**
> I mean, at least my son is in the Youthy band. What's your excuse?

> **FLEABAG**
> (to camera)
>
> UGHGHHGHGH.

She looks over her shoulder. Martin is standing over her, smirking, with a bruised nose and eye. The band play.

> **FLEABAG**
> I'm helping the Priest.

> **MARTIN**
> (laughs)
> Wow! You do like a challenge, don't you.
> (beat)
> Hey, I just wanna say something—

> **FLEABAG**
> It's from River Island, I got it last week.

> **MARTIN**
> No, I just want to say I'm sorry. For saying what I said. I'm sorry for what you went through. I'm sorry.

> **FLEABAG**
> I know what you are doing.
> (to camera)
> Not gonna say it.

> **MARTIN**
> I'm just saying sorry.

> **FLEABAG**
> (to camera)
> I'm not going to say it.

> **MARTIN**
> I'm sorry.

Fleabag shakes her head at the camera. Martin waits. But she's not going to say it.

                    MARTIN
Ok! And thank you. She and I have never been better.
You had a big part in that.

Beat.

                    FLEABAG
                  (laughing)
I'm happy for you.
                    (beat)
I'm happy you've found a way to deflect from your
pitiful, self-sabotaging, ego-driven, masturbatory —
                  (to camera)
I can't believe how well this is coming out.
                  (to Martin)
— pawing, insidious —
                  (to camera)
Insidious!
                  (to Martin)
— overwhelming mediocrity, by finally figuring out that
at your very core, you are a weaky.
                  (to camera)
DAMN.

                    MARTIN
A 'weaky'?

The band finishes and everyone applauds. Adding insult to
injury. Both Fleabag and Martin applaud as they keep
speaking.

                    FLEABAG
                  (to camera)
DAMN DAMN.

                    MARTIN
Wow. A 'weaky'?

Beat.

                 MARTIN (CONT'D)
Well in that case, I just wanted YOU to know that, I'm
impressed with how you just keep bouncing back. I really
am.
                    (beat)
You're a strongy.

He laughs. Jake comes over. He looms over them looking for
Claire.

                    MARTIN
That was awesome, man.

FLEABAG
(to camera)
Creepy Jake. Mainly says things like—

JAKE
Where's Claire?

FLEABAG
(to camera)
And—

JAKE
Where's Claire?

MARTIN
She couldn't make it, man. Lucky for us your aunt is such an avid churchgoer.

JAKE
Hi. Thanks for watching.

FLEABAG
You were excellent.

Jake smiles and gives her a hug suddenly.

MARTIN
Careful there buddy, you could go down for that sort of behaviour these days.

JAKE
It was just a hug.

MARTIN
(mimicking)
'It was just a huuuggg!'
(beat)
You gotta do better than that these days, boy.
(laughs)
Specially round this firecracker.

JAKE
But I didn't—

MARTIN
Come on.
(to Fleabag)
I don't want to be an asshole. I just want her to be happy. And she has been really happy. Until she saw you. Just saying.

He winks at her but it's painful with his black eye. He walks off with Jake.

Fleabag turns to look for the Priest. He is surrounded by women again. He doesn't look at her.

Suddenly, from behind, Jake appears again.

> **FLEABAG**
> Hi Jake?

> **JAKE**
> (whispers in her ear)
> Tell her to leave him.

Beat.

> **FLEABAG**
> What?

> **JAKE**
> (whispers)
> Tell her to leave him.

He walks off.

> **FLEABAG**
> (to camera)
> He's going to kill someone one day.

EXT. CHURCH — DAY

Fleabag is walking away with a coconut from the fête.

> **PRIEST (O.S.)**
> Hey!

She turns around. It's the Priest.

> **FLEABAG**
> (to camera, thrilled)
> Yes, Father!
> (to Priest, innocent)
> Yes, Father?

> **PRIEST**
> I can't believe I'm saying this, but —

> **FLEABAG**
> (to camera)
> Oh my God.

> **PRIEST**
> — can I get that coconut back? They're actually on hire. I don't think all of them are real actually which is morally a bit dubious, but we've got to make money somehow...

                    FLEABAG
Oh. Sure, here.

She hands the coconut back. Their hands brush as she does.
She looks at the camera.

                    FLEABAG
          (to camera, bit breathless)
Knuckle brush.

                    PRIEST
And um... Listen, I hope you don't mind but...

He pulls out a bible.

                    PRIEST
I've marked some pages in here that...

                    FLEABAG
Oh, erm, I —

She laughs nervously, horrified.

                    PRIEST
No, no, no — I'm not trying to... they're just words.

                    FLEABAG
Ok, it's just, I think I know what happens.

He smiles but doesn't rise to it.

                    PRIEST
Classic. Well, have a read. I'd like to know what you
think. And if you ever want to talk about stuff, I'm
here. With a G&T, of course.
          (beat)
You can come here whenever you want.
          (beat)
I'd like you to come.

She smiles.

                PRIEST (CONT'D)
If it helps.

He leaves. What was that? She looks at us briefly —
dismisses it.

She walks away, thumbing through the bible thoughtfully.

                  END OF EPISODE 2

EPISODE 3

INT. FLEABAG'S FLAT. BATHROOM — MORNING

Fleabag is in the bath reading the bible.

Beat.

She gasps, shocked by a twist in the tale.

She looks to camera.

TITLES: FLEABAG

INT. POSH BUSINESS LIFT — DAY

Claire and Fleabag are in a lift. Fleabag is holding trays and trays of cling-filmed canapés.

Beat.

> **CLAIRE**
> Just don't — talk too much, or try and pretend that you know anything about the company.

> **FLEABAG**
> Ok.

> **CLAIRE**
> And don't be funny... Or clever or... Just don't be the centre of attention. These people are very important to me so just don't—

> **FLEABAG**
> Ok.

> **CLAIRE**
> Don't... be yourself.

> **FLEABAG**
> I won't.

Fleabag does a little fart. Claire hears it and immediately closes her eyes with the stress of it.

> **CLAIRE**
> For fuck's sake.
> (covering her mouth)
> I know people in this building. Anyone could—

The lift stops. The doors open. An immaculate businesswoman, LESLIE walks in smiling.

LESLIE

Hi Claire.

CLAIRE

Hello Leslie.

Claire does not introduce Fleabag. Leslie presses her button, then stops and sniffs slightly. Claire looks mortified.

LESLIE
(genuine)

Oo that's lovely, what is that?

Fleabag looks at Claire, smug.

INT. POSH BUSINESS ENTRANCE HALL — DAY

Moments later. Claire and Fleabag walk through the entrance hall of a Very Serious Business Building.

CLAIRE

We have a load of vegetarians so make sure it's clear which ones have meat in them.

FLEABAG
(to camera)

Loves a crisis.

CLAIRE

We have a couple of waitresses... for the drinks so if you could hand round the food —

FLEABAG
(to camera)

Put her in a quiet room with a nice breeze and she'll have a panic attack.

Claire looks around, still walking at pace.

CLAIRE

Where is everyone?

FLEABAG
(to camera)

She's so happy.

CLAIRE

God, this is stressful. Don't be weird about how big my office is.

They walk into her office.

INT. CLAIRE'S OFFICE — DAY

Fleabag and Claire enter. Fleabag is astonished at the size of it.

> **FLEABAG**
> What the fuck.

> **CLAIRE**
> I know.

> **FLEABAG**
> Are you—

> **CLAIRE**
> It's over the top, I know. Ok.
> (indicating the canapés)
> Put them on the table.

Fleabag tries to.

> **CLAIRE**
> Not that table.

> **FLEABAG**
> Are you Ok?

> **CLAIRE**
> Of course. It's just — it's a big night and the Finnish partners are here so it's all a bit...

Claire gives her a look.

> **CLAIRE**
> Check the award.

> **FLEABAG**
> Why?

> **CLAIRE**
> Just to make sure it's not pink or anything horrifically female. She'll loathe that. Be careful with it. It's worth thousands.

Fleabag checks opens the award box.

> **FLEABAG**
> It's not pink.

> **CLAIRE**
> Good.

> **FLEABAG**
> It's perfect, it looks like a sperm. Your hair looks nice.

Claire hurries around her desk.

> **CLAIRE**
> Shut up. Ok—

Fleabag sits down.

> **CLAIRE**
> DON'T SIT ON THAT!

Fleabag jumps up.

> **CLAIRE**
> Ok, put those on the posh plates, put the award behind
> the microphone. Oh and um... thank you. You've really,
> er. Thank you.

Claire turns, goes to leave. As she goes Fleabag sneaks
another peek at the award. Over her shoulder —

> **CLAIRE**
> Don't play with that.

Claire leaves.

Fleabag takes the award out of the box. Looks at it.

> **FLEABAG**
> Oooo, heavy...

It immediately slips out of her hands and crashes to the
floor. Smashed to pieces.

She looks at the camera. Fuck.

EXT. POSH BUSINESS BUILDING — DAY

Fleabag runs out of office in a panic. She passes a HANDSOME
MAN — checks him out quickly and runs on.

EXT. LONDON SQUARE/STREET — DAY

Fleabag runs across City Square/Street.

EXT. LONDON SQUARE/STREET — DAY

Fleabag runs back across the City Square/Street.

EXT. POSH BUSINESS BUILDING — DAY

Fleabag runs back into the office building. Gives thumbs-up as she passes us.

INT. POSH BUSINESS ROOM — DAY

Fleabag makes her way through the guests with the award box. She places the award box on the table on the stage. She is sweating. She sees two stand-up banners that say: 'BEST WOMAN IN BUSINESS'.

Fleabag frowns at them. She steps down off the stage and grabs a tray of canapés to hand round. Claire appears behind her.

                    CLAIRE
        Where have you been?!

                    FLEABAG
        I forgot the vegetarian bites — but it's all fine.
        You're gonna love them.

                    CLAIRE
        You're sweating *so* much.

                    FLEABAG
        Sorry.

                    CLAIRE
        It's attention-grabbing.

                    FLEABAG
        It's only on one side.

Claire rushes her through the crowd to introduce her to a smart businesswoman.

                    CLAIRE
        Sorry,this is Sylvia, she is going to be presenting the
        award, so you need to give it to her before she goes
        up, Ok.

                    FLEABAG
        Hi.

                    SYLVIA
                  (canapés)
        Has this got shellfish in it?

                    FLEABAG
        No.

                    SYLVIA
        Fine.

She takes one and eats it. Claire spots BELINDA.

                              SYLVIA
     Four CEOs have been fired. Two are being taken to court.

Women laugh.

                              SYLVIA
     It's just sad. We felt like a family.

                              FLEABAG
     Especially sad when you have to tell your family not to
     touch each other up by the photocopier.

The women laugh.

                              CLAIRE
                            (quietly)
     Stop making jokes.

                              FLEABAG
     I'm sorry, I can't help it.

                              CLAIRE
     You can.

Belinda approaches.

                              CLAIRE
     Belinda's coming. Don't speak to Belinda.

Belinda arrives.

                              BELINDA
     Hellooo Claire!

                              CLAIRE
     Hellooo Belinda!

                              BELINDA
                        (to Claire's dress)
     God you're tasteful.
                        (to Fleabag's canapés)
     Are these meaty?

Huge pause. Fleabag doesn't say anything.

                              CLAIRE
     SAY SOMETHING.

                              FLEABAG
     I think they have courgette in them?

BELINDA

Oh I love courgettes... You can treat them appallingly and they still grow.

Belinda takes three and walks off with a smile.

FLEABAG

She seems lovely.

CLAIRE

Yes, she's great.

FLEABAG

So who are you so nervous about—

CLAIRE

I'm not nervous — I'm being completely—

A man approaches: this is KLARE. He is Finnish. Claire instantly goes weird.

KLARE

Claire!

CLAIRE

Hi!!

(beat)

Hi.

They have an enthusiastic/awkward hello and try to air kiss but end up kissing on the lips. Fleabag watches with a grin.

CLAIRE

I'm so glad you could come.

KLARE

Of course! It's my job!

CLAIRE

This is my catering, she's the sister.

FLEABAG

Hi!

KLARE

I ate a sausage over there thinking it was a prune. Fifteen years of vegetarianism. Gone! Like bang, bang.

He mimes eating two on each 'bang'.

FLEABAG

We actually call them bangers.

>   **KLARE**
>   (laughs)
>   That's funny.

Claire looks at Fleabag.

>   **CLAIRE**
>   Yes. It was.
>   (to Fleabag)
>   Don't be funny.

>   **FLEABAG**
>   How do you know each other?

>   **KLARE**
>   We're partners. She's been working with me in Finland
>   and it's — oh — yes — exactly — I'm a big fan!

>   **CLAIRE**
>   (simultaneously)
>   We're partners. Business partners — in — yes. We don't
>   see each other that much, but I'm a huge — thank you —
>   admirer.

Beat. They both laugh.

Awkward beat. Fleabag grins.

>   **KLARE**
>   I'm going to get a drink. Do you want anything?

>   **CLAIRE**
>   Oh, erm. Champagne please.

>   **KLARE**
>   Oo, off the wagon?

>   **CLAIRE**
>   Just when I'm with you!

He starts walking off. Claire tries to say her next line in
time, but he's gone too far.

>   **CLAIRE**
>   (laughing)
>   Let's go fucking crazy tonight, then.

He catches the end of it and turns and comes back. Claire is
mortified. She shakes her head.

>   **KLARE**
>   (friendly)
>   What did you say?

                           CLAIRE
No I just said... it's not—

                            KLARE
No, what did you say?

                           CLAIRE
Erm, er. I just said let's go fuck like crazy tonight.

Fleabag looks at the camera. 'WHAT?'

                      CLAIRE (CONT'D)
Oh God.

Fleabag smiles. Scared to say anything. Klare starts
laughing.

                            KLARE
Ha! Ok!

They laugh. Klare walks off smiling, touching Claire's
shoulder. She looks at Fleabag, embarrassed.

                           CLAIRE
Shut up.

                          FLEABAG
Oh my God.

                           CLAIRE
He's a very good businessman. He's just very, socially
sort of —

She does a gesture that is indecipherable.

                          FLEABAG
What's erm —

Fleabag repeats the indecipherable gesture.

                           CLAIRE
Shut up.

                          FLEABAG
                          (laughing)
Claire...

                           CLAIRE
Please don't. Please don't. I can't cope, Ok.

                          FLEABAG
Ok. What's his name?

Nothing.

> **FLEABAG**
> What's his name?

Beat.

> **CLAIRE**
> Klare.

> **FLEABAG**
> What?

> **CLAIRE**
> His name is Klare.
>   (beat)
> Don't.

Fleabag grins a bit.

> **CLAIRE**
> Oh God, I have to announce. Ok. Mingle. But don't talk
> to anyone.

> **FLEABAG**
> Ok.

> **CLAIRE**
> I'm not in love with him.

> **FLEABAG**
> Ok.

Fleabag watches her go. She notices Klare watching Claire
too. She raises her eyebrows to the camera.

HARD CUT TO: INT. POSH BUSINESS ROOM — DAY

Another part of the room. Claire is up at the front. Fleabag
is in the crowd.

> **CLAIRE**
>   (on mic)
> Hi everyone. I'm very proud to announce the nominees
> for the Women in Business award, sponsored by us here
> at Hurbots. Amongst our exceptional women we have:
> Georgina Franks.

There is clapping.

> **CLAIRE**
>   (on mic)
> Belinda Friers.

More claps.

>   CLAIRE
>   (on mic)
>   And another extraordinary woman, Klare Korhonen.

Everyone claps and turns to a very confused Klare, who sort of waves.

>   CLAIRE
>   (on mic)
>   Sorry I think there's been a mistake, here... and er,
>   Elizabeth Sawkin.

More claps.

>   CLAIRE
>   (on mic)
>   Congratulations to you all and have a wonderful evening!
>   We will be presenting the award very soon.

CUT TO: INT. POSH OFFICE CORRIDOR — DAY

Fleabag and Claire are walking quickly.

>   CLAIRE
>   I'm going to introduce Sylvia, who is going to intro-
>   duce Belinda. When you hear me introducing Sylvia get
>   her on stage. It has to go like cockwork.

>   FLEABAG
>   Like what?

>   CLAIRE
>   Cockwork.

>   FLEABAG
>   Claire your brain is somewhere else right now.

>   CLAIRE
>   Sylvia, go!

Fleabag runs off.

INT. LADIES' BATHROOM — DAY

Fleabag looks for Sylvia in the loo.

>   FLEABAG
>   Sylvia.

She sees Sylvia is in a stall vomiting. Clearly allergic to the shellfish canapé Fleabag served her earlier.

                         FLEABAG
                        (to camera)
        Crab.

INT. POSH BUSINESS ROOM — DAY

Moments later. Claire is on stage about to introduce Sylvia.
Fleabag weaves her way through the crowd.

                          CLAIRE
                         (on mic)
        A huge thanks to Matthew, Mark, Luke and John for coming
        up with this award. And Link-y-din for connecting us all
        this evening and beyond. I'm so excited to introduce
        Sylvia Hamber, this year's winner of 'Women Who Work',
        who will announce this year's Best Woman in Business.

Fleabag mouths at Claire desperately, trying to get her
attention.

                          CLAIRE
        Sylvia.

Claire turns. Fleabag gets her attention and shakes her head
and acts slicing her throat. Claire looks HORRIFIED. They mime
a bit to and fro. Fleabag points to herself 'I can do it'.
Claire considers for a second. Then turns back to the mic.

                          CLAIRE
                (to Fleabag but through the mic)
        I'LL DO IT.
                        (to herself)
        I can do it.
                    (back to the audience)
        I'm sorry, it appears that Sylvia is busy... Which
        shouldn't come as a surprise really.

Claire grimaces.

                     CLAIRE (CONT'D)
                         (on mic)
        This has been a big year for business.
                         (beat)
        Particularly women in business. Men have been pretty
        hands-on the past few decades.

Fleabag lets out a laugh. Everyone else is silent.

                     CLAIRE (CONT'D)
        I'd like to thank all the brilliant men and women who
        have supported each other here at Hurbots. We're a
        family, really. And if we've learned anything over the
        past 12 months it's that family really shouldn't touch
        each other up next to the photocopier.

Everyone laughs. Claire looks at Fleabag who mouths 'funny!'
She turns back to the crowd.

>   **CLAIRE (CONT'D)**
>   (on mic)
> I'm honoured to present this award to this year's 'Best
> Woman in Business'... Belinda Friers.

CUT TO: ELIZABETH SAWKIN in the crowd.

>   **ELIZABETH SAWKIN**
> Fuck's sake.

Huge amount of clapping. Claire turns to open the box with
the award on it, on a small table behind her. Her face
drops. Inside, in place of the expensive glass sperm, is
Godmother's sculpture from the first season: Just a gold
headless woman with boobs.

Fleabag sees it. She grimaces slightly. Claire looks at her
aghast, she's not happy. She turns, the statue in hand.

Belinda walks up and joins Claire.

Claire hesitates to give her the award.

Claire passes her the award. Belinda looks very surprised.

The moment she does, a PHOTOGRAPHER takes a photo of them
both holding it. Claire looking horrified.

>   **BELINDA**
>   (about the award, on mic)
> Thank you, thank you, um, thank you. Well, I was going
> to say this is a bit on the nose, but she doesn't seem
> to have one.

Everyone laughs.

INT. LIFT CORRIDOR — DAY

Later. Claire is furious with Fleabag.

>   **CLAIRE**
> What were you thinking?

>   **FLEABAG**
> It'll be fine.

>   **CLAIRE**
> It is not fine, I awarded her with a pair of tits.

Claire frantically presses buttons to call a lift.

> **CLAIRE**
> Chase her down.

> **FLEABAG**
> Chase her down?

> **CLAIRE**
> It's a stolen piece of art. I will deal with the
> photographer.

Klare approaches.

> **KLARE**
> CLAIRE!! You were brilliant! My God!

They kiss on the cheek.

> **CLAIRE**
> Thank you, Klare.

> **KLARE**
> I loved your joke.

> **CLAIRE**
> (pointed to Fleabag)
> Oh well, I didn't think it was that funny.
> (to Fleabag, pretending to be fun)
> Can you go, my love!

Fleabag indicates the lift and presses the button again.

> **FLEABAG**
> I'm just gonna—

> **CLAIRE**
> Take the stairs.

EXT. STREET — EVENING

Fleabag follows Belinda down the street.

Belinda looks over her shoulder, suspiciously.

She crosses the road. Fleabag crosses too.

After a couple more yards, Belinda suddenly turns. Fleabag
stops.

> **BELINDA**
> I'm trained in martial arts. Just the basics, but it's
> enough.

Beat.

> **FLEABAG**
> Um... I work at Harbots —

> **BELINDA**
> Hurbots. Yes, I ate a courgette off your tray.

> **FLEABAG**
> Yes.

> **BELINDA**
> It was delicious.

> **FLEABAG**
> Thank you.

> **BELINDA**
> What do you want?

Beat. Fleabag points to the award.

> **FLEABAG**
> That. I need to take... your award back.

> **BELINDA**
> Why?

> **FLEABAG**
> It's a stolen piece of art. It's not an award. It's all
> my fault. I can explain.

> **BELINDA**
> Is it a long story?

> **FLEABAG**
> Sort of.

Long pause.

Belinda looks at her.

INT. POSH HOTEL BAR — EVENING

Later. Fleabag is with Belinda in the bar of her hotel. They
are drinking enormous martinis. She feels a little out of
place.

> **BELINDA**
> (laughing)
> And she still doesn't know you have it? Oh that's
> glorious, and you did exactly the right thing.

                              FLEABAG
I think you're the only person who thinks that.

She looks at the statue between them.

                              BELINDA
God. 'Women's awards'.

                              FLEABAG
Congratulations.

                              BELINDA
It's infantilising bollocks.

                              FLEABAG
What? Don't you think it's good that...

                              BELINDA
No. No. It's ghettoising. It's a subsection of success.
It's the fucking children's table of awards.

                              FLEABAG
                              (laughing)
Why did you go?

                              BELINDA
Because I'd be an arsehole not to.

A WAITER delivers another two martinis.

                              BELINDA
Thank you darling.
                      (looking at the statue)
God, she's hot.

                              FLEABAG
Yep.

                              BELINDA
Are you a lesbian?

                              FLEABAG
Not strictly. You?

Belinda nods.

                              BELINDA
Do you like old movies?

                              FLEABAG
Some.

                              BELINDA
What's your favourite period film?

> **FLEABAG**
> *Carrie.*

Belinda roars with laughter.

> **BELINDA**
> God, you're a tonic. What do you do? Are you a 'woman in business'.

> **FLEABAG**
> I run a café.

> **BELINDA**
> Oh! Good for you. Did you make the canapés?

> **FLEABAG**
> No actually, I stole them.

Belinda laughs again.

> **FLEABAG**
> How old are you?

> **BELINDA**
> Fifty-eight. You?

> **FLEABAG**
> Thirty-three.

> **BELINDA**
> Oof. Don't worry. It does get better.

> **FLEABAG**
> You promise?

Beat. Belinda smiles at her.

> **BELINDA**
> I promise. Listen. I was on an aeroplane the other day and I realised... well I've been longing to say this out loud.
> (beat)
> Women are born with pain built in. It's our physical destiny. Period pains, sore boobs, child birth, you know. We carry it within ourselves throughout our lives. Men don't. They have to seek it out. They invent all sorts of gods and demons and things so they can feel guilty about things, which is something we do very well on our own. Then they create wars so they can feel things and touch each other, and when there aren't any wars they play rugby. We already have it all going on in here, inside. We have pain on a cycle for years and years and years and then, when you feel like you've made peace with it all... you know what happens? The MENOPAUSE comes. The fucking MENOPAUSE comes and it is —

Fleabag's face is contorted in horror.

> **BELINDA (CONT'D)**
> — the most WONDERFUL fucking thing in the world. Yes,
> your entire pelvic floor crumbles and you get fucking
> HOT and no-one cares, but then you're free. No longer a
> slave, no longer a machine, with parts. You are just a
> person. In Business.

> **FLEABAG**
> I was told it was horrendous.

> **BELINDA**
> It is horrendous. But then it's magnificent.

Fleabag stares at her.

> **BELINDA**
> Something to look forward to.

Fleabag smiles. Belinda finishes her martini.

> **BELINDA**
> You better get back to that party.

> **FLEABAG**
> *Your* party.

> **BELINDA**
> It's not a party until someone flirts with you.
> (beat)
> Now that's the only truly shit thing about getting
> older. People don't flirt with you anymore. Not for
> real. Not with danger. I miss walking into a room and
> not knowing... There's a sort of energy. A dare. Do not
> take that for granted. There is nothing more exciting
> than a room full of people.

> **FLEABAG**
> Except most people are —

> **BELINDA**
> What?

> **FLEABAG**
> Shit.

> **BELINDA**
> Look at me.
> (beat)
> Listen.
> (beat)
> People are all we've got.
> (pause)

People are all we've got. So grab the night by the
nipples and go and flirt with someone.

Pause. They smile at each other. Fleabag suddenly leans
forward and kisses her.

Belinda stops her.

> **BELINDA**
> No, that is not what I meant.

Fleabag hovers near her face.

Then kisses her anyway.

A couple of people notice and watch. Not gawping. Just
watching.

Belinda pulls away and holds Fleabag's face.

> **BELINDA**
> Oh, I wish you were my type.
> (beat)
> Take this tart back to my party and find someone to
> actually do that with.

She hands her the statue back.

> **FLEABAG**
> I want to do that with you.

> **BELINDA**
> No.

> **FLEABAG**
> Why not?

> **BELINDA**
> Honestly?

> **FLEABAG**
> Yeah.

> **BELINDA**
> I can't be arsed darling.
> (beat)
> I'm going to go back to my room, have ONE more martini
> and —

She pulls out her card.

> **BELINDA**
> If you need anything, you call me. Anything.
> (beat)
> You can have whoever you want at your age.

> **FLEABAG**
> Except for the Best Woman in Business.

> **BELINDA**
> Yes, but that's just because she's exhausted.

> **FLEABAG**
> Thirty-three isn't exactly—

> **BELINDA**
> What had Jesus done by thirty-three?

> **FLEABAG**
> Died?

> **BELINDA**
> Exactly. So get out there and *flirt*.

She floats off. Fleabag looks at the business card. She
looks at the camera.

INT. CLAIRE'S OFFICE — NIGHT

Fleabag walks in.

> **FLEABAG**
> Here you are!

> **CLAIRE**
> Oh, hi!

> **FLEABAG**
> I thought you might be snogging Finland.

> **CLAIRE**
> No. Just sorting a few things!

> **FLEABAG**
> (holds up statue)
> I got her! And Belinda gave me her card!

> **CLAIRE**
> (happy)
> Oh, that's great!

Beat.

> **FLEABAG**
> What?

> **CLAIRE**
> (lightly)
> Nothing.

FLEABAG
(to camera)
She's furious.
(to Claire)
Really?

CLAIRE
(totally convincingly)
Yes! It was a great night! Everything went smoothly in the end and everyone loved the canapés.

FLEABAG
Really.
(to camera)
I'm a dead woman.

FLEABAG
Really?

CLAIRE
Yes! It was a great night.

FLEABAG
(to camera)
She's going to blow.
(to Claire)
I just have a feeling that—

CLAIRE
I WOULD HAVE COME UP WITH MY OWN JOKE IF YOU HADN'T PUT THAT ONE IN MY HEAD. I HAVE MY OWN JOKES. I AM FUNNY. I AM INTERESTING. I KNEW I SHOULDN'T HAVE BROUGHT YOU HERE.

FLEABAG
What do you mean 'interesting'?!

CLAIRE
You think you can just do whatever you like, say whatever you like, steal whatever you like, kiss whoever you like.

FLEABAG
He kissed me!

CLAIRE
I KNOW.

FLEABAG
YOU *KNOW*? Then why are we spending the whole time—

CLAIRE
Because you're fine. You'll always be fine. You'll always be interesting. With your quirky café and your

dead best friend. You just — make me feel like I've...
failed.

Wide of the big office.

> **FLEABAG**
> Claire.

> **CLAIRE**
> If you mention the size of my office I will scream.

Fleabag mouths 'it's huge' to camera.

Pause.

> **FLEABAG**
> I just thought we were hanging out... just as friends.

> **CLAIRE**
> We're not friends. We are sisters.
> (beat)
> Get your own friends.

Fleabag looks at her. Ouch.

EXT. PRIEST'S HOUSE. FRONT DOOR — NIGHT

Fleabag rings the big hanging bell.

The Priest opens the door. He is in a t-shirt and pyjama
bottoms.

> **PRIEST**
> Oh, hi.

> **FLEABAG**
> Oh. Sorry — I didn't have your number and you said come
> round any time with G&Ts.

She holds up a carrier bag of G&Ts.

> **PRIEST**
> Yeah, yeah, yeah, sure. I just — this is a bit embar-
> rassing but recently I've been really enjoying going to
> bed at 9:30.

> **FLEABAG**
> Oh shit.

> **PRIEST**
> No no, it's fine, I can see the G&Ts! You Ok?

> **FLEABAG**
> Yes I just... fancied a drink.

                    (to camera)
And a priest.
                    (to Priest)
And a chat maybe.

                          PRIEST
That's my whole job. We might have to be quiet though
because Pam is a sound tyrant in the evenings.

                          FLEABAG
Pam lives here?

                          PRIEST
Yeah, Pam lives here.

He beckons her in.

INT. PRIEST'S HOUSE. LIVING ROOM — NIGHT

Priest sits with Fleabag in the drab living room. They have
opened the G&Ts.

                          FLEABAG
So I read your book.

                          PRIEST
Go on then.

                          FLEABAG
It's got some great twists.

                          PRIEST
True.

                          FLEABAG
I couldn't help but notice —

                          PRIEST
Come on, spit it out.

                          FLEABAG
Just one or two inconsistencies...

                          PRIEST
Sure.

                          FLEABAG
So, the world was made in seven days. And on the first
day LIGHT came and then a few days later the SUN came?

Beat.

> **PRIEST**
> Yeah, that's ridiculous.

> **FLEABAG**
> But you believe that?

> **PRIEST**
> It's not fact... It's poetry. It's a moral code. It's for interpretation. To help us work out God's plan for us.

> **FLEABAG**
> So, what's God's plan for you?

Beat.

> **PRIEST**
> I believe God meant for me to love people in a different way. I believe I am meant to love as a father.

> **FLEABAG**
> We can arrange that.

> **PRIEST**
> A father of many.

> **FLEABAG**
> I'll go up to three.

> **PRIEST**
> (laughs)
> Not going to happen.

> **FLEABAG**
> Two then.

> **PRIEST**
> Ok, two.

They smile. Suddenly there's a bang from upstairs.

> **PRIEST**
> Oops. Shit, Pam, she's not happy. We should go outside

EXT. PRIEST'S HOUSE. GARDEN — NIGHT

> **FLEABAG**
> Do you think I should become a Catholic?

> **PRIEST**
> No, don't do that. I like that you believe in a meaningless existence. You're good for me. You make me question my faith.

>   **FLEABAG**
> And?

Beat.

>   **PRIEST**
> I've never felt closer to God.

They laugh. She gives him a look. He laughs.

>   **FLEABAG**
> Fuck you.

There is a rustle in a bush. The Priest is instantly terrified.

>   **PRIEST**
> What was that? It wasn't a fox, was it?

>   **FLEABAG**
> I don't know.

He stands up quickly.

>   **PRIEST**
> Is it a fox? Shine something.
>   (into the night)
> BOO. BAAA! Oh God, I bet it's a fox.

Fleabag is laughing.

>   **PRIEST**
> No, I'm not being funny, foxes have been after me for
> years. It's like they have a pact or something. I'm not
> kidding, I was on the toilet. A TOILET of a TRAIN. And
> when the train stopped, a fucking FOX tried to get through
> the window. OF A TRAIN. ITS FACE WAS IN THE WINDOW.

Fleabag is laughing.

>   **PRIEST**
> And once when I was at a monastery, I woke up just
> feeling a bit weird like there might be a fox about and
> A FOX was sitting under my window just looking up like
> this —
>   (beat)
> — pointing at me like — you. We're watching you. We're
> having you.

>   **FLEABAG**
> Lucky God got there first.

>   **PRIEST**
> Well yeah.

> **FLEABAG**
> You could be a fox boy by now.

> **PRIEST**
> And we all know what happens to them.

He tentatively sits back down.

Beat.

> **FLEABAG**
> Are you Ok?

> **PRIEST**
> I'm Ok.
> (beat)
> Do you think I'm mad?

> **FLEABAG**
> Because of the fox thing or because of the God thing?

He laughs.

> **PRIEST**
> You're obsessed.

> **FLEABAG**
> Do you ever have doubts?

> **PRIEST**
> Sure, every day. It's part of the deal.

> **FLEABAG**
> I just don't think I could do it. Especially the —

He looks at her.

> **PRIEST**
> What?

> **FLEABAG**
> The celibacy thing.

There's a rustle.

> **PRIEST**
> IT'S A FUCKING FOX.

> **FLEABAG**
> CHILL OUT ABOUT THE FOX.

> **PRIEST**
> Sorry. I just... don't know what they want from me.
> (beat)
> I'm sorry. Celibacy. Go.

He smiles.

> **FLEABAG**
> I just couldn't give up sex forever. It's just too, it's too —

> **PRIEST**
> Celibacy is a lot less complicated than romantic relationships.

> **FLEABAG**
> But what if you meet someone you like?

> **PRIEST**
> I talk and drink and laugh and give them bibles and hope they eventually leave me alone.

> **FLEABAG**
> What if you meet someone you love?

They hold eye contact.

> **PRIEST**
> We're not going to have sex.

Fleabag glances at the camera.

> **PRIEST**
> I know you think that's what you want from me. But it's not. It won't bring anything good.

They laugh, there's a spark.

> **FLEABAG**
> Well, it might —

> **PRIEST**
> It won't. I've been there many times. Before I found this. Many, many times.

> **FLEABAG**
> How many times?

Beat.

> **PRIEST**
> Many.
>   (beat)
> I'd really like to be your friend though.

> **FLEABAG**
> I'd like to be your friend too.
>   (to camera)
> We will last a week.

                           PRIEST
What was that?

                           FLEABAG
What?

                           PRIEST
Where did... Where did you just go?

                           FLEABAG
What?

                           PRIEST
You just went somewhere.

Fleabag looks at the camera in panic.

                           PRIEST
There. There. Where did you just go?

                           FLEABAG
Nowhere.

He looks at her, uncertain.

                           PRIEST
Ok...

Pause. He turns away. Fleabag looks at the camera. Where do
we go from here?

Suddenly a rustle in the bushes again — they both turn and
jump in fear.

                     PRIEST/FLEABAG
AGH!!

                     END OF EPISODE 3

EPISODE 4

INT. CLERICAL DRESS SHOP — DAY

Fleabag sits waiting. The Priest is in the dressing room.

> **PRIEST (O.S.)**
> I dunno.

> **FLEABAG**
> Just come out.

Beat. He pulls the curtain and steps out wearing an over-the-top wedding vestment.

Fleabag looks at him, considering the outfit.

Beat.

> **FLEABAG**
> I prefer the last one.

> **PRIEST**
> Me too. Bit more / subtle.

> **FLEABAG**
> Elegant, / yeah.

> **PRIEST**
> It's these bits, / isn't it?

> **FLEABAG**
> Yep, last one, definitely.

> **PRIEST**
> Yep. Great.

He turns round and goes back in.

She gives us a fleeting, coy look, before turning back to her phone.

TITLES: FLEABAG

EXT. NOISY STREET IN CENTRAL LONDON — DAY

Fleabag and the Priest are walking down the road, they've just come from the clerical shop.

He is raving about his choice of vestments — clearly pleased. She is listening to him, enjoying it. She only talks to camera when she is sure he can't see.

                              PRIEST
I'm really pleased with that — once it's nipped in there —

He indicates his arms, squeezing them slightly.

                         FLEABAG
     Oh, it'll be perfect.
                         (to camera)
     His arms.

                              PRIEST
     Do you prefer weddings or funerals?

                         FLEABAG
     Weddings.
                         (to camera)
     His arms.

                              PRIEST
     I think there's something humbling about funerals.

                         FLEABAG
     Really?

She can't help looking at his arms.

                              PRIEST
     Yeah, it's good to dwell on the next life.

                         FLEABAG
     You really think there's a next life?

                              PRIEST
     What do you believe? Worm food?

She nods.

                              PRIEST
     Why?!

                         FLEABAG
     Why what?
                         (to camera)
     His neck!

                              PRIEST
     Why would you believe in something awful, when you can
     believe in something WONDERFUL!

                         FLEABAG
                         (laughing)
     Don't make me an optimist, you will ruin my life!

They laugh. A beat.

                              PRIEST
        Have you been to many funerals?

INT. FLASHBACK — FLEABAG'S MUM'S FUNERAL. CHURCH — DAY

A quick flash of Claire and Fleabag in black, standing at
the entrance to a church — greeting MOURNERS.

EXT. SAME NOISY STREET IN CENTRAL LONDON AS BEFORE — DAY

                              FLEABAG
        A couple.
                          (to camera)
        His neck.

                              PRIEST
        And you never felt them... go somewhere?

                              FLEABAG
                     (accidentally to camera)
        No, they were already gone.
                     (accidentally to Priest)
        His beautiful neck.

Beat.

                              PRIEST
        What?

Fleabag, panicked look to camera.

                              FLEABAG
        What?

                              PRIEST
        You just said 'his beautiful neck'.

                              FLEABAG
                          (covering)
        No... No I said 'they were already gone'.

                              PRIEST
        Ok. Weird.

They continue walking. He stops suddenly outside an old
ornate building.

                              PRIEST
        Oh right, so — this might be —

He touches her arm to guide her in. She notices, looks at
us.

                    PRIEST (CONT'D)
— your idea of hell. But I think it's kind of special.

He turns and heads in. As he does —

                    FLEABAG
                  (sighs to camera)
    His beautiful neck.

HARD CUT TO: INT. QUAKER HALL — DAY

Silence.

There is a circle of chairs with a table in the middle. Some
QUAKERS sit there.

On the table is a jug of water, a vase of flowers and
various religious texts including the Quran and the Bible.

It's very calm.

The Priest sits on a chair. Fleabag sits across the other
side.

                    FLEABAG
                   (to camera)
    Quaker meeting. You're not allowed to speak. If the
    spirit moves you to speak you have to stand up and share
    it in front of everyone. It's very intense, it's very
    quiet and it's very, very erotic.

Fleabag looks over at the Priest. They smile at each other.
A QUAKER MAN stands up.

                    FLEABAG
    Oop.

                   QUAKER MAN
    I think... I'm going to go home... in November.

Silence.

                   QUAKER MAN
    ... I think.

The Quaker Man sits down.

Fleabag looks to camera — fair enough. More silence. She
glances over at the Priest. He's deep in thought.

                    FLEABAG
                   (to camera)
    What's he thinking?

She looks back to the Priest.

> **FLEABAG**
> (to camera)
> What's he thinking?

He's still lost in thought. She looks back to us.

> **FLEABAG**
> (to camera)
> I don't really think it's... I'm not really
> feeling... I don't think it's really affecting me—

She slowly begins lurching forward.

> **FLEABAG**
> (to camera, surprised at herself)
> ... oh my God.

She begins slowly to stand, involuntarily. She's more
surprised than anyone.

> **FLEABAG**
> (to camera)
> Oh my God, oh my God. What am I going to say, what am I
> going to say... ?
> (to the room)
> I sometimes worry —
> (beat)
> — that I wouldn't be such a feminist if I had bigger
> tits.

Silence. A small cough.

The Priest stifles a laugh.

EXT. NOISY STREET IN CENTRAL LONDON — DAY

Fleabag and the Priest walk slowly out of the Quaker
building.

> **PRIEST**
> Well it's good you felt something.

> **FLEABAG**
> Is it?

> **PRIEST**
> *Something* moved you.

> **FLEABAG**
> I'm not sure I needed to be moved to discover that about
> myself... What were you thinking?

                   PRIEST
Well, I was thinking about how peaceful I felt and then
for some reason I was thinking about your tits which
kind of ruined it.

                  FLEABAG
               (laughing)
Oh, my tits ruined your peace?

                   PRIEST
               (smiling)
Yeah — you could say that.

They laugh briefly.

Beat.

The chemistry between them builds.

It's too much.

                  FLEABAG
I should probably open the café.

                   PRIEST
          (simultaneously)
I've got a confession, actually, in a little bit.

                   PRIEST
Oh! Can I see it?

                  FLEABAG
Oh! Yeah... it's a bit...

                   PRIEST
What?

                  FLEABAG
It's a bit...

                   PRIEST
WHAT?!

HARD CUT TO: INT. HILARY'S CAFÉ — DAY

Priest and Fleabag sit in the café. The Priest is holding
Hilary aloft — astounded:

                   PRIEST
THE. FUCK.

He is instantly in love with her. She is making happy little
squeaking noises as he cuddles her into his chest.

                           PRIEST
          You gorgeous little thing!

Fleabag watches him holding her — she turns to camera and
bites her lip. It's too much.

                           PRIEST
                         (laughing)
          Can I ask, why so many guinea pigs?

                          FLEABAG
          Oh I um, I just um —

FLASHBACK FROM SERIES ONE. INT. HILARY'S CAFÉ — DAY

Boo putting up a picture of a guinea pig.

                            BOO
          THIS is an excellent one.

EXT. BACK IN HILARY'S CAFÉ AS BEFORE — DAY

Back with Priest and Fleabag. She continues.

                          FLEABAG
          — I just thought it would be a unique selling point.

                           PRIEST
          Yeah? Which came first, the guinea pig or the guinea
          pig café?

                          FLEABAG
                         (laughing)
          That is a... big old question.

                           PRIEST
          Fair enough. What do guinea pigs do?

                          FLEABAG
          They're born, they shit themselves with fear and then
          they die.

                           PRIEST
                         (laughing)
          Can I use that at the wedding? Seriously, I need
          material. Tell me about your stepmother to be...
          what's she like?

                          FLEABAG
          Oh, erm. She's...

She searches.

                              FLEABAG
... She's from Exeter.

                               PRIEST
                              (smiles)
Umm. Ok, thank you, that's very helpful. How did she
meet your dad?

                              FLEABAG

Through my mother—

                               PRIEST
Right.

                              FLEABAG
She was my mother's student at one point. Do your
parents get on?

                               PRIEST
No. Were you close to your mum?

                              FLEABAG
Yeah. Are you?

                               PRIEST
Not really. / So that must've been a bit weird—

                              FLEABAG
How come / Well, I don't really think about it.

Silence. Hilary squeaking away.

                              FLEABAG
So do you go back a lot to...

                               PRIEST
                           (simultaneously)
So you run...

                               PRIEST
No no no... Do you run this place on your own?

                              FLEABAG
No I opened it with a friend.

                               PRIEST
Oh cool, right, so you run it together?

                              FLEABAG
No. She's... she, uh—

                               PRIEST
She what?

INT. FLASHBACK, HILARY'S CAFÉ — DAY

Boo eating a sandwich by the window.

INT. HILARY'S CAFÉ AS BEFORE — DAY

Back with Fleabag. She looks at us.

INT. FLASHBACK, HILARY'S CAFÉ — DAY

Boo shaking her head, enjoying her sandwich.

INT. HILARY'S CAFÉ AS BEFORE — DAY

Back with Fleabag. She breaks her look to us.

                         PRIEST
          What?

                         FLEABAG
          What?

                         PRIEST
          She... she, what?

                         FLEABAG
          She...
                    (laughs then turn to camera)
          He's a bit annoying actually.

The Priest notices her turn. He looks where she was looking,
right at us.

                         PRIEST
          What is that?

                         FLEABAG
          What?

                         PRIEST
          That thing. That you're doing... it's like you
          disappear.

                         FLEABAG
          What?

                         PRIEST
          What are you not telling me?

                         FLEABAG
          Nothing!

PRIEST

Tell me what's going on underneath there!

FLEABAG

Nothing!

PRIEST

Tell me! Come on, you can tell me.

FLEABAG
(to Priest)

No!

(to camera)

Nothing!

He immediately looks where she is looking, right down the barrel at us.

PRIEST

Ah! What are you doing?

FLEABAG

Stop being so churchy!

PRIEST

I'm not being churchy, I'm just trying to get to know you.

FLEABAG

Well I don't want that.

A long silence.

PRIEST

Listen, I'm just, I'm just trying to help you.

Fleabag looks at him.

FLEABAG

What?

PRIEST
(backpedalling)

No, no. I didn't mean—

FLEABAG

Oh, I know what you mean, Father. Thank you so much for your guidance—

PRIEST

— come on. I didn't mean, I didn't mean—

FLEABAG

— I really should get back to work. A customer is bound
to turn up any minute. You should probably be getting
back to God. Don't you think?

He looks at her, slightly lost for words.

FLEABAG

I think you've played with my guinea-pig long enough.

She takes Hilary from him.

She stands and puts her back in her hutch, with her back
turned to the Priest.

PRIEST

Ok.

He stands and looks at her.

PRIEST (CONT'D)

All right, bye.

He leaves. The door shuts firmly behind him.

HARD CUT TO: EXT. LONDON STREET — DAY

Fleabag walks sadly down the street. Smoking.

JUMP CUT TO: EXT. SAME LONDON STREET BUT LATER — DAY

She's still walking and smoking, trying to avoid the
camera's eye.

**EXT. FLASHBACK, FLEABAG'S MUM'S FUNERAL. CHURCH GROUNDS —
DAY**

Fleabag and Boo share a cigarette.

EXT. SAME LONDON STREET AS BEFORE — DAY

Fleabag still avoiding us.

CUT TO: EXT. A NEW LONDON STREET, LATER — DAY

Fleabag still avoiding us, looking over her shoulder.

INT. FLASHBACK, FLEABAG'S MUM'S FUNERAL. CHURCH BACK ROOM — DAY

Fleabag, Boo and Claire are all standing in the back room, they look up as they hear Godmother's voice.

> **GODMOTHER (O.S)**
> Sorry girls, people are starting to arrive.

EXT. A NEW LONDON STREET, LATER — DAY

Back to the last street, Fleabag avoiding us, looking over her shoulder as we pursue her. She begins to run away.

INT. FLASHBACK, FLEABAG'S MUM'S FUNERAL. CHURCH — DAY

We had a glimpse of this earlier, before the Quaker Meeting. Fleabag and Claire stand, dressed in black, greeting mourners.

> **FAMILY FRIEND 3**
> She was a spectacular woman.

INT. FLEABAG'S FLAT. HALLWAY — DAY

Fleabag walks in. Alone. We are waiting for her. She avoids us again.

INT. FLASHBACK, FLEABAG'S MUM'S FUNERAL. CHURCH — DAY

A glimpse of Dad sitting alone in a pew.

INT. FLEABAG'S FLAT. HALLWAY — DAY

Fleabag takes off her coat. Sighs heavily.

INT. FLASHBACK, DAD'S HOUSE. MUM'S WAKE — DAY

Fleabag and Dad hold hands. He stands up and leaves her.

INT. FLEABAG'S FLAT. BATHROOM — DAY

Fleabag looks at her reflection.

INT. FLASHBACK, FLEABAG'S MUM'S FUNERAL. CHURCH BACK ROOM — DAY

Close up of Boo's face looking at us. Fleabag's POV.

We see nothing of the background. She looks concerned.

>   **BOO**
> Don't worry. We can sort this out.

INT. FLEABAG'S FLAT. BATHROOM — DAY

Back with Fleabag looking at her reflection. She runs the tap, washes her face. She starts scrubbing her face hard, really hard. We hear Boo's voice:

>   **BOO (O.S.)**
> Stop doing that —

CUT TO: INT. FLASHBACK, FLEABAG'S MUM'S FUNERAL. CHURCH BACK ROOM — DAY

Fleabag is standing in front of a mirror rubbing her face hard, the exact same way. Boo continues:

>   **BOO**
> — to your face.

>   **FLEABAG**
> I have to. I don't know what's wrong. I look so *good*.

>   **BOO**
> It's Ok, we can sort it out. Just take some of your make-up off.

>   **FLEABAG**
> I'm not wearing any make-up.

>   **BOO**
> What? What has happened? I have never seen you look so good —

>   **FLEABAG**
> I don't know. I just woke up looking amazing and now everyone's going to think I got a fucking facial for my mother's funeral.

Fleabag is teary, Claire enters.

>   **CLAIRE**
> Oh, what the hell, you look incredible.

>   **BOO**
> We're trying to mess her up.

>   **FLEABAG**
> I don't know, no matter what I do with my hair, it just
> keeps falling in this really chic way.

>   **CLAIRE**
> Oh God.

>   **FLEABAG**
> You look perfect.

>   **CLAIRE**
> Thank you.

Godmother pops her head in.

>   **GODMOTHER**
>   (gently)
> Sorry girls, but people are starting to arrive.

The sisters smile. They liked her then.

>   **CLAIRE**
> Thank you.

>   **GODMOTHER**
> You don't have to greet them if it's too —
>   (to Fleabag)
> Gosh, you look gorgeous.

>   **FLEABAG**
>   (depressed)
> Thank you.

INT. FLASHBACK, FLEABAG'S MUM'S FUNERAL. CHURCH — DAY

Back with Fleabag and Claire, greeting mourners.

People are filing in.

Boo stands a little way down handing the guests the Order of
Service booklets.

Fleabag and Claire speak to each other as people arrive.

All the guests are impressed by Fleabag looking so good. A
series of FAMILY FRIENDS pass.

>   **FAMILY FRIEND 1**
> I'm so sorry.

                         CLAIRE
Thank you.

                     FAMILY FRIEND 1
You look glorious.

                         FLEABAG
Thank you.

                         CLAIRE
                     (to Fleabag)
Have you spoken to Dad?

                         FLEABAG
No, not yet. He's avoiding me.

                     FAMILY FRIEND 2
My deepest condolences, girls. She was magnificent.

                     FLEABAG/CLAIRE
Thanks so much. / Thanks so much.

                     FAMILY FRIEND 2
                   (noticing Fleabag)
My God, you look well.

                         FLEABAG
Thank you.
                     (to Claire)
Have you?

                         CLAIRE
He's not really engaging.

                     FAMILY FRIEND 3
She was a spectacular woman.

                         FLEABAG
Thanks.

                     FAMILY FRIEND 4
Darling, you look wonderful.

                         FLEABAG
Oh my God.

                     FAMILY FRIEND 5
Hi Claire.

                         CLAIRE
Hi.

                     FAMILY FRIEND 5
Gosh! Grief clearly agrees with you!

>
>   **FLEABAG**
>   Thank you, Jeremy.

They look over at their Dad, who is at the front, sitting
alone. A few PEOPLE are thinking about whether or not to sit
with him. They decide not to. Then Godmother approaches him.

>   **FLEABAG**
>   Oop — incoming.

They watch Godmother put her arm around Dad.

>   **FLEABAG**
>   My God, she is shameless.

>   **CLAIRE**
>   Can you not think the fucking worst of someone for just
>   a split fucking second?

Fleabag looks at her.

>   **CLAIRE**
>   Not everyone is after cock.

Claire storms off into the church.

Boo and Fleabag exchange a look. Fleabag walks over to Boo.
They look at Godmother, kneeling and talking to Dad.

>   **FLEABAG**
>   She's definitely trying to fuck my Dad.

>   **BOO**
>   She ain't made o' wood.

Beat. Fleabag laughs in spite of herself.

>   **BOO**
>   Do you want a ciggie?

**EXT. FLASHBACK, FLEABAG'S MUM'S FUNERAL. CHURCH GROUNDS —
DAY**

Boo and Fleabag having a ciggie.

>   **BOO**
>   Ooh! Incoming...

Harry, wearing extremely tight trousers, approaches. He's
behaving in a very funereal fashion.

>   **BOO**
>   Hi Harry.

                         HARRY
        Hi. Hi. You Ok?

He kisses her.

                        FLEABAG
        Um hm. You? Do you need anything?

                         HARRY
        No I'm good thanks, I've just had a large glass of
        water.

Beat.

                        FLEABAG
        Are your trousers Ok?

                         HARRY
        Yeah, sorry. I left them in the drier.

                          BOO
        Ah, mate.

Harry starts welling up.

                         HARRY
        Shit, sorry.

                        FLEABAG
        It's Ok.

                         HARRY
        It's just funerals, when you actually knew the
        person... well, they're so...

Fleabag hugs Harry.

                         HARRY
        It just doesn't feel real. I'm just going to miss her
        so much. Have you cried yet?

                        FLEABAG
        Yes.

He looks at Fleabag.

                         HARRY
        I didn't see you cr— Wow. You look —
                        (studying her face)
        Have you had your eyebrows done?

Fleabag looks to Boo.

INT. FLASHBACK, FLEABAG'S MUM'S FUNERAL. CHURCH — DAY

Claire and Fleabag walk down the aisle with Godmother in the middle.

She is arm in arm with both of them.

> GODMOTHER
> Hi girls. How are you doing?

> FLEABAG
> Ok thanks.

> CLAIRE
> Alright.

> GODMOTHER
> You know the hard bit is going to be in a few weeks. When it all calms down.

> CLAIRE/FLEABAG
> Yup. / They do say that, yes. Yup.

> GODMOTHER
> People start to forget, and the flowers and the cards stop turning up.

> CLAIRE/FLEABAG
> Yes. / Uh huh.

> GODMOTHER
> And people just disappear. Because it spooks them to be around someone perpetually in pain.

> FLEABAG/CLAIRE
> Ok / right.

> GODMOTHER
> And your lovely boyfriends might not be able to cope.

> CLAIRE/FLEABAG
> Well, he's my husband / I'm sure they'll push through.

> GODMOTHER
> I just want you to know that I will always be there. Always.
> (beat)
> Always.

> CLAIRE
> Thank you.

                              GODMOTHER
Always.
                              (beat)
Always. I'm going to check on the sausage rolls.

She smiles and holds each of their cheeks affectionately.
She trots off.

                               CLAIRE
See.

                              FLEABAG
Ok.

INT. FLASHBACK, DAD'S HOUSE. WAKE — DAY

There are People milling around the wake.

The house looks different. More homely. Brighter. Less art.
Less grand.

Fleabag eats a finger sandwich. Claire approaches.

                              FLEABAG
Hey.

                               CLAIRE
I don't know how you're eating.
                              (beat)
Do something.

INT. FLASHBACK, DAD'S HOUSE. BEDROOM — DAY

Fleabag finds her Dad in the bedroom changing his shoes.

                              FLEABAG
Hi.

                                DAD
Hello darling.
                          (his shoes—)
Bit tight.

                              FLEABAG
Oh yeah, tell me about it.

Beat.

                                DAD
I found her very difficult you know.

                              FLEABAG
I know.

                                DAD
I lo— I loved her, but —

Beat.

                              FLEABAG
That's all that really matters.

                                DAD
No, I don't think it is. Her instincts...
were...
                             (beat)
She just knew how to be fun. And how to be kind. She
just knew.
                             (beat)
I'm just... guessing.

                              FLEABAG
You're fun, Dad!

                                DAD
No — I — I didn't like that about her. I loved her but
I didn't like that she was... For a long time I —
                             (beat)
And today —
                             (beat)
— I was jealous of her.

He smiles at Fleabag.

                              FLEABAG
That's a lovely thing to say, really.

Godmother pokes her head in.

                            GODMOTHER
Oh sorry.
                             (beat)
I'll leave you two.

She waits for a beat then leaves.

                                DAD
She's a bit annoying isn't she?

Fleabag smiles.

                                DAD
Let's go and find your sister.

                    FLEABAG
Yeah, I don't think she wants to see me —

                    DAD
She loves you. She just didn't get the fun gene.

Fleabag is suddenly overwhelmed with emotion.

                    FLEABAG
I just, I don't know what to—

                    DAD
I know. Buck up. Smile. Charm. Off we go. We'll be Ok.

He stands up. They are holding hands. He drops her hand gently.

                    FLEABAG
I'll follow you.

He goes to leave. As he does:

                    DAD
You look lovely by the way.

                    FLEABAG
Thank you.

INT. CHURCH — NIGHT

Back in the present. Fleabag sits in a pew in utter silence.

She is staring ahead of her.

She is lost.

We hear her voice and Boo's off screen, a memory.

                  FLEABAG (O.S.)
I don't know what to do with it —

                  BOO
With what?

CUT TO: INT. FLASHBACK, DAD'S HOUSE. WAKE — DAY

Boo and Fleabag sit together at a table. The wake seems over.

                  FLEABAG
                  (tearful)
With all the love I have for her. I don't know... where
to — put it now.

Pause.

                              BOO
                         (matter of fact)
         I'll take it.

Fleabag laughs.

                              BOO
         No, I'm serious. It sounds lovely.

She looks at Boo. She means it.

                              BOO
         I'll have it.
                              (beat)
         You have to give it to me.

                           FLEABAG
         Ok.

                              BOO
         It's gotta go somewhere.

INT. CHURCH AS BEFORE — NIGHT

Fleabag in the pew. She begins to kneel.

She brings her hands up to a prayer position.

She bows her head to her hands.

Just then a BLAST of music comes from the back of the
church.

It's Jennifer Lopez or something really incongruous.

She gets up.

She starts walking. She eyes the camera. But we follow her.

She pushes a door.

INT. VESTRY — NIGHT — CONT.

Fleabag enters. She sees the Priest standing there, reaching
high into a cupboard.

He is drunk.

Fleabag stops the music.

PRIEST
FUCK!

He turns and sees Fleabag.

PRIEST
FUCK! JESUS!

FLEABAG
Woah! Why are you awake? It's 9.45 p.m.!

PRIEST
Oh my God, I thought you were just in my head. Then. I
— I mean you were in my head then. But then you were
there.

FLEABAG
You Ok, Father?

PRIEST
Fuck you, calling me Father, like it doesn't turn you
on just to say it.

Beat.

PRIEST
Do you want a drink?

FLEABAG
Ok...

PRIEST
Don't move.

He gets glasses.

PRIEST
Are you a nostalgic person?

FLEABAG
Yeah.

PRIEST
Do you like Winnie the Pooh?

FLEABAG
Yes.

PRIEST
I fucking love Winnie the Pooh. I can't read a Winnie
the Pooh quote without crying. Fuck. Piglet.

He brings his palm to his heart. She repeats the gesture.

> **FLEABAG**
> Piglet.

> **PRIEST**
> Why are you here? Sorry but — I mean why are you here?
> Were you looking for me?

> **FLEABAG**
> I was on the verge of having a little prayer actually.

Beat.

He can't help but laugh.

> **PRIEST**
> No no, no no no... Don't...
> (beat)
> Don't you dare. That's *my* thing. What were you praying
> about? Please say you were praying for me. I could do
> with the extra pair of hands. Mine don't seem to have
> the fucking reach anymore.

He jumps up at the cupboard again.

> **PRIEST**
> GOD, HELP ME.

He knocks the cupboard and the whiskey bottle falls into his
hand.

> **PRIEST**
> (quietly to God)
> Thank you.
> (beat)
> You know, there was a man who wanted to be a saint SO
> BADLY that he castrated himself to stop himself, y'know.
> Whack.

> **FLEABAG**
> Wow.

He pours two drinks. Hands her one. He holds his glass up.

> **PRIEST**
> Here's to peace.
> (beat)
> And those who get in the way of it.

She clinks glasses with him.

They drink. She watches him.

He looks at her.

We hold it.

                    FLEABAG
    I'm sorry about today.

                     PRIEST
    Forget it. Look at this.

He opens a cupboard and pulls out his clerical outfit for
Mass. He loves this garment.

                     PRIEST
    Look at it. That's the first one I ever got. I went all
    the way to Rome for that.
                   (laughs)
    Such a nerd! Two years before I was allowed to wear it,
    but I just. Couldn't. Wait. I couldn't wait. I knew I
    wanted a bold, y'know — this colour, but proper *plum*.
    You can only get proper plum in Italy.
                    (beat)
    Sometimes I worry I'm only in it for the outfits.
                 (he looks at her)
    It's so beautiful, isn't it.
                    (beat)
    I mean. Your stuff is lovely too.

She smiles. Thank you.

                     PRIEST
    What were you praying about?

Beat. She doesn't say anything.

                     PRIEST
    You don't like answering questions. Do you?

Silence.

                     PRIEST
    Ok. Come with me.

He walks out of the vestry with his glass.

                     PRIEST
    I know what to do with you.

INT. CHURCH. CONFESSIONAL — NIGHT

They stand outside the confession box, holding their
glasses.

                     PRIEST
    You go in there, and I go in there.

> **FLEABAG**
> And you make me tell you all my secrets so you can ulti-
> mately trap and control me?

He laughs.

> **PRIEST**
> Yeah. No. You tell me what is weighing on your heart
> and I listen without judgement and in complete confi-
> dence.

> **FLEABAG**
> Sounds dodgy.

> **PRIEST**
> I just listen. At the very least it would shut me up
> for a minute.

> **FLEABAG**
> I'm not a Catholic.

> **PRIEST**
> Tonight that doesn't matter.

> **FLEABAG**
> Won't I catch on fire or something?

> **PRIEST**
> If you did, it would confirm my faith, so let's try it.
> Go on.

She doesn't move.

> **PRIEST**
> Go on.

Beat.

She takes the challenge.

> **FLEABAG**
> Alright.

She moves into the box. He closes the door/curtain.

She hears him get into his side.

We stay on her the whole time.

> **PRIEST (O.S.)**
> Ok, now you say 'Bless me, Father, for I have sinned—'

> **FLEABAG**
> I'm not going to say that.

PRIEST (O.S.)

Very good! It's been — enter days, years, months since my last confession.

FLEABAG
(shakes her head)

Nope.

PRIEST (O.S.)

Then I say that's Ok, blah blah blah, 'til you tell me what's on your mind. Tell me your si—

FLEABAG

Sins?

PRIEST (O.S.)

Sins.

PRIEST (O.S. CONT'D)

If you want.

FLEABAG

Why would I tell you my—

PRIEST (O.S.)

Because it will make you feel better. And because —
(playfully)
I want to know.

FLEABAG

Ok.

Pause. She takes a swig of her drink.

FLEABAG

I lied.

PRIEST (O.S.)

Ok.

FLEABAG

To you.

PRIEST (O.S.)

About...

FLEABAG

About... the miscarriage.

She winces, expecting a reaction. Silence.

FLEABAG

I was just covering for my sister who actually had the miscarriage because her husband didn't know that she was pregnant and it just...

> ### PRIEST (O.S.)
> (gently)

Ok.

> (beat)

Keep going.

> ### FLEABAG

And I've stolen things. I've had a LOT of sex outside of marriage. And... Once or twice inside someone else's. There's been a spot of sodomy... There's been much masturbation. A bit of violence and then of course the endless fucking blasphemy.

> ### PRIEST (O.S.)
> (laughs)

And?

> ### FLEABAG

And —

> ### PRIEST (O.S.)

Go on.

> ### FLEABAG

AND —

EXT. FLASHBACK, PARK — DAY

Boo laughing and walking with us.

INT. CHURCH. CONFESSIONAL — NIGHT

Back with Fleabag and the Priest.

> ### FLEABAG

And I — I can't . . .

EXT. FLASHBACK TO LONDON STREET. SERIES ONE — DAY

Boo in tears, about to step in front of the traffic.

INT. BACK IN CHURCH AS BEFORE. CONFESSIONAL — NIGHT

Back with the Priest and Fleabag.

> ### PRIEST (O.S.)

It's Ok, go on.

Beat.

> **FLEABAG**
Frightened.

> **PRIEST**
Of what?

> **FLEABAG**
> (not easy for her to say)
Of forgetting. Things. People.
> (beat)
Forgetting people.

Beat. She drinks.

> **FLEABAG**
And I'm ashamed of not knowing what I—

> **PRIEST (O.S.)**
Want? It's Ok not to know what you want.

> **FLEABAG**
No, I know what I want, I know exactly what I want, right now.

> **PRIEST (O.S.)**
What's that?

Pause.

> **FLEABAG**
It's bad.

> **PRIEST (O.S.)**
That's Ok.

> **FLEABAG**
I want someone to tell me what to wear in the morning.

Pause.

> **PRIEST (O.S.)**
Ok. Well I think there are people who can do that—

> **FLEABAG**
No, I want someone to tell me what to wear every morning... I want someone to tell me what to eat, what to like, what to hate, what to rage about, what to listen to, what band to like, what to buy tickets for, what to joke about, what not to joke about. I want someone to tell me what to believe in, who to vote for, who to love and how to... tell them.
> (beat)
I just think I want someone to tell me how to live my life, Father, because so far, I think I've been getting it wrong.

                              (beat)
     And I know that is why people want people like you in
     their lives. Because you just tell them how to do it.
     You just tell them what to do. And what they'll get out
     of the end of it. And even though I don't believe your
     bullshit and I know that scientifically nothing I do
     makes any difference in the end anyway, I'm still
     scared, why am I still scared?
                              (beat)
     Just fucking tell me what to do, Father.

Silence.

She looks to the grate. She can't make out his expression. A
long pause.

                         PRIEST (O.S.)
     Kneel.

Beat.

                           FLEABAG
     What?

Beat.

                         PRIEST (O.S.)
     Kneel.

Beat.

Fleabag is stunned.

Beat.

                         PRIEST (O.S.)
                           (gently)
     Just kneel.

She kneels.

The curtain opens and he stands over her.

She looks up at him.

He kneels in front of her.

He gently takes her face in his hands.

They are breathing nervously.

He holds her face in front of his for a moment. Deciding.

She moves her lips forward and they kiss.

It's a gentle, loving kiss. It's nothing short of fucking beautiful.

They stop. They look at each other.

They kiss again.

They kiss more passionately.

It becomes more physical.

She starts hiking his skirts.

They grab at each other.

She gets him against the door of the confessional and keeps hiking his skirts up.

She eventually gets underneath, but quickly discovers he also has trousers on UNDER HIS SKIRT!

> **FLEABAG**
> Skirt *and* trousers?

> **PRIEST**
> Sorry.

They keep kissing. The passion builds and builds...

But then—

A painting of Jesus falls off the wall. It hits the church flagstones with a crash.

They immediately stop. They both turn to look at it.

Beat.

Fleabag looks to the Priest. She tries to smile. He holds her gaze. Then turns, mortified, and walks away from her. Out of the church.

She watches him go.

Beat.

She looks at us.

END OF EPISODE 4

EPISODE 5

INT. BUSINESS BAR — NIGHT

Fleabag sits with Hot Misogynist.

They are a few cocktails down.

Fleabag has lipstick on and is wearing a little more make-up than we've seen before.

She is tipsy and very flirty.

> **HOT MISOGYNIST**
> I thought I wouldn't see you again unless you were in trouble.

> **FLEABAG**
> Oh, I'm in trouble.

> **HOT MISOGYNIST**
> Oh, you mean this kind of trouble.

He gestures around his face and body. She roars with laughter.

> **FLEABAG**
> (to camera)
> Isn't he GREAT. He's so great. He's funny. He makes jokes —

> **HOT MISOGYNIST**
> She turned around and it was the golden one!

She roars with laughter.

> **FLEABAG**
> (to camera)
> Sort of needed to hear the top bit.

> **HOT MISOGYNIST**
> I love word play.

> **FLEABAG**
> (to camera)
> He's clever.

> **HOT MISOGYNIST**
> Shakespeare uses word play.

> **FLEABAG**
> (to camera)
> He says things like —

> **HOT MISOGYNIST**
> I've got a big case tomorrow.

                    FLEABAG
                  (to camera)
He's a little bit controlling —

              HOT MISOGYNIST
Don't eat that.

                    FLEABAG
                  (to camera)
— but it's manageable.
                  (to Hot Misogynist)
I'm going to.

              HOT MISOGYNIST
Ok.

                    FLEABAG
                  (to camera)
He's a feminist.

              HOT MISOGYNIST
I have a sister.

                    FLEABAG
                  (to camera)
And he's unpredictable.

              HOT MISOGYNIST
I'm just gonna go for a shit.

He winks at her and stands up.

                    FLEABAG
I'm ignoring that.

              HOT MISOGYNIST
Actually. Do you wanna go have sex?

                    FLEABAG
                  (to camera)
That's better!

              HOT MISOGYNIST
I'm really good at it.

                    FLEABAG
            (to camera, with a sigh)
He won't be.

              HOT MISOGYNIST
I'm really good at it.

                    FLEABAG
                  (to camera)
He won't be.

INT. FLEABAG'S FLAT. BEDROOM — NIGHT

Fleabag is having sex with Hot Misogynist.

>   **FLEABAG**
>   (to camera)
>   He's really good at it.

>   *TITLES: FLEABAG*

EXT. DAD'S HOUSE — MORNING

Fleabag, looking a hungover, shagged mess, is walking up the
street to Dad's house.

>   **FLEABAG**
>   Oh God.
>   (to camera)
>   I'm not gonna be sick.
>   (to camera)
>   I'm not gonna be sick.

Coming from the opposite direction is Claire, carrying an
enormous wedding arch garland thing, and a bassoon in a
case.

They both reach the gate at the same time.

>   **FLEABAG**
>   Hi.

>   **CLAIRE**
>   Hi.

Claire struggles through the gate.

>   **FLEABAG**
>   Do you need a hand with any of...

>   **CLAIRE**
>   No, no, no, no.

>   **FLEABAG**
>   I can at least take the bassoon.

>   **CLAIRE**
>   I'm perfectly balanced, thank you.
>   (beat)
>   Big night last night?

                              FLEABAG
    Is it obvious?

Claire's look indicates it definitely is obvious.

                              CLAIRE
    Well, at least someone's having fun.

They reach the front door, Claire struggling to reach the
doorbell.

                              FLEABAG
    I can get the bell.

                              CLAIRE
    NO, NO, I'VE GOT IT.

She rings it and they stand in the doorway. Fleabag lets out
an unhealthy groan.

                              CLAIRE
    Are you going to be sick?

                              FLEABAG
                    (pulling herself together)
    No.

                              CLAIRE
    She'd better be quick today. I have a serious appoint-
    ment later that I can't miss. It's very important.

                              FLEABAG
                        (concerned)
    What kind of appointment?

                              CLAIRE
    A serious one. I can't miss it, Ok?

                              FLEABAG
    Do you need me to—

                              CLAIRE
    I don't need you.
                        (beat)
    To do anything, thank you.
                        (beat)
    Unless you can find a way to stop this horrendous
    wedding from happening —

Dad opens the door.

                              DAD
    Girls, come in!

INT. DAD'S HOUSE. HALLWAY — DAY

Claire and Fleabag follow Dad inside. Claire struggles in with the garland and a bassoon case. Fleabag keeps getting hit by it.

> **DAD**
> You can just leave it there for now— would you like a quick cup of tea before you start? / It's already in a pot—

> **CLAIRE**
> I have to be out of here pretty quickly. / Ok.

> **FLEABAG**
> (hungover)
> Just some water or some gin would be—

> **DAD**
> Come through, we have a whole tray of —

They walk into the living room as they are talking.

INT. DAD'S HOUSE. LIVING ROOM/HALLWAY — DAY

Dad, Fleabag and Claire file in.

> **DAD**
> — sweet chocolatey things, our lovely friend has just dropped round.

Beat. Priest is there. So is Godmother.

> **GODMOTHER**
> Hello darling.

> **PRIEST**
> Hello.

> **FLEABAG**
> (to camera)
> I'm going to be sick.

> **GODMOTHER**
> (to Fleabag)
> Oh, are you alright? You look horrendous.

> **FLEABAG**
> Oh — er, thanks. Just a big night. Hello.

> **PRIEST**
> Hey! I only meant to be quick, I don't need to — wasn't expecting the whole family! Wow!

> **DAD**
> They're being painted. Isn't that fun!

> **PRIEST**
> So fun! I um... I can come back later.

> **GODMOTHER**
> No no!

> **FLEABAG**
> No.
> (to camera)
> No.

The Priest looks at her.

> **GODMOTHER**
> Come on, fill us in. Probably better actually that we should all hear the plans.

> **PRIEST**
> Right. Well I just wanted to pop in actually to say that — um —

Beat. They all look at him.

> **PRIEST (CONT'D)**
> I've been called away this weekend and I'm afraid I won't be able to officiate at the wedding tomorrow.

Beat. Silence.

> **CLAIRE**
> Oh, Christ.

> **FLEABAG**
> Why?

> **PRIEST**
> My brother is ill. I have to go and see him.

> **FLEABAG**
> What is he ill with?

> **PRIEST**
> A lorry. Accident.

> **FLEABAG**
> Right.

> **GODMOTHER**
> Oh God.

CLAIRE
Is he alright?

PRIEST
He's in a bit of a state to be honest. But er —

He stumbles. He looks at Fleabag.

PRIEST (CONT'D)
I just — can't do it. I can't do it.

Fleabag holds his gaze.

GODMOTHER
Well... Well.

Everyone looks at Godmother, waiting for her to blow.

FLEABAG
(to camera)
Oh. This is going to be spectacular.

GODMOTHER
Oh...
(beat)
... You...
(beat)
... *poor* man. Of course you must go.

PRIEST
Really?

DAD
Really?

GODMOTHER
Of course! Family first!
(grasping Claire's shoulder a little too
tightly)
Always family first. You must go, get straight to him.
Send me all the details of what you've worked out so
far. We'll sort something out.

PRIEST
I've put the feelers out for someone else and—

DAD
Well, I think we might have to—

GODMOTHER
Don't worry about a thing. This is far more important.
You must go! Go, go, go.

PRIEST

Oh, Ok. Well thank you so much for understanding.

DAD

Well sure, sure, sure.

Godmother ushers the Priest out of the room to the front door. He catches Fleabag's eye as he walks out. We stay with Fleabag and Claire as they hear —

PRIEST (O.S.)

Well, all the best and — I'm sorry. And good luck.

GODMOTHER (O.S.)
            (sweetly)
Bye darling and good luck!
We hear the front door close firmly behind him.

GODMOTHER (O.S.)

What... a... CUNT. What A *CUNT*!!

DAD (O.S.)

Now, now, I don't—

GODMOTHER (O.S.)

BASTARD, FUCKING BASTARD.
            (beat)
Don't. Touch me. Christ, I need to paint. I need to paint, right now.
            (as she storms upstairs)
Send them away!

Dad re-enters the living room.

DAD

Um... I think you should, er...

CLAIRE

Yes. Ok.

Claire exits. Fleabag follows.

FLEABAG

Bye Dad.

CLAIRE

Bye Dad.

EXT. DAD'S HOUSE — DAY

The door closes behind Claire and Fleabag. They walk down towards the gate, Claire still with the bassoon.

                              CLAIRE
    Well, that solves that problem. I'm relieved for him.

Beat.

                              CLAIRE
    Are you alright?

Fleabag races past her.

                             FLEABAG
    Yeah.
                         (to camera too)
    Just late for the café.

She races off. Claire looks after her, confused.

                              CLAIRE
    Right.

EXT. BUS STOP NEAR DAD'S — DAY

Fleabag sits with her head in her hands.

She looks up. The Priest is sitting next to her. She jumps
in shock—

                             FLEABAG
    OH MY GOD!

                              PRIEST
    Sorry, sorry!

                             FLEABAG
    Jesus. How long were you there?!

                              PRIEST
    Literally, three seconds.

Beat.

                             FLEABAG
    You can't just cancel a wedding.

                              PRIEST
    I don't have a choice.

                             FLEABAG
    But you have the dress!

He laughs despite himself. He puts his head in his hands.

> **PRIEST**
> I can't and I—

> **FLEABAG**
> Can I just say—

> **PRIEST**
> No I don't want to—

> **FLEABAG**
> How do you know what I'm going to say?

Pause. They look at each other for a long moment.

> **PRIEST**
> Please don't come to the church again.

Beat.

> **PRIEST**
> I mean that with the greatest of compliments.

She looks at him. He stands and walks away.

She watches him go. She turns and looks at us. Left alone at the bus stop.

INT. HILARY'S CAFÉ — DAY

The café is busy and Fleabag is still hungover. Chatty Joe is following her around, chatting relentlessly.

> **CHATTY JOE**
> I strongly advised taking out insurance. The problem is —

> **FLEABAG**
> (to camera)
> I can deal with it.

> **CHATTY JOE**
> It was about seven foot tall...

> **FLEABAG**
> (to camera)
> I can deal with it.

> **CHATTY JOE**
> ... a very large armchair...

> **FLEABAG**
> (to camera)
> I can't deal with it.

                              CHATTY JOE
    ... chinchilla, suffocating underneath him...

                              FLEABAG
    It's Tuesday, Joe.

                              CHATTY JOE
    No. It's Chatty Wednesday.

He points to the sign saying 'Today is Chatty Wednesday'.

                              FLEABAG
    No. It's Quiet Tuesday.
                              (to camera)
    It's Chatty Wednesday.

                              CHATTY JOE
    It was a very small chinchilla...

                              FLEABAG
    CAN YOU JUST STOP CHATTING JUST FOR A SECOND PLEASE
    JOE!

The café goes quiet. Other customers stare. Joe looks
surprised.

                              FLEABAG
    Joe, I...

He smiles, mimes zipping up his mouth and walks off.

The bell on the café door rings and in walks the BANK
MANAGER in his bank clothes.

                              FLEABAG
    Hi.

                              BANK MANAGER
    You Ok?

                              FLEABAG
    Yeah, are you Ok? You look like something bad's
    happened.

                              BANK MANAGER
    Do I? I thought I was looking jolly.

                              FLEABAG
    Oh! Erm, why?

                              BANK MANAGER
    I've been offered a new job.

                    FLEABAG
Oh... congratulations!

                 BANK MANAGER
But I just wanted to say... goodbye. And — to give you
this.

He hands Fleabag a small box. She opens the lid.

                 BANK MANAGER
It's a guinea pig.

                    FLEABAG
                  (to camera)
It's a hamster.
                 (to Bank Manager)
Thanks.

Fleabag's phone starts buzzing. She looks at who's calling.

                    FLEABAG
Sorry, it's my sister, she's a bit mental. Do you mind
if I —

                 BANK MANAGER
Sure. I wasn't gonna stay so —

Fleabag answers her phone.

                    FLEABAG
Claire?

Claire sounds like she is in utter crisis.

                 CLAIRE (O.S.)
                  (crying)
Something's happened, something awful has happened.

                    FLEABAG
What? Where are you, do you need me to come?

                 CLAIRE (O.S.)
No, no, no, I fucked it up, I've fucked everything up.
Can you come?

                    FLEABAG
I have to close the café but — Just tell me where you
are.

                 CLAIRE (O.S.)
Don't close — I'm so sorry, but, but...

                 BANK MANAGER
I can look after the place, if you want?

                              FLEABAG
Really?

                         BANK MANAGER
Well, I don't start 'til Monday.

                              FLEABAG
Then why are you...

She looks at his suit.

                         BANK MANAGER
I just like it.

                              FLEABAG
Could you do me a favour and give Hilary and...

She looks at the hamster.

                         BANK MANAGER
Stephanie.

                              FLEABAG
Stephanie some cucumber at 2.30?

                         CLAIRE (O.S.)
Who's Stephanie?

                              FLEABAG
Thanks!

She hands him the keys and heads out, phone pressed to her
ear.

                              FLEABAG
Claire, just tell me where you are. And what the HELL
has happened???

HARD CUT TO: EXT. CITY SQUARE — DAY

CLOSE on Claire. She has a very short, weird hair-cut,
sitting under a tree on a bench, with the bassoon case.

She has teary eyes.

Fleabag stares at her.

Pause.

                              CLAIRE
Tell the truth.

                          FLEABAG
                       (to camera)
It's horrendous.

                          CLAIRE
It's horrendous.

                          FLEABAG
It's modern.

                          CLAIRE
Don't lie!

                          FLEABAG
I'm not!

                          CLAIRE
I look like a pencil.

                          FLEABAG
                       (laughing)
You don't look like a...

                          CLAIRE
DON'T LAUGH!

                          FLEABAG
It's Ok!

                          CLAIRE
It's not! It's not Ok. I'm going to lose my job.

                          FLEABAG
You're not going to lose your job, it's cool!

                          CLAIRE
IT'S NOT COOL!

                          FLEABAG
It's edgy!

                          CLAIRE
FUCK OFF!

                          FLEABAG
It's chic!

                          CLAIRE
IT'S UNSALVAGEABLE!

                          FLEABAG
CLAIRE, IT'S FRENCH.

Beat.

                              CLAIRE
    Really?

                              FLEABAG
    Yes.

Fleabag gives us a look — no.

                              FLEABAG
    Have you been drinking?

                              CLAIRE
    Oh, he gave me champagne before he RUINED MY LIFE.
                         (deadly serious)
    That's how they get you.

                              FLEABAG
    Did you go to Anthony?

Claire looks at her guiltily.

                              FLEABAG
    Claire!

                              CLAIRE
    I KNOW.

                              FLEABAG
    What! Remember what happened to me?!

INT. FLASHBACK, HAIRDRESSER'S — YEARS EARLIER

Fleabag in the hairdresser's chair. A HAIRDRESSER (man, 30s,
stylish) stands behind her. She has long hair on one side.
He has mindlessly cut all the way up the other side of her
head.

She looks horrified as he cuts further and further up her
hair.

                              HAIRDRESSER
    I honestly thought it was the last time I was ever going
    to see him —

                              FLEABAG
    Um... That's just awful but —

He cuts a huge chunk.

                              HAIRDRESSER
    His little face was just—

> **FLEABAG**
> ANTHONY!

EXT. CITY SQUARE — DAY

Back in the present. Fleabag and Claire, as before, on the bench with the bassoon.

> **FLEABAG**
> Is this what you asked for?

> **CLAIRE**
> NO! Of course not. He's just a bastard.

Beat.

> **FLEABAG**
> Right. Fuck it.

> **CLAIRE**
> What?

> **FLEABAG**
> Come on.

Fleabag stands and marches off. She grabs the bassoon case as she leaves.

> **CLAIRE**
> No, no, no! It's alright... slow down!

INT. HAIRDRESSER'S — DAY

Moments later Fleabag storms into a posh hairdresser's, followed by Claire with the bassoon. The Hairdresser from the flashback is doing a WOMAN's hair. There are five other CUSTOMERS in the salon.

> **FLEABAG**
> Hey!

Hairdresser sees Fleabag and Claire coming and steels up. He talks to her like a dog trainer. Not pissed off. Just deadly serious and very strong.

> **HAIRDRESSER**
> NO.

> **FLEABAG**
> Anthony!

                              HAIRDRESSER
NO.
                    (pointing to Claire)
That is EXACTLY what she asked for.

                              FLEABAG
No it's not. We want compensation.

                              HAIRDRESSER
Claire?

                              CLAIRE
I've got two important meetings and I look like a
pencil.

                              HAIRDRESSER
NO. Don't blame me for your bad choices. Hair isn't
everything.

                              FLEABAG
Wow.

                              HAIRDRESSER
What?

                              FLEABAG
Hair. Is. Everything. We wish it wasn't so we could
actually think about something else occasionally. But
it is. It's the difference between a good day and a bad
day. We're meant to think that it is a symbol of power,
a symbol of fertility, some people are exploited for it
and it pays your fucking bills. Hair is everything,
Anthony.

                              CLAIRE
Show her the reference.

                              HAIRDRESSER
Claudia. Bring me the bin.

An employee, CLAUDIA, brings him the bin. He pulls out a
picture of a model with exactly Claire's current haircut.

                              HAIRDRESSER
If you want to change your life. Change your life.
                    (beat)
It's not going to happen in here.

                              FLEABAG
Sorry Anthony... see you next week.

                              CLAIRE
Sorry Anthony, I didn't... think it would turn out like
that.

EXT. CITY SQUARE — DAY

Claire and Fleabag are back on the bench from earlier, with the bassoon.

> CLAIRE
> Have you got any cigarettes?

> FLEABAG
> No.

> CLAIRE
> Good.

> CLAIRE
> Thank you for being there.

> FLEABAG
> It was very cathartic.

> CLAIRE
> At the hospital.

Beat.

> FLEABAG
> S'Ok. Shame you couldn't keep that doctor.

Claire smiles.

> FLEABAG
> I'm sorry you lost it.

Claire looks out, consumed by guilt.

> CLAIRE
> (filled with guilt)
> I just felt relief.
> (beat)
> I didn't want my husband's baby. Isn't that awful?

Fleabag reaches for Claire's hand. She understands.

Beat.

> CLAIRE
> I haven't even asked you how you are.

Beat. Fleabag looks at her, waiting for her to ask it.

> CLAIRE
> How are you? What's going on with you?

                         FLEABAG
   I —

Fleabag looks to camera briefly.

                    FLEABAG (CONT'D)
   — met someone.

Beat.

                          CLAIRE
   What?! Really?!

                         FLEABAG
   Yep.

                          CLAIRE
   Oh my God, that's amazing! What does he do?

                         FLEABAG
   He's a priest.

Claire lets her head fall forwards and holds her temples.
For ages.

Ages.

Then she looks up, realising.

                          CLAIRE
   Is it — oh my God —

Fleabag nods.

                          CLAIRE
   You are joking.

                         FLEABAG
   Nope.

                          CLAIRE
                      (laughing)
   Oh God, I'm sorry — it's just—

                         FLEABAG
   I know.

                          CLAIRE
   I'm sure it's very complicated. It's just—

                         FLEABAG
   I know.

Beat.

                              CLAIRE
God, you're a genius.

Fleabag laughs in spite of herself.

                              CLAIRE
You're my fucking hero.

                           KLARE (O.S.)
CLAIRE! Is that you?

Klare is there, with a Finnish BUSINESS MAN and BUSINESS
WOMAN. Claire looks up. Mortified.

                              CLAIRE
Oh God. Oh God oh God.

                              KLARE
CLAIRE. Oh my GOD, CLAIRE, I LOVE YOUR HAIR! It's so
cute and edgy and cool. Like superstar — popstar. Listen
— these penguins are taking me to this amazing London
music thing. Are you free?

                             FLEABAG
                           (to camera)
Yes.

                              KLARE
Do you want to come?

                              CLAIRE
I — I have to take my stepson his bassoon, I — wish I
could —

                              KLARE
Ah. Well — I leave tomorrow. So.

                             FLEABAG
I'll take the bassoon! I've got it!

Beat.

                              CLAIRE
No. I — he's expecting me to—

                             FLEABAG
Tell Jake it's with me at the café. Honestly, it's fine.

                              KLARE
Hey — I'm not going to get in the way of your family
days.

                             FLEABAG
I'll take it. Please get in the way of her family days.

Just tell Jake I've got it.

Claire shoots her a look — Fleabag prises the bassoon off
Claire.

> **FLEABAG**
> No biggie.

Claire nods.

> **FLEABAG**
> Bye Claire. Bye Klare.
> > (to camera)
> Bye Claire.

Klare and Claire walk away, Fleabag watches them go.

> **KLARE**
> > (at her hair)
> I can't believe your hair! It's just so chic. And cute!
> It's all the things! It goes so well with your top.

> **CLAIRE**
> Oh that's so sweet of you. Honestly, I've had such a
> day with it.

Fleabag checks her watch — fuck! She runs off, frantically.

EXT. HILARY'S CAFÉ — DAY

Bank Manager is tidying up outside, he is wearing a
'Hilary's Café' pinny. He hands Fleabag the keys. She still
holds the bassoon case.

> **BANK MANAGER**
> That was exhausting. The new guinea pig —

> **FLEABAG**
> > (to camera)
> Hamster.

> **BANK MANAGER**
> — is in with Hilary. They shared the cucumber Ok which
> was... quite sweet.

> **FLEABAG**
> Thanks!

> **BANK MANAGER**
> Well, I'd say anytime, but. Um —

> **FLEABAG**
> You have a new job.

> **BANK MANAGER**
I will be back though. My wife would love Chatty
Wednesdays.

> **FLEABAG**
> (smiling)
Oh!

> **BANK MANAGER**
You have a visitor. I let him wait in there.

Fleabag looks to camera. Who is it? She shakes hands with
Bank Manager.

> **FLEABAG**
Pleasure doing business with you.

> **BANK MANAGER**
Bye.

He turns and walks away.

> **FLEABAG**
> (to camera)
He took the pinny.

INT. HILARY'S CAFÉ — DAY

She walks into the café. Standing there by Hilary's hutch is
her visitor.

> **FLEABAG**
> (to camera)
Ugh.

It's Martin. He's holding Hilary, stroking her — it's
sinister.

> **MARTIN**
Hey!

> **FLEABAG**
> (to camera)
He's going to make a bassoon joke.

> **MARTIN**
Is that a bassoon in your hand or are you just pleased
to see me?

> **FLEABAG**
Would you say that to your son?

MARTIN
When he has his bassoon, sure.
(laughing)
But he's never pleased to see me.

FLEABAG
It doesn't even make sense. Why would a bassoon in my
hand—

MARTIN
Like a dick in your hand.

FLEABAG
Right, so if I was walking towards you with an amputated
dick in my hand, you would assume it was because I was
horny.

MARTIN
Well I'd assume that you had been! Certainly wouldn't
put it past you to chop a dick off.

FLEABAG
Put the guinea pig down.

MARTIN
Where is she?

FLEABAG
Why?

MARTIN
Well she was meant to drop that off and she's not at
the office.

FLEABAG
Well, I don't know where she is.

MARTIN
(the bassoon)
So you just found that?

FLEABAG
Please don't hurt the guinea pig.

MARTIN
I would never hurt the guinea pig.

He turns to the hutch.

MARTIN (CONT'D)
(seriously)
I wouldn't do that.

He mumbles sweetly to Hilary as he replaces her in her hutch — Fleabag looks to the camera. Disturbed.

> **FLEABAG**
> Are you sure we should even be talking? Aren't you supposed to be getting me arrested or something—

> **MARTIN**
> Wow — she really tells you everything, doesn't she. Cute tables.

He pulls a small bottle of whiskey out of his pocket.

> **FLEABAG**
> Jesus, Martin.

> **MARTIN**
> FUCK OFF.
> > (beat. He points at her)
> You are the problem, you know that. You are the problem in my perfect life.

> **FLEABAG**
> I haven't seen you in a year.

> **MARTIN**
> And yet stiiiilllll...
> > (laughing, pointing at her face)
> Off she runs into the night for you... I can't even get the woman pregnant and then you come in, showing off about your miscarriage like you didn't even want the one you had. I WAS JUST TRYING TO MAKE HER FEEL BETTER.

Beat. He looks at her.

Beat.

Her phone rings in her bag.

> **MARTIN**
> Give me your phone.

> **FLEABAG**
> No.

> **MARTIN**
> Give me your phone.

> **FLEABAG**
> No.

> **MARTIN**
> Is she leaving me?

FLEABAG

Hope so.

MARTIN

Don't let her leave me.
(he stifles a sob)
Don't let her leave me. Please.

Beat. Fleabag looks at him. She looks at the camera and
pulls a mock sad face.

FLEABAG

I hope she doesn't come home tonight.

Martin laughs bitterly. Then reaches and grabs Fleabag by
the collar.

FLEABAG
(to camera)
Argh! Cashmere, cashmere, cashmere!

MARTIN

I will take you down, fucker.

FLEABAG

I will take YOU DOWN, fucker.

Martin laughs again, bitter. He lets her go.

MARTIN

FUCK YOU!

FLEABAG

FUCK YOU!

MARTIN

FUCK YOU!

FLEABAG

FUCK YOU!

MARTIN

FUCK YOU, YOU BETTER START SLEEPING WITH A LAWYER!

FLEABAG

I'M ALREADY SLEEPING WITH A LAWYER!

MARTIN

Oh yeah? LUCKY LAWYER.

Beat. Slightly confused by what he just said, and realising
the argument is over, Martin exits the café and drunkenly
runs down the street.

Fleabag sighs.

> **FLEABAG**
> (to camera)
> Better call my lawyer.

**HARD CUT TO: INT. FLEABAG'S FLAT. HALLWAY/FRONT DOOR —
NIGHT**

Fleabag is standing facing her front door. Now in her coat.

> **FLEABAG**
> You know that feeling when the Hot Misogynist who might
> not be a misogynist is turning up to your house for the
> second time in 48 hours to give you an orgasm you don't
> want, just so you can do something to get your head out
> of the fact that the only person in the world you want
> to see is the Priest that you—

The buzzer goes.

> **FLEABAG**
> So you pick yourself up, cover yourself in coconut oil
> and hope that he doesn't notice that you haven't shaved
> your—

She opens the door.

The Priest stands there.

> **PRIEST**
> Hey.
> (beat)
> Your sister gave me your address.

She just stares at him in shock. He sees her outfit.

> **PRIEST**
> Are you on your way out?

> **FLEABAG**
> No, I... just got in.
> (to camera)
> I've only got underwear on under this coat.

> **PRIEST**
> Cool. Can I come in?

> **FLEABAG**
> Yeah. Sure.

INT. FLEABAG'S FLAT. LIVING ROOM — NIGHT

The Priest walks into her living room.

> PRIEST
>
> It's, uh, nice—

> FLEABAG
>
> Thank you.

He paces the room slightly. Fleabag glances at the camera —
what is he going to say?

> FLEABAG
>
> Water?

> PRIEST
>
> Um. No thanks. I wanna... keep a clear head.
> (quickly)
> I changed my mind about the wedding. I can't let them
> down like that. And apparently no one else will wear
> the outfit.

> FLEABAG
>
> That's good of you.

> PRIEST
>
> Do you want to take off your coat?

> FLEABAG
>
> No, I'm good. Bit chilly.

He looks at her. Beat.

> PRIEST
>
> I sacrificed a lot for this life. I gave a lot of things
> up. So—

The doorbell rings.

Beat.

> PRIEST
>
> Do you want to get that?

> FLEABAG
>
> I don't like opening the door to people I don't know.

> HOT MISOGYNIST (O.S.)
> I'm baaaaacckkk!!

The doorbell rings again. Beat.

> ### PRIEST
> Look, if there's someone you need to see or — let in—

Fleabag sits down.

> ### FLEABAG
> No, no, no... Honestly it's fine.

Beat. He settles.

> ### PRIEST
> When I was a child, I—

The doorbell rings again. Hot Misogynist shouts through the door.

> ### FLEABAG
> I'll just be —

She goes to the door.

INT. FLEABAG'S FLAT. HALLWAY / FRONT DOOR

Fleabag opens the door. Hot Misogynist is there, ready to go.

> ### HOT MISOGYNIST
> So you're in trouble again, huh?

> ### FLEABAG
> Listen, I'm sorry, but you can't come in.

> ### HOT MISOGYNIST
> Ok! You wanna do it on the doorstep?

The Priest overhears the conversation.

> ### FLEABAG
> I'm so sorry, but my Priest is here and he really needs some guidance.

> ### HOT MISOGYNIST
> What? Is he Ok?

> ### FLEABAG
> No — I think he's having an emotional crisis.

> ### HOT MISOGYNIST
> Shall I wait? You said you wanted to see me.

> ### FLEABAG
> Yes, I did want to see you and now I don't want to see you.

HOT MISOGYNIST
Did I do something wrong? You seemed to like what I
did?

FLEABAG
Yes I did.

HOT MISOGYNIST
I'm really good at it.

Meanwhile the Priest overhears — and stands, awkwardly.

FLEABAG
Yep.

HOT MISOGYNIST
I'm really good at it.

FLEABAG
Yep. I know you are. You're really good at it.

HOT MISOGYNIST
Well, clearly I'm not. If you don't want it.

FLEABAG
Oh for God's sake. You're the best sex I've ever had.

HOT MISOGYNIST
What?

FLEABAG
You're the best sex I've ever had.

HOT MISOGYNIST
Really?

FLEABAG
Honestly. You made me come nine times.

HOT MISOGYNIST
Honestly?

Fleabag nods. He smiles, proud and relieved.

HOT MISOGYNIST
Ok, cool. Do you want me to go?

FLEABAG
Yeah.

HOT MISOGYNIST
I'll take this somewhere else.

                              FLEABAG
        Ok, good. Good for her.

He touches her cheek.

                         HOT MISOGYNIST
        Nine times. You're a saint.

He leaves. She closes the door behind him.

INT. FLEABAG'S FLAT. LIVING ROOM — NIGHT

Fleabag walks back in.

                              FLEABAG
        I'm sorry, that was just—

                               PRIEST
        No, it's Ok, I won't ask.
                              (beat)
        Nine times...

                              FLEABAG
                            (quickly)
        I just had to get rid of him.

                               PRIEST
        Sure.
                              (beat)
        I can't be physical with you.

                              FLEABAG
        We can't even wrestle?

He laughs awkwardly. He looks at her.

                              FLEABAG
        Priests have sex, you know. A lot of them actually do.
        They don't burst into flames, I googled it.

                               PRIEST
        I can't have sex with you because I'll fall in love with
        you and if I fall in love with you, I won't burst into
        flames, but... my life will be fucked.

                              FLEABAG
                          (to camera)
        We're going to have sex.

                               PRIEST
        I'm meant to love ONE thing.

Beat.

> **FLEABAG**
> (to camera)
Oh my God, we're going to have sex.

> **PRIEST**
> (noticing her talk to us)
FOR FUCK'S SAKE STOP THAT. I don't think you want to be told what to do at all. I think you know exactly what to do. If you really wanted someone to tell you what to do, you'd be wearing one of these.

> **FLEABAG**
Women aren't actually allowed—

> **PRIEST**
Oh, fuck off, I know.

He looks at her.

Pause.

> **PRIEST**
We're going to have sex, aren't we?

She nods. He nods too.

> **PRIEST**
Yeah.

> **FLEABAG**
Yeah.

> **PRIEST**
Ok.

He moves towards her, begins undoing her coat. Sees the underwear underneath.

> **PRIEST**
Oh. Um, Ok.

> **FLEABAG**
Listen, I had a — uh.

He shakes his head gently.

She falls quiet. He opens her coat. She leans forward and kisses him gently. He suddenly goes for it. He's a pro... he just needed permission.

INT. FLEABAG'S FLAT. BEDROOM — NIGHT

Fleabag and the Priest are in bed. He is on top of her, it's passionate.

She looks to the camera, then pushes it forcefully away.

END OF EPISODE 5

EPISODE 6

INT. FLEABAG'S FLAT. BEDROOM — MORNING

Fleabag is lying in bed awake.

The Priest is lying with his back to her.

She strokes the back of his neck.

> **PRIEST**
> (gently, without turning)
> What?
> (beat)
> What are you thinking?

> **FLEABAG**
> I just —

> **PRIEST**
> (gently)
> Go on.

He turns. He looks at her.

He smiles at her.

She smiles at him.

> **FLEABAG**
> I just —

> **PRIEST**
> (gently)
> Go on.

Beat.

> **FLEABAG**
> I just can't believe you did that.

Beat. He smiles.

> **PRIEST**
> I know.

TITLE CARD: THE WEDDING

EXT. DAD'S HOUSE. GARDEN — DAY

JUMP CUTS OF: Fleabag and Claire in the garden welcoming GUESTS.

                    CLAIRE / FLEABAG
So good to see you!

— as they hug various family friends.

                         CLAIRE
We're over the moon.

                        FLEABAG
Heyyy, good to see you.

                         CLAIRE
Love the shirt.

                        FLEABAG
                       (to Claire)
Who is that?

JUMP CUT TO: Fleabag gestures to Claire's clip-on ponytail.

                        FLEABAG
Is this the—

                         CLAIRE
Don't. It'll come off.

JUMP CUT TO: The portrait of Fleabag and Claire is prom-
inently displayed. Fleabag and Claire look over at
Godmother and Dad.

                         CLAIRE
What's happened with the priest?

JUMP CUT TO: Fleabag and Claire greet Harry and Elaine.
Fleabag and Elaine accidentally kiss on the lips.

JUMP CUT TO: Back with Fleabag and Claire.

                        FLEABAG
Nothing.

JUMP CUT TO: Dad approaches Claire and Fleabag.

                          DAD
Ohhh, so good of you to come and get me.

                        FLEABAG
Get you?

                    DAD
    See me.

JUMP CUT TO: Jake arrives with his bassoon.

                  FLEABAG
    Hi Jake.

                   JAKE
    Where's Claire?

                  FLEABAG
    Just there.

She points to Claire right next to her.

                  CLAIRE
    Your Dad's just down there.

JUMP CUT TO: Back with Dad, Fleabag and Claire.

                    DAD
    Nice skirts.

Fleabag and Claire are both wearing dresses.

                    DAD
    Do you need me to say anything... emotional about
    today?

               FLEABAG/CLAIRE
    No no, we're good. / I think we're fine, thanks.

JUMP CUT TO: Fleabag and Claire on their own.

                  CLAIRE
    Do you want tequila? I'm gonna get one.

JUMP CUT TO: More guests arrive.

               FLEABAG/CLAIRE
    Hi, hi, nice to see you!

JUMP CUT TO: Back with Fleabag and Claire.

                  FLEABAG
    How's Klare?

> **CLAIRE**
> Well, he's crazy about me, so...
> (beat)
> That's a nightmare.

> **FLEABAG**
> Nightmare.

> **CLAIRE**
> He's back to Finland today anyway which is good. It's fine, it's totally fine.

> **FLEABAG**
> Sounds like it's fine.

> **CLAIRE**
> It is.

Fleabag gives the camera a look.

> **CLAIRE**
> (sighs)
> It's going to be a lovely day, isn't it.

> **FLEABAG**
> (sighs)
> I'm afraid so.

EXT. DAD'S HOUSE. GARDEN, ELSEWHERE — DAY

Fleabag (holding the present) is being introduced to Godmother's fascinating friends: DANIEL, FRANCINE and ASIF. Dad hovers. Claire, Martin and Jake stand by.

> **GODMOTHER**
> This is my very interesting friend Daniel, who's *deaf*. I picked him up at a student gallery opening. Utterly fascinating. Can't hear a thing, but is a fabulous physical communicator through hands and lips.

Daniel signs something. Godmother is enchanted.

> **GODMOTHER**
> Oh I love that! And this is my extraordinary friend Francine. She's a *lesbian* —

> **FLEABAG**
> (to camera, mouthing simultaneously)
> Lesbian.

> **GODMOTHER**
> And this is Asif, my bisexual Syrian *refugee* friend —
> (to Dad)

— who you haven't actually met yet darling. And Asif, this is um —
              (to Dad, forgetting his name but horrified
                    with herself for it)
— oh my God. This is... This is... God, how extra-ordinary — I always call you darling!
                    (beat, recovering)
This is the love of my life!

Even she is horrified. She kisses him.

                    FLEABAG
              (holding her present up)
Is there somewhere I can put this?

                    GODMOTHER
We said no presents! Oh you're such a sweetheart. She's a natural rule breaker.

                    DAD
Not today!

                    FLEABAG
Well I've been trying to get rid of it for ages, so —

Godmother takes it. She touches Fleabag's cheek.

                    GODMOTHER
              (sincerely)
Ohhhh. Thank you.

Beat.

                    GODMOTHER
I'm going to open it over a bin, so I've got somewhere to put the paper.

She smiles and walks inside.

Beat. Godmother turns back.

                    GODMOTHER
              (pointing at Fleabag)
Come with me!

Fleabag goes in.

INT. DAD'S HOUSE. KITCHEN — DAY

Godmother and Fleabag walk in.

                    FLEABAG
Are you short on staff or... Do you need me or...?

Godmother turns round to face her while opening the present over the bin.

> **GODMOTHER**
> No, I just wondered if you had a little show planned?

> **FLEABAG**
> What?

> **GODMOTHER**
> Well, you normally do. And I wondered if there was anything I might need to know about that might happen later?

> **FLEABAG**
> No.

> **GODMOTHER**
> Good. Well let me know if you change your mind. Because today is the most important day of my life, and I love your father very much and I imagine you'd rather have me looking after him in the years to come than having to do it yourself. So.
> (beat)
> No more miscarriages.

She looks down and opens the box, seeing the statue.

Godmother looks up at her in shock.

> **FLEABAG**
> It's worth a lot. So...

She strokes her face. She accepts the significance of the gift.

> **GODMOTHER**
> Thank you.
> (beat)
> I'll go and put her straight back on her shelf.

She turns and walks to the door, then turns.

> **GODMOTHER**
> (beat)
> Do you know, I often thought it strange that of all my pieces you chose to take her.

> **FLEABAG**
> Why?

Godmother looks at the statue in her hand. She smiles.

> GODMOTHER

She was based on your mother.

Fleabag frowns.

> GODMOTHER
> (she squeezes the statue to her chest)

So nice to have her back in the house.

She smiles sweetly and exits.

Fleabag burns with rage.

EXT. DAD'S HOUSE. SIDE ALLEY — DAY

Fleabag rushes to the side of the house, with a packet of cigarettes. She looks up to find the Priest.

> FLEABAG

Oh—

> PRIEST

Oh FUCK!

> FLEABAG

Oh my God, FUCK, you're here.

> PRIEST

Jesus. I thought you were a fox.
> (beat)

You're not.

> FLEABAG

No — are you — I didn't know you were —

> PRIEST

No no, I'm fine, sorry — I know — I just didn't want to — I'm practising the homily.

> FLEABAG

How's it going?

> PRIEST

Not good. I can't — I can't...
> (beat)

You look lovely.

> FLEABAG

Thank you. So do you.

> PRIEST

Wait till you see me in the full shebang. You're going to lose your fucking mind.

Fleabag laughs. A beat.

> **PRIEST**
> We just need to get through this bit. Then we can... we can —

> **FLEABAG**
> Yeah.

Beat.

> **PRIEST**
> Better get changed.

> **FLEABAG**
> Yeah. Good luck.

He goes to leave, then suddenly they're kissing, passionately, up against the wall. They stop, smiling.

> **FLEABAG**
> Oh my God. You have lipstick all over you—

> **PRIEST**
> Fucking hell!
> (wiping his mouth)
> That would not look good. Is it gone? Oh fucking hell. I don't know — I don't know — oh I don't know what this feeling is.

> **FLEABAG**
> Is it God or is it me?

> **PRIEST**
> I don't know...
> (beat)
> I don't know.

He slowly walks away. He turns back to her but decides he can't. He walks away.

> **FLEABAG**
> Fuck you then.

They laugh, and he goes.

EXT. DAD'S HOUSE. GARDEN, ELSEWHERE — DAY

Later. Fleabag is outside. Godmother is with a group of GUESTS introducing everyone. Martin and Jake are stood nearby. Claire approaches Fleabag.

> ### CLAIRE
> Where's your priest?

> ### FLEABAG
> I don't know. Are you Ok?

> ### CLAIRE
> Yes, well... I hate my husband and the man I love is on his way to Finland, so... Pretty weird.

> ### GODMOTHER
> OH! Way to upstage the bride!

They all turn to see the Priest walking towards them, in his robes. He and Fleabag share a look. She smiles at him, he smiles back.

Godmother is thrilled he's worn the whole thing.

> ### PRIEST
> I did my best!

> ### GODMOTHER
> Oh look!

She tries to twirl him.

> ### GODMOTHER (CONT'D)
> This is our very chic Priest—

> ### PRIEST
> I was aiming for chic!

He smiles at Fleabag.

> ### FLEABAG
> It's particularly good around the —

She indicates the arms.

> ### PRIEST
> Thank you —

Godmother continues her introductions.

> ### GODMOTHER
> Father, you remember Martin!

> ### MARTIN
> Hey, how're you doing man?

> ### PRIEST
> Bit nervous Martin!

They shake hands. Martin laughs.

> **GODMOTHER**
> You know Jake.

> **PRIEST**
> Yes, hello Jake, how're you?

Jake silently shakes the Priest's hand.

> **GODMOTHER**
> This is my very interesting friend Lucy who is a surrogate.

Priest shakes hands with Lucy.

> **PRIEST**
> Hello, nice to meet you.

> **MARTIN**
> Weird!

> **GODMOTHER**
> And this is my unstable stepdaughter who's had a miscarriage.

Everyone lets out a quiet mumble of 'Oh no, I'm so sorry' etc. together.

Priest and Fleabag shake hands.

> **PRIEST**
> Nice to see you again.

> **FLEABAG**
> You too.

> **GODMOTHER**
> You knew that, you were there.

> **CLAIRE**
> (laughing)
> It was my miscarriage.

Everybody laughs. Thinking it was a joke.

> **MARTIN**
> What?!

> **CLAIRE**
> It was my fucking miscarriage!

Everyone laughs more. Martin laughs particularly loudly.

                    CLAIRE
                 (to Martin)
      Yes, I thought you'd find that funny.

He stops.

                   GODMOTHER
      How interesting.

                    CLAIRE
      She was just covering for me.

                    MARTIN
      We were pregnant?

                    CLAIRE
      For a few weeks. Yes.

                    MARTIN
      It was my baby?

                   GODMOTHER
                 (to Fleabag)
      Sorry, so you haven't had a miscarriage?

                   FLEABAG
      No, sorry.

                    MARTIN
      Wait, what the fuck is going on here? It was my baby?

                    CLAIRE
      I guess it was your baby's way of saying it didn't want
      you as its father.
                 (beat, pointed)
      Like a goldfish out the bowl, sort of thing.

Fleabag looks at the camera. Godmother laughs nervously.

                   GODMOTHER
      Sorry, but whoever had a miscarriage, could you take it
      to the kitchen?

Claire goes to leave. Jake starts to follow.

                    CLAIRE
      No. Don't follow me Jake.
                 (to Martin)
      Oh and, this is over.

Claire leaves. Fleabag follows her, shortly followed by
Martin.

INT. DAD'S HOUSE. KITCHEN — DAY

Claire enters the kitchen, and Fleabag and Martin follow shortly. A WAITRESS is leaving the kitchen with a tray of champagne and Fleabag gratefully takes one.

Claire is breathing heavily.

> CLAIRE
>
> You're leaving me.

> MARTIN
>
> No, no, no.

> CLAIRE
>
> YES.

> MARTIN
>
> Are you drunk?

> CLAIRE
>
> Yes.

> FLEABAG
>
> Are you sober?

> MARTIN
>
> A bit.
> (to Fleabag)
> Could you fuck off for—

> FLEABAG
>
> Ok, no, no, I'm staying right here.

> CLAIRE
> (simultaneously)
> Oh absolutely not.

> CLAIRE
>
> I want you to leave me.

> MARTIN
>
> Listen to me. I just, I have —

> FLEABAG
> (to camera)
> I think he has a little speech—

> MARTIN
>
> — I have a little speech that's building here.

Fleabag holds her champagne to the camera.

                              MARTIN
Now, I know you look at me and you see a bad man with a
big beard.

                              CLAIRE
You're an alcoholic, and you tried it on with my sister—

                              MARTIN
Fine, I tried to kiss your sister on her birthday—

                              CLAIRE
MY birthday.

                              MARTIN
FINE, I mix up birthdays and I have an alcohol problem
just like everyone else in this fucking country. But I
am here and I do things. I pick up Jake from shit, I
make dessert for Easter, I organise the downstairs
toilet, I fired the humming cleaner—

                              CLAIRE
You enjoyed that.

                              MARTIN
I hoover the car, I put up all your certificates and I
don't make you feel guilty for not having sex with me.
I AM NOT A BAD GUY, I just have a bad personality. It's
not my fault. Some people are just born with fucked
personalities. Look at Jake. He is so creepy. It's not
his fault. Why the bassoon?! You wanna know what the
bassoon is?! It's a CRY FOR HELP.
                             (pause)
The main fucking problem here, is that you don't *like*
me.
                             (beat)
And that has been breaking my fucking heart for eleven
years. I love you. I make you laugh. I'm a douche, but
I make you laugh. You said that was the most important
thing!
                        (she says nothing)
I think the thing that you hate the most about yourself
is that you actually love me! So I am not going to leave
you until you are down on your knees begging me.

Beat. Fleabag looks at Claire.

Claire gets on her knees.

                              CLAIRE
     Please leave me.

Beat.

>   **MARTIN**
> Oh man. I didn't think you'd do that in that dress.
>   (beat)
> Right. Well.
>   (beat)
> I guess the only thing left for me to say is...
>   (to Fleabag)
> Fuck you.

>   **FLEABAG**
> Fuck you.

Beat. He goes.

Fleabag looks at Claire. She offers her hand. Claire takes it.

EXT. DAD'S GARDEN. SIDE ALLEY — LATER

Fleabag is having a cigarette. We see a flash of her and the Priest kissing earlier.

EXT. DAD'S GARDEN — LATER

Later. Godmother and the Priest are waiting nervously. Jake is preparing his bassoon. Fleabag and Claire are eating cake. Godmother approaches them nervously.

>   **GODMOTHER**
> What have you done with him?

>   **FLEABAG**
> Who?

>   **GODMOTHER**
> Your father. The wedding is about to start and no one
> can find him anywhere. Can you do something?
>   (meaning it)
> Please. Please.
>   (beat)
> Please.

Fleabag looks at the camera smugly.

>   **FLEABAG**
>   (to Claire, pointing)
> Garden.

>   **CLAIRE**
> Upstairs.

                         FLEABAG
   Ok.

They go.

INT. DAD'S HOUSE. LANDING — DAY

Fleabag rushes up the stairs to the landing, and finds the
ladder to the attic. She calls up the ladder.

                         FLEABAG
   Dad?

She climbs up the ladder, pulling her dress down as she
goes.

INT. DAD'S HOUSE. ATTIC — DAY

Fleabag finds Dad up there crouched in a corner.

                         FLEABAG
   Dad.

                         DAD
   I can't get out.

Beat. She climbs in. He is sat in the corner, crouched over,
clearly in a crisis.

                         FLEABAG
   Ok, Dad. You can.

                         DAD
   I can't!! It's a trap. I'm stuck. There's nothing I can
   do!

                         FLEABAG
   No, Dad, everyone will understand — just give them all
   a bottle to take home. Honestly, they will be relieved.

She gets close enough to discover him with his foot stuck
between floorboards.

He stares at her.

                         DAD
   My foot. Is stuck.

Beat.

                         FLEABAG
   Oh.

> **DAD**
> Everyone will understand?

> **FLEABAG**
> Um.

He stares at her. Then he pulls his foot. He groans at the pain.

> **DAD**
> Will you help me please?

> **FLEABAG**
> How is it stuck?

She gets on her knees. She investigates the shoe.

> **DAD**
> Just — just help me get it out. I am going to be in so much trouble.

> **FLEABAG**
> What are you doing up here?

> **DAD**
> I — I just remembered that I'd left a — a friendly mouse trap up here a few weeks ago and I hadn't checked it. I wanted to make sure that one little chap hadn't got trapped in it and was suffocating up here.

He looks at her.

> **FLEABAG**
> I think I've worked out what we need to do.

> **DAD**
> Do it.
> > (she doesn't)
> Do it.
> > (she doesn't)
> Darling!

> **FLEABAG**
> I'll do it if you tell me why you're up here. Just one honest answer.

> **DAD**
> I... What... What... I — I don't think...

> **FLEABAG**
> One full sentence.

Beat.

                    DAD
I was checking on the mouse.

                 FLEABAG
Dad.
                   (beat)
Do you want to make a run for it? I can smuggle you out
in one of Mum's dresses.

                    DAD
You would as well.

They both laugh.

The music starts outside. He starts to panic.

                    DAD
I know she's not...
                   (beat)
Everyone's cup of tea.

Fleabag laughs. He laughs.

                    DAD
And neither are you, darling.
                   (beat)
I mean... I'm sorry... I love you — but I'm not sure
that I like you.
                   (beat)
All the time. Sorry.

                 FLEABAG
Hey, you created this monster...

He smiles.

                    DAD
You're not the way you are because of me.

                 FLEABAG
I know.

                    DAD
You're the way you are because of her.
                   (beat)
And it's those bits that you need to cling to.

She nods.

                    DAD
Could you... get my shoe out?

She takes his foot out of his shoe.

                              DAD
I just want you all to be proud of me.

                          FLEABAG
We are proud of you Dad. You have two daughters who love
you, even if you don't like them.

She removes the shoe from the floorboard.

                              DAD
I like Claire.

                          FLEABAG
                         (laughing)
Jesus, Dad.

He laughs. She puts the shoe back on his foot, ties his
shoelace.

                              DAD
Thank you.

He looks at her, not sure what to do.

                          FLEABAG
Come on.

                              DAD
I don't think I can...

                          FLEABAG
Come on. Buck up. Smiles. Charm. Off we go.

They stand.

                              DAD
I think you know how to love better than any of us.
That's why you find it all so painful.

Beat. He moves off. She is moved, then...

                          FLEABAG
                   (to camera, bemused)
I don't find it painful.

EXT. DAD'S HOUSE. GARDEN — DAY

Fleabag leads limping Dad into the garden.

Godmother is at the end of her aisle with Priest. She looks
up and sees them. She holds her heart with relief and mouths
'thank you' at Fleabag.

She and Dad get to the top of his aisle. She begins to let
go of his arm.

> **FLEABAG**
> (whispering)
> Ok Dad.

He grabs her hand and presses it into his arm.

> **DAD**
> No — stay a moment. Stay.

Beat. She doesn't let go. She starts leading him down his
aisle.

Godmother is walking down her aisle, slightly perturbed by
what she is seeing, but mainly relieved that he is there.

It's almost as if Fleabag is giving Dad away.

The Priest stands at the front.

Once she's brought him to the front, Fleabag tries to go
again but Dad hangs onto her hand.

> **GODMOTHER**
> (sharp)
> Darling.

> **DAD**
> Sorry.

He lets go of Fleabag's hand. Fleabag goes and joins Claire,
who's seated at the back. Claire and Fleabag share a look
and perhaps a hand squeeze.

> **PRIEST**
> Good afternoon, everybody. Thank you for coming today
> to celebrate the love between... these two very special
> people. Before we start, Jake has asked to play another
> piece on his bassoon.

Jake starts to play the bassoon. Fleabag sees Martin
standing morosely at the back.

> **CLAIRE**
> I can't do this reading.

> **FLEABAG**
> Don't do it.

> **CLAIRE**
> What?!

> **FLEABAG**
> I'll do it. You go and get him.

> **CLAIRE**
> I can't go and get him!

> **FLEABAG**
> Why not?

> **CLAIRE**
> It's too late. I can't... leave my father's wedding.
> He's called Klare for God's sake and he's already at
> the airport anyway.

> **FLEABAG**
> Well there you go. Is it running through the airport
> kind of love?

> **CLAIRE**
> I'm not going to the airport. He'd think I was insane.

> **FLEABAG**
> I'm just sayi—

> **CLAIRE**
> The *airport*. How would I even find him? You can't get
> through security without a boarding pass.

> **FLEABAG**
> I wasn't suggesting you—

> **CLAIRE**
> I'd have to buy a dummy ticket, just to get through the
> gate. I don't know when his flight is, or which
> terminal. Imagine if I knew that. Imagine him finding
> out I knew all that. Imagine if he was just in Boots,
> buying a pair of tweezers in Terminal 5, and suddenly I
> was there: 'Hello Klare.'

> **FLEABAG**
> Yeah, that would be intense.

Beat.

> **CLAIRE**
> The only person I'd run through the airport for is you.

They look at each other.

Jake finishes his piece and everyone applauds.

> **PRIEST**
> Thank you Jake for that beautiful bassoon piece...
> written specially for today. I believe it's called...

                    (he reads from a paper)
'Where's Claire?'

The guests applaud.

                    PRIEST
I think what you guys are doing is amazing. Sorry —
                    (he gets emotional)
Fuck me! Sorry — I didn't get much sleep last night.

Claire and Fleabag give each other a look.

                    PRIEST
So it turns out it's quite hard to come up with something original to say about love. But I've had a go.

Long pause.

                    PRIEST
Love is awful! It's awful. It's painful. It's fright-
ening. It makes you doubt yourself, judge yourself,
distance yourself from the other people in your life.
Makes you selfish. Makes you creepy. It makes you
obsessed with your hair. Makes you cruel. Makes you say
and do things you never thought you would do.

                    CLAIRE
                (quietly, to Fleabag)
There's something wrong with your priest.

Fleabag looks at her, then at us. Concerned.

                    PRIEST
It's all any of us want and it's hell when we get there.
So no wonder it's something we don't want to do on our
own.

Priest and Fleabag catch eyes.

                    PRIEST
I was taught that if we're born with love, then life is
about choosing the right place to put it. People talk
about that a lot. It 'feeling right'. 'When it feels
right, it's easy.' But I'm not sure that's true. It
takes strength to know what's right.
                    (beat)
And love isn't something that weak people do. Being a
romantic takes a hell of a lot of hope. I think what
they mean is... When you find somebody that you
love... It feels like hope.

Claire is on the verge of tears.

> FLEABAG
> (whispering)
> Go out the side way. Now.

Claire smiles. She puts her hand to her head and unclips her ponytail and puts it on her seat as she goes. Jake and Martin watch her go.

> PRIEST
> So thank you for bringing us all together here today. To take words from this book of love — be strong and take heart, all you who hope... in the Lord. Amen.

Beat. He looks at Fleabag.

> PRIEST
> And now, let's get on with the big bit!

He turns to Godmother and Dad.

EXT. DAD'S HOUSE. FRONT DOOR — DUSK

Music is blaring from the house. The party is now in full swing.

Fleabag comes out the front door and lights a cigarette.

The front door behind her opens and Dad comes out.

> DAD
> Oh! There you are.

He stands next to her. He smiles. She smiles. They break out into laughter.

She offers him the cigarette. He first refuses it, but then —

> DAD
> Oh, fuck it.

He takes it. He has a drag. He blows the smoke out. The day is done. He's happy and relieved.

> DAD (CONT'D)
> (about the cigarette)
> Thank you.

She smiles.

> DAD (CONT'D)
> (about the day)
> And thank you.

He touches her cheek and turns to go back inside. He turns
before he leaves.

> **DAD**
> Oh... The uh... Priest is looking for you.

> **FLEABAG**
> Oh.

> **DAD**
> Don't break his heart.

He smiles and goes back in.

Beat.

Fleabag puts out her cigarette and walks inside.

EXT. DAD'S HOUSE. GARDEN — NIGHT

Party in full swing. Godmother and Dad are happy newlyweds,
standing with the Priest. Fleabag approaches with her bag.

> **PRIEST**
> Oh, are you leaving?

> **FLEABAG**
> Oh, actually, well I — I thought you were —

> **PRIEST**
> I was changing.

> **FLEABAG**
> (laughing)
> Oh yeah.

> **PRIEST**
> What do you do — do you get the — get the bus, or...?

> **FLEABAG**
> Yeah, I get the bus.

> **PRIEST**
> On the road?

> **FLEABAG**
> Just on the road. I get on the bus.

> **PRIEST**
> Well that's nice.

Dad interrupts.

> **DAD**
> Bye, my daughter.

                    FLEABAG
                 (to Dad)
    Bye, Father.
                      (to Priest, flirty)
    Bye, Father.

Everyone laughs.

                    FLEABAG
               (to Godmother, polite)
    Goodbye.

                    GODMOTHER
    Bye.

She goes.

EXT. LONDON. STREET. BUS STOP — NIGHT

Fleabag sits at the bus stop. She looks up the road.

He's not there.

She looks up the road again. She smiles.

The Priest approaches.

                    FLEABAG
    You nailed it.

He laughs. He sits. They look up at the screen. It's 46
minutes until the next bus.

                    PRIEST
    Ugh. They always lie. It'll magically come in a
    minute.
                 (beat)
    They're really into each other, those two. It's nice.

                    FLEABAG
    They really pulled it off.

                    PRIEST
    Was your sister Ok? She seemed —

                    FLEABAG
    Yeah she — er — she — had to do a work thing...

                    PRIEST
    — a bit on edge.

                    PRIEST
    Wow, dedicated!

                    FLEABAG
    Addicted.

They look at each other. Pause.

                    FLEABAG
    It's God, isn't it?

Beat.

                    PRIEST
    Yeah.

Fleabag smiles and nods.

                    FLEABAG
    Damn.
                    (pause)
    Damn.

               FLEABAG (CONT'D)
    You know the worst thing is... That I fucking love you.

Beat.

               FLEABAG (CONT'D)
    I love you.

Beat. He takes a breath, but she interrupts.

                    FLEABAG
    No no don't, let's just leave that out there for a
    second on its own.

Beat.

               FLEABAG (CONT'D)
    I love you.

They sit with the words.

Pause. She looks at him.

He takes her hand.

                    PRIEST
                    (gently)
    It'll pass.

Beat.

She smiles.

Beat.

FLEABAG

This bus is not magically coming.

PRIEST
(getting up)

I think I'll walk.

FLEABAG

Ok.

PRIEST

See you Sunday?

She laughs.

PRIEST

I'm joking. You're never ever allowed in my church again.

They laugh.

Beat.

PRIEST

I love you too.
(beat)
Ok.

He turns and walks away.

Soon, he is gone.

Fleabag inhales sharply.

She looks up at the digital bus timer. It says: Cancelled.

Beat. Fleabag sits there.

After a few moments a FOX passes her in the middle of the road.

It stops and looks at her.

She points in the direction the Priest walked.

FLEABAG

He went that way.

The fox trots off after him.

Fleabag sits there.

She opens her bag and pulls out the STATUE.

She looks at it... Her golden mother, sat with her at a bus stop in the middle of the night. Just the two of them.

She looks at us.

A hint of a smile.

She stands up, puts her bag over her shoulder and, holding the statue of her mother in her hand, she turns to walk.

The camera moves with her for a couple of steps.

She stops, feeling it follow her. She looks at us. She smiles slightly with an almost imperceptible shake of her head.

She's asking us not to follow her.

She turns and walks again up the street.

The camera remains where it is.

When she gets almost out of sight she turns and gives us a smile and a little wave.

Then turns and walks off into the night.

Goodbye.

                          THE END.

Who is Fleabag?

I was twenty-seven and in a cynical spiral. Convinced my work and my brain carried less value than my desirability, a rage grew in me at the invisible lectures I felt I was getting all the time about how to be a woman, how to be a feminist. That the world measured a female's worth only by her desirability. I read an article once that said that a woman's prime was at age twenty-five, because that is when she was considered at her most sexually attractive. Everywhere I looked there were inexplicably naked women – posters on the Tube, adverts for toothpaste, dog food. Someone would have their tits out. Porn was something that people gorged on rather than dabbled with. We were becoming numbed by it, and I was teetering on the edge of a depression. From there I looked down into the abyss and at the bottom of it was Fleabag looking up at me, in lipstick.

Her attitude. Her humour. Her ability to sum a person up and eviscerate them with a single, brutal insight is was drove me to write her. She said the unsayable, but it was the truth, albeit bent with cruelty. She was in her custom-tailored coat of pain wrapped around a broken heart. The bitter author of her own tragedy. It was her fault. She could not complain, she couldn't blame it on anyone. She didn't feel sorry for herself and she didn't attribute her flaws to any one event or ordeal that she had experienced. One day she woke up with an audience watching her so she did the only thing she could . . . she put on a show.

Post-script

Fleabag's Beginning

Fleabag began as a ten-minute monologue written for a short-form storytelling night at the Leicester Square Theatre in London, put together by a fellow fringe theatre hustler at the time, Deborah Frances-White. Thanks to the enthusiasm of the crowd there and the ambition of our producer Francesca Moody we soon had a spot at the Underbelly venue in Edinburgh in August. We raised four thousand pounds on Kickstarter and off we went. A month later we were standing in our living-rooms with our hair tousled and the wrong shoes on, clutching a Fringe First and wondering if the whole thing was just a crowd-funded acid-trip. We'd sold out, had great reviews, confirmed a slot at the Soho Theatre and the BBC had asked me to write a pilot. It took me just under a year to crack the adaptation. We nearly lost the commission because it took so long. But my producers Jack and Harry Williams fought for it and it became a Comedy Feed on BBC3.

The Love Stories

These scripts are a result of the most important collaborations of my life and have, in some way, proven to me that your work is only as strong as the people in your team and the gin in your tonic. These two series came about as a result of many late nights, many doubts, and the constant support, rallying, inspiration and faith of a group of people who have grown to feel like family.

Vicky Jones

Director and dramaturg of the stage show,
script editor for Series One, eternal touchstone.

There's a scene in series one where Fleabag is annoyed with herself and Boo dresses up in Fleabag's clothes and forces her to 'have a go at herself'. That was Vicky Jones in my living room, in my coat, in my stupid hat, in 2014.

I left drama school with no job and little confidence, but with the enduring, insatiable need to find ways to make work. Meeting Vicky changed everything. She was a director also on the fringes of the industry trying to make her way, and with the power of two we were galvanised to actually step out and make something ourselves. We created our theatre company, *DryWrite*, and put up monthly new writing nights in a pub in East London. After some time, Vicky and I encouraged (forced) each other to write. With Vicky's faith I felt totally unafraid. My writing became very focused. I just wanted to make *her* laugh, make *her* cry, make *her* gasp. When I was asked to write a monologue for the London Story Festival, I applied the same focus. Vicky read the early draft, helped me hone it, sat front and centre at the show, cheered the loudest, and the rest is Fleabag's history. Her insight, emotional rigour, dogged instinct for the truth and ability to see what you are trying to write before you know yourself defined Fleabag's story.

Vicky helped me develop the play from the very first word, to the opening night, to the first series of the TV show. It would not exist without her. Beyond her incredible talent as a director and writer, she is the kind of friend people write storybooks about. She was my inspiration for Boo, my reason for writing and my soft-landing when I failed. Knowing she was there made me take bigger risks because I knew if it went tits-up there would be a bottle of wine and a healthy 'AAAH FUCKIT' before we jumped into the next thing.

When trying to crack the pilot episode, Vicky filmed me on her phone as I walked around my kitchen. I was making tea and experimenting talking to the camera. After five minutes she pulled the phone down and grinned: 'It works.'

Harry Bradbeer

Director

First interview with Harry:

PHOEBE (28ish, female)
So, what do you make of Fleabag?

HARRY (49ish, male)
Oh, for God's sake darling I AM Fleabag!

Harry is the most profoundly empathetic person I have ever met. He treats every character as if they are the main part and he was right at the heart of the writing process. He is my 'Truth Hound'! He is only interested in what is going on deep inside the characters, their conflicts, their desires. He gave me language for what I otherwise couldn't articulate.

During the first season he taught me about 'Visual Sentences'. I didn't know how to remind the audience of what happened to Boo and I didn't want Fleabag to have to explain it more than once as it's not something she would ever talk about to anyone, other than drunkenly to cab drivers she doesn't know the middle of the night. Harry described the image of Boo standing across the street with cars zooming past her. He said that was all we needed. A new part of my brain opened up. That was the way into Fleabag's pain. She has such a formidable armour of wit and self-awareness, but drop that in at any point – her laughing at a party, her during sex, her walking down the street feeling 'great' – and we'd know that she isn't OK. That she is still haunted. It was a huge step in my learning about writing for the screen and one of many, many lessons from Harry.

Harry empowers people. He allowed me my vision. He listened to every idea I had, however ludicrous or wrong, and fought back only when he felt something didn't feel true. Even though I was twenty-eight and had next-to-no experience, and he was a BAFTA winning, hasn't-stopped-working TV director, I never felt patronised. I spent many hours in his kitchen – more wine – talking out the twists and turns of the characters. We'd wrestle over what he needed to be able to tell the story visually to match what I had already had in my head. He can be moved to tears by a character. He's the best person to pitch an idea to. He will laugh until he cries if it's funny, furrow his brow and shake his head if it's terrible and shed tears if it's moving.

While writing the second series, I lost faith in it so many times. I really felt

Fleabag's story had ended and that we had already seen and heard the most interesting thing about this woman. Harry was adamant that I was wrong. 'If she has something else to learn, then we have more story to tell'. Harry was convinced that the greatest love story we had to tell was that between Fleabag and herself. I shuddered at the sentimentality of it, but I knew it was true.

Jenny

Story producer, Series Two

Jenny is my lifeline. She was the story producer on *Fleabag Two*. We met and worked together on *Killing Eve* and it was a life-changing partnership. I need to talk things out. A LOT. When I spoke to Jenny, it felt like my brain was expanding. Whether we were talking about hair dye or story arcs, it all ended up in the show one way or another.

Jenny was with me every step of the way writing Series Two. We would sit in the office all day putting up post-its of all the ideas I'd had over the last few years. We'd go for lunch, go for dinner, go to Cornwall, go to LA, always talking. I HATE showing a first draft to anyone and I'm incredibly last-minute because of it. But I would show Jenny everything. She is the reason this series is so good. I can't imagine working on a show without her brain, her wit, her heart and her hornet-infested house.

Seconds after we wrapped the final scene of Series Two we were in the kitchen at 'Dad's' house. Everyone quietly left me and Jenny alone for a moment. We just sat in a daze staring at each other. We did it. We know it's only a TV show, but it's what we had been pouring our hearts into for endless days and nights for months. Up until that day, for us it had been everything. We cried and laughed and shook hands, agreeing to always dig that deep and push that hard on everything else we do together.

Sian Clifford

Claire

Sian and I have known each other since drama school. She was as extraordinary then as she is now. I value her opinion and talent deeply. She was relentlessly supportive of my writing, attending every short writing night, acting in anything I begged her to be a part of. She played a sort of prototype Claire in a short play I wrote years before *Fleabag*. Once I saw her embody that character I just wanted to write and write for her. I still do. Giving Sian more to do was one of the main incentives to come back for the second series. I just wanted to see her really get her teeth in to something. Knowing how limitless her range is inspired so much of Claire's emotional journey. I talked Sian through all the ideas before each series to gauge how it landed and would be twitching with anticipation for her reaction to each script. She's been a loyal, supportive friend and collaborator and has delivered the most moving portrait of Claire I could have imagined. Extraordinarily, we never really had to talk 'about' Claire. Sian just knew who she was. She's an exquisite actress and has an instinct for story that I relied on often in my wobbly moments. There were a few times I tried to change the lines on set, and she would quietly stop me. 'It's good. Stop it.'

Father William

I spoke to a few priests while researching the show, but the conversations with Father William impacted me far beyond character research. He spoke candidly about the struggles and rewards of giving one's life to a faith. We had long meandering conversations covering topics from the mundane to the controversial, which all fed their way into the fabric of the second series in one way or another. He was deeply cultured and met every challenging question with great humour, consideration and a brilliant biblical reference. I was most interested in, if a little shy to ask about, his experience with celibacy. He spoke eloquently about the pull between the loneliness, and the freedom of it, at one heart-stopping moment describing it as a 'wound'. He was a great influence on the character. Many of the Priest's lines were inspired by things Father William had said.

The Cast

This cast was a goddam gift. Even though the scripts were 'completed', there were always changes on set. Bill Paterson and Fiona Shaw had scenes reworked minutes before we filmed it, Olivia Colman often had new lines whispered to her mid-scene and Andrew and I once performed a scene I hadn't even had time to write down! Every member of the cast faced it with it with kindness and chutzpah, but no-one was thrown more of a curveball than Brett Gelman. In honour of all of them having to occasionally wing it last minute, I'm going to tell his story.

While sitting with Brett in the car on the way to his climactic final scene I asked him to read out the speech from the script. He did. Something wasn't right. I knew I had to rewrite it, but we only had eleven minutes until we arrived on set. I started writing and talking it through with Brett. I was frantically writing while he read it out in the car. By the time we got to the set, there was a new speech. He had thirty seconds to learn it before he hit the location. Everything was set up. I explained to Harry what I had just put Brett through and the whole crew were behind him. He hit his mark, took a breath then belted out a word-perfect, on point, INCREDIBLE performance of the speech. Then he did it again. And again. He got a round of applause every time, and my heart soars whenever I see that scene!

Olivia came to see the play of *Fleabag* and afterwards told me that if I ever wanted her to be in anything, I just had to ask. I ASKED IMMEDIATELY. I then ran to my producers, cracked open the pilot script, rewrote the end and created the part of Godmother specifically for her. She was there at the very first read-through for the BBC in the basement of a café in Soho, and she's moved mountains to be there for us ever since. If it wasn't for her the part of Godmother would have never existed.

Andrew Scott

Priest

I met Andrew in 2009. We were playing fast-talking, sassy bankers in *Roaring Trade* at the Soho Theatre. It was a formative acting experience for me. I'd worked with one of the best actors in the world on my first job. Acting with him raised my bar of what it should feel like, look like and sound like to be a performer. He was electric to work with and glorious to spend time with.

As the idea of the Priest was forming, I resisted it. I was too aware of the potholes and pitfalls of TV comedy priests. There were iconic parts in history that loomed over the idea and in some ways it seemed too obvious to put Fleabag with a man of God. Then Andrew stepped to the front of my mind and suddenly the character roared into existence. The pitfalls and the potholes became the marks on a treasure map of how find a new way to bring a priest into the conversation. This challenge intensified: I didn't just have to write a good part. He had to be good enough for Andrew.

I asked Andrew to meet for a coffee in Soho Theatre. 'I want you to be in Fleabag Two.' He was open... 'Go on...' I pitched him the character. I told him I wanted to write a kind but complex man who was a match for Fleabag. She has spent her life being able to reduce people to a "Bus Rodent" or an

"Arsehole Guy" but this would be a man she couldn't dismiss. This would be a man whose faith is given real consideration and respect in the show, someone who we took seriously. This would be a love story. His eyes lit up. He told me he'd been wanting to play love for a long time.

For the next four hours Andrew and I spoke about love, life, sex, religion, fear, lust, faith, sexuality, need, family, belonging . . . everything. His perspective on the world was already influencing the character as we idled through Soho. My inner voice was screaming *'if he poured a shot-glass' worth of whatever magic he has is in real life into this show, we'd have a heart-stopping character.'* He turned to me: 'I want to show you something'. He walked me down Haymarket and we turned into a small door that boasted a sign: *Quaker meeting.* There was no-one there, just a few signs to remind you not to talk in the meeting room. We walked into the room, sat there alone, the two of us, breaking their only rule for another hour.

When we eventually left, he turned to me: 'Let's do it.' We filmed the Quaker scene in the same place we'd met that day. Andrew brought more to this character than can be summed up in words. He brought a soul to the character, that I believe we all could feel when watching him. He even insisted on the character saying 'I love you too' to Fleabag at the end, and thank God he did.

Iso

Composer

Iso wrote the music for both series, giving the show it's defining sound. There was minimal music in the first series, bar the burst of discordance over the titles, and the rock guitar credit music became the sound of *Fleabag* instantly. However, her score for the second series elevated the story from the page and filled every emotional corner of the story.

One of my favourite memories from making *Fleabag* was when Iso and I stayed up horrendously late in her studio watching the opening episode again and again trying to find the right sound. I had handed over impossible references of enormous choirs and orchestras. We knew it had to sound epic, but we just didn't have that kind of budget. She would not be defeated. After hearing all the references she nodded, got up and went out for a cigarette. When she came back she said she needed to ignore everything I had played her and just write from her gut. Agreed. I watched her sit at her keyboard, switch on Episode 1, and improvise live on the keyboard pretty much exactly what you hear in the final result. We practically screamed with excitement all the way through it. She's a genius.

Gary Dollner

Editor

Editing is essentially the final draft of the script and Gary sculpts the story just as much as I have to. I LOVE cutting and Gary is never spooked by a brutal slashing of a scene. We try *everything*, but often end up with his first instincts. We tried taking all the asides out of the first episode. We spliced and cut and sewed things together with Harry as if the whole show was a free-for-all. Gary is a magician. If a joke doesn't land or a scene is sticky, he will find a way to rearrange, break it up, tweak it, turn it round until it sings. He can restructure a scene, transform a performance, make a funny moment heartbreaking and vice-versa. He and Iso have a special and specific bond. In moments of panic he'll wave his hand and say 'just wait til Iso gets her hands on it . . . wait for her music.' Strangely, her score often fit perfectly with his cuts even though she hadn't seen them yet. We spent days on that final scene at the bus stop. All of us crammed into that tiny editing space until 3am, shaving *seconds* off a reaction shot. Gary freaking out at the mouse scurrying around beneath us. Even though we were blurry-eyed and exhausted, he wouldn't stop until it was as close to perfect as we could get it. He has no poker face. He got emotional, or roared with laughter or just as frankly stared me right in the eye with a 'nah, it's just not funny mate'. He's as huge-hearted as he is quick-witted and can cut a diamond out of anything. At the end of the second series Fleabag looks up at the bus stop which reads *Dollner Avenue*. A small tribute to a total hero.

Producers

Jack and Harry Williams commissioned a show from me after I recited the ten-minute monologue to them over a pint. It was the most relaxed meeting I had ever had with producers and it's been that way ever since. They trusted me and championed me, and never forced their presence. They optioned me on the basis of a few jokes. 'You're funny.'

Lydia Hampson and Sarah Hammond were the producers and engines at the heart of the show. They probably slept the least and worried the most besides me. They had very little budget and absolutely no time, yet were eternally patient with mad last-minute delivery and were across the story lining all the way. Whatever was needed – a fox that can look at me in a very specific way – they made it happen. They gently talked me down from *terrible* ideas many times and put blood, sweat and tears into this show. They were vital collaborators at scripting stage, and are at the very heart of *Fleabag*.

BBC and Amazon were incredibly supportive and gave us so much space and support: without them I wouldn't have written these scripts or been able to have found this team.

My Family

Most of all, I would like to thank Mum, Dad, Iso and Jasp. Their notes, jokes, instincts, love, encouragement and support have been the fire underneath Fleabag from beginning to the end. Thank you for being there every step of the way. I love you.

(And thank you for calling me Flea)

x

The Confessional Kyrie

Composed by Isobel Waller-Bridge

Kyrie

by

Isobel Waller Bridge

2

"Write like you're not afraid"